The

COMPLETE GUIDE

to

CONTRACT
LAWYERING

OTHER BOOKS BY DEBORAH ARRON

What Can You Do with a Law Degree?

A Lawyer's Guide to Career Alternatives Inside,
Outside and Around the Law

NICHE PRESS

(See page 318 for more information.)

Running from the Law

Why Good Lawyers Are Getting Out of the Legal Profession

TEN SPEED PRESS

The
COMPLETE GUIDE
to
CONTRACT
LAWYERING

What Every Lawyer and
Law Firm Needs to Know about
Temporary Legal Services

DEBORAH ARRON & DEBORAH GUYOL

Published by:

Niche Press

P.O. Box 99477

Seattle, WA 98199

(206) 285-5239; (800) 359-9629

Copies of this book are available at quantity discounts. Please contact the publisher for further information.

Library of Congress Cataloging-in-Publication Data

Arron, Deborah L., 1950-

    The complete guide to contract lawyering: what every lawyer and law firm needs to know about temporary legal services / by Deborah Arron & Deborah Guyol

    p.   cm.

    Includes bibliographical references and index.

    ISBN 0-940675-45-5 (pbk . : alk. paper)

    1. Legal services—United States. 2. Lawyers—United States.

    3. Temporary employment—Law and legislation—United States.

    I. Guyol, Deborah, 1946-   . II. Title.

KF315.A97 1995

340' .023—dc20   95-23796

                                                    CIP

Designed and typeset by Elizabeth Watson

Printed in the United States of America

ISBN 0-940675-45-5

ACKNOWLEDGMENTS

This book was a true collaboration from start to finish, not only between the two of us, but with the help of the hundreds of people across the country who gave us their input. We'd like to acknowledge the special contributions of the following people:

Everyone who volunteered to be interviewed, with special thank you's to Ellen Alexander, Lee Archer, Elizabeth Bottman, Daniel K. Edwards, Katherine Foldes, Samuel A. Frederick, Richard Kaplan, Nadine Rhodes, Sue Samuelson, Linda Gill Taylor, Robert Thomas, Cynthia Vranizan and Tom Watters;

Those contract lawyers, hiring lawyers and contract lawyer placement agency owners we interviewed who also passed on names of other contract and hiring lawyers, including Eric Ebel, Liz Elliott, Lesley Friedman, Shawn Mathis Isbell, Werner Lewin, Susan Shulenberger, Shelley Wallace, and Robert Webster;

The law school career services directors who aided us in our research by providing names of contract lawyer placement agencies, hiring lawyers and contract lawyers in their areas, including Beth Cohen Besner of Nova University, Carolyn Bregman of Emory University, Jean E. French of Boston College, Amanda Harding of the University of North Carolina at Chapel Hill, Deborah Hirsch of the University of Houston, Annette Jones of the University of Texas, Stephanie W. Jumonville of Loyola New Orleans, Audrey Koscielniak of State University of New York at Buffalo, Jane Thomson of the University of California at Davis, Jo-Ann M. Verrier of the University of Pennsylvania, and Mark A. Weber of the University of Illinois at Urbana-Champaign;

The insurance carrier representatives who so forthrightly shared information about company policies toward contract lawyers;

The career counselors who provided input about the market for contract lawyers in their areas including Lew Gumper of Billings, Montana, Leslie Messman of Denver and Kathy Meija Morris and Sheila Neilson of Chicago;

The experts who reviewed, corrected and commented upon the content of our manuscript including Laura Black of Special Counsel, Jeff Crawford of the Oregon Professional Liability Fund, Eugene Hardy, Lewis M. Horowitz of Lane Powell Spears

Lubersky, S. Diane Rynerson of Oregon Women lawyers, and Sylvia Stevens of the Oregon State Bar;

Those who cannot as easily be categorized but were instrumental in helping us write a comprehensive book, including Don Bradley, Larry Bodine of Sidley & Austin, Lisa Horowitz, Dan Keppler, Kent Larson, Teri Powers, Jackie Krasas Rogers, and Dov Seidman;

Mark Jaroslaw, who once again learned more than he'd anticipated about the practice of law;

Michael Sweeney of the Oregon Attorney Assistance Program who brought the two of us together;

And especially each other, as neither of us could—or would—have written this book without the support, wisdom and enthusiasm of the other.

CONTENTS

Appendices

INTRODUCTION

"Big Companies Hire "More Lawyer-Temps," read a *Wall Street Journal* headline in September 1994. "Temporary Attorneys Bring a Permanent Change to Firm Staffs," noted the *Chicago Daily Law Bulletin*.

How did the shift to greater use of temporary attorneys—or contract lawyers, as we refer to them—evolve? Is the shift a positive or negative development for the legal profession? Does it reflect systemic changes in the legal profession or parallel reforms in the business world? More important, how can you—as a practicing lawyer, law firm administrator or recent law school graduate—take advantage of its benefits? How can you avoid its drawbacks?

The Complete Guide to Contract Lawyering is organized in four parts, with supplemental appendices. Part I explains the larger social and economic forces at work in the growth of this form of practice. Part II speaks to the individual lawyer interested in working as a contract lawyer, and provides the financial and mechanical details necessary to establish a successful practice. Part III addresses the needs of hiring lawyers, emphasizing the value of contract staffing and offering suggestions for the nuts and bolts of hiring and supervising contract lawyers. You'll find the most significant changes in this second edition of the book in Part IV. It analyzes the complex ethical and business issues that affect the relationship between contract lawyer and hiring lawyer: conflict of interest and client notification; independent contractor status; malpractice liability and coverage; written agreements and the involvement of contract lawyer placement agencies. The appendices provide profiles of contract lawyer placement agencies nationwide, summaries of ethics opinions, and input on organizing an office.

Although the book is a resource for the legal profession, we've done our best to keep it from being too dry or prescriptive. Much of the information is conveyed through the personal experiences of lawyers around the country—those who work with contract lawyers, those who work as contract lawyers, and those who act as intermediaries between the two. Many of the lawyers are identified by their full names; some have pseudonyms or are composites of the many lawyers we interviewed. With the help of all these resources, we assembled as complete as possible a picture of the world of contract work. We hope you can learn from their experiences, as well as from our observations.

Deborah Guyol's work as a contract lawyer and as coordinator of the Oregon Women Lawyers' Contract Lawyer Referral Service introduced her firsthand to many of the issues this book addresses. Deborah Arron's knowledge came from her ten years of private law practice experience as well as the stories she has heard in her new career as a national speaker and consultant on career development issues for lawyers. Together we sought to prepare a comprehensive overview of this emerging practice option.

Both of us see contract lawyering as a solution to many current problems in the profession. It can help entry-level lawyers get experience in a demanding job market; it can afford relief to lawyers who dislike aspects of practice that other lawyers love; it can enable busy practitioners to preserve their sanity while protecting their bottom line; it can even rescue law firms and legal departments that downsized too enthusiastically and are now short-handed.

While we wanted to write an entirely supportive book about contract lawyers, our research did reveal some negative aspects of the phenomenon. We learned that the growth of temporary services is related to decreased loyalty and commitment among lawyers; that many lawyers are forced to accept temporary positions when they're looking for the security of something more permanent; that the popularity of the concept among hiring lawyers can make it hard for new lawyers to find jobs and could ultimately result in a gradual decline in ethics and standards of practice.

Despite the acknowledged negative social consequences, temporary work is here to stay—at least for the foreseeable future—and contract legal work has advantages that outweigh its drawbacks. The legal profession, like the general business environment, is shifting to a new practice model, one in which permanent associations of lawyers (firms) will be smaller and more flexible, and temporary associations with other lawyers (as well as other professionals) will be more common. This new model mirrors the existing state of attorney/client relationships as well. Where clients once signed on for life, now lawyers must prove themselves anew for each project. Everything is temporary: lawyer to client, partner to partner, employer to employee relationships. Only the contract lawyer work option freely acknowledges— and makes good use of—the impermanence of our professional environment.

Deborah Arron and Deborah Guyol

Part 1

THE
RISE
OF
CONTRACT
LAWYERING

I

SETTING THE STAGE

Contract lawyers perform legal services for other lawyers on an intermittent or impermanent basis. Their rise in prominence in the legal profession coincides with tremendous growth in the entire temporary services industry.

All indicators point to temporary work as *the* fastest growing category of American employment today. Consider these statistics:

- *Temporary employment generated over $50 billion in 1997, a 700 percent increase since 1986. The number of temporary workers is expected to grow by 20 percent a year, and by the year 2000 will include some 10 million individuals.*
- *The National Association of Temporary and Staffing Services reports that temporary work assignments nearly tripled between 1980 and 1994, while the rest of the country's employment expanded by only about 20 percent.*
- *Manpower, Inc., the nation's first temporary staffing agency, employed 560,000 workers in 1993, overtaking General Motors and IBM as the nation's largest employer.*
- *Temporary employment of medical, legal, managerial, and technical professionals exploded in the 1990s, and accounts for a fifth of all regular temporary workers.*

"People who study employment trends say legal professionals were among the last group to turn to independent contracting, but their numbers are now growing fast," observes Samuel Frederick, a Philadelphia corporate lawyer and co-founder of contract lawyer placement agency Assigned Counsel, Inc. The *Wall Street Journal* agrees:

*As recently as two or three years ago, temporary legal help was used
mostly by small businesses and tiny law firms, and legal piecework was
considered an offbeat option for the mother with young children or for
burnt-out associates who wanted to spend more time writing
screenplays. But ever since the recession forced companies to cut costs
and poured hundreds of top-notch attorneys into the market, the use of
legal temps has gone mainstream.[1]*

In 1988, when a mere 1,300 attorneys were estimated to be involved in temp
work around the country, Lesley Friedman, founder of contract lawyer placement
agency Special Counsel International, compared the use of contract lawyers to "the
situation ten to 15 years ago when paralegals were new to law office management."[2]
Just six years later, contract lawyer placement agencies were working with an
estimated 10,000 lawyers—an eight-fold increase—and had some $40 million in
revenues to show for their efforts. Friedman's receipts alone were indicative of the
astonishing growth of this industry, more than tripling to $3 million between 1991
and 1993, and exceeding $10 million in 1994. Those numbers don't begin to reflect
the thousands of other contract lawyers who have found a comfortable niche
marketing themselves outside the agency sphere. This less publicized revolution is
replacing space sharing, overload, staff attorney and other "down-the-food-chain"
referrals with contract lawyer relationships.

WHAT IS CONTRACT LAWYERING?

Here are five "snapshots" of contract lawyers, practitioners who perform legal
services for other lawyers on an intermittent or impermanent hourly or project—as
opposed to salaried—basis.

- *Angela is a former commercial litigation associate at several large Los
  Angeles law firms who handles discrete legal research and drafting
  projects such as motions for summary judgment. Her clientele includes
  partners at mid-sized law firms and solo practitioners. She charges
  between $50 and $70 per hour, sometimes trimming the hours she bills for
  self-perceived inefficiency. Both Angela and her clients recognize her as a
  contract lawyer.*

1. Amy Stevens, "Big Companies Hire More Lawyer-Temps," *Wall Street Journal*, September 22, 1994.
2. "Lesley Friedman, Esq.: Her Concept," *South Shore Tribune*, March 10, 1988.

- *Derek used to be an associate of a large Manhattan law firm but now works through a temporary placement agency. A typical assignment for Derek involves two months of work for a mid-sized law firm, assisting with a major case right before trial. He puts in 60 to 90 hours each week, organizing the trial notebook and drafting motions* in limine, *the trial brief and jury instructions. Derek's agency pays him an hourly rate of $48 (out of the $74 per hour it bills the firm), and he must provide his own benefits package. Derek calls himself a freelance lawyer; the agency calls him a project attorney; the firm where he does contract work calls him a "blessing."*

- *Louise clerked for the Illinois Supreme Court and spent ten years practicing in law firms before deciding she wanted to be her own boss. She set up a practice in her home, soliciting appellate assignments from other lawyers. Now, she has a full-time contract law practice, and her schedule is often so booked she has to subcontract work to other contract lawyers. Although she refers to herself as an appellate specialist, Louise is in fact a contract lawyer who limits her practice to handling appeals for other lawyers' clients.*

- *Martin is a solo practitioner in Houston who works on an as-needed or on-call basis for several busier practitioners with whom he shares office space. Martin checks in regularly with the other lawyers to see if there's overload available. The lawyers hand him discrete projects for their existing clients, and occasionally send him cases they don't want to handle. They all refer to the relationship as a space-sharing arrangement. In fact, much of it fits the definition of contract work.*

Although contract lawyer arrangements vary widely, they have two factors in common. First, *the contract lawyer is always hired by another lawyer*—whom we refer to as the hiring lawyer—to do work for the hiring lawyer's client. Second, *both parties intend the relationship to be temporary or irregular.* Whether hired by a law firm, solo practitioner, government agency or in-house legal department; whether compensated as an independent contractor or employee; whether paid an hourly rate or a flat fee; whether working on a project, rush or as-needed basis; whether employed full-time, overtime or part-time; and whether completing a two-hour assignment or one that involves two years of work, neither the contract lawyer nor the hiring lawyer has any guarantee that the relationship will continue beyond a specified period or project.

Titles such as temporary lawyer, contingent lawyer, free-lance attorney, consulting lawyer, staff attorney, of counsel and special counsel are used interchangeably these days. In this book, we use one term—"contract lawyering"—to describe all intentionally temporary lawyer-to-lawyer relationships. We believe it best embodies the professionalism of the role, and is more inclusive than terms like "consulting lawyer," "special counsel," "independent contractor" and "contingent lawyer." It also avoids the negative baggage attached to the words "temporary" and "temp." (Appendix 1 explains various terms and the distinctions among them.)

WHAT CONTRACT LAWYERING MEANS TO YOU

If you're concerned about law practice economics, you can call upon contract lawyers to help you compete in today's market by giving your firm greater flexibility and versatility at a reasonable cost. Rather than staffing up with lawyers whose specialties are in fashion one season and out the next, you can give temporary assignments to contract lawyers who have the precise type and degree of training required for whatever shift in client needs may develop.

If you manage an in-house legal department, you can achieve a more cost-effective operation and minimize outside counsel costs—without increasing permanent staff—by using contract lawyers at busy times.

If you're experiencing diminished career satisfaction, contract lawyering may be a welcome option, whether you're burned out by the time commitments of your practice or itching to concentrate on tasks that draw upon your strengths while offloading those that don't.

If you're a new lawyer—or reentering the legal job market—and your job search does not consider temporary assignments with other lawyers, you're conducting a 20th Century job hunt in a 21st Century market. Many law firms, still suffering from the recession of the late 1980s and early 1990s or worried about the next one, are hesitant to hire more permanent lawyers. Offering these firms a contract work option will expand your prospects.

If you're pursuing a dual career or making a transition out of the legal profession, switching to a contract role, or bringing in contract assistance, can give you the time and money to build another business or accomplish a career change.

What does the contract lawyer trend mean for the legal profession itself? For tens of thousands of lawyers, law firms and in-house legal departments, the growth of contract lawyering reflects a deep restructuring of the law practice environment and coincides with a larger national workplace movement toward use of contingent workers. The next chapter explores some of the forces that have contributed to the growth of this new work option.

2

CONTRACT LAWYERING IN CONTEXT

Three trends have converged to encourage the growth of today's market for contract legal services: the end of the job, the rise and fall of the megafirm and the billable hour, and individual lawyers' rejection of the existing law practice model.

Some would argue—and they would be correct—that contract lawyering is not a new phenomenon, but a return to a pre-World War II system in which megafirms didn't exist and office sharing and mentoring arrangements were even more common than law firms. Dick Maizels, a Portland, Oregon, solo practitioner, began using "contract lawyers" when he started his practice more than 20 years ago. In those days, recent graduates who couldn't find full-time jobs would provide several hours a month of legal research or other services in exchange for the use of one of his extra offices, phone and secretarial assistance.

"Law firms, since the dawn of creation, have always brought in somebody when they got overloaded, typically through the old boys network," says Robert Webster, co-founder of The Lawsmiths temporary placement agency in San Francisco. Yet another form of contract lawyering occurs when corporate law departments hire outside law firms on a project basis, says Samuel Frederick. Other well-accepted variations on the temporary or contingent theme include "of counsel," consulting specialist and summer law clerk arrangements. Although the relationship has been around for a long time, it's taking on new prominence as changes in the world of work collide with a legal profession in its own transition.

THE END OF THE JOB

Although today we regard corporate employment of most of the work force as the norm, a century ago almost 90 percent of all Americans were self-employed.

Before World War I, farmers made up the largest single group of workers in every country. The second largest group was servants.[1]

The job itself, says William Bridges, author of *JobShift*, is a "social artifact" that emerged in the early 19th Century to fuel the Industrial Revolution. By the 1950s, corporations had transformed the population of farmers and servants into one of prosperous blue-collar workers. These industrial workers made up the largest segment of the work force in all developed countries, and enjoyed job security and a comfortable income supported by the oversight of a substantial managerial class.

Now *Fortune* magazine announces "The End of the Job," noting that "in a fast-moving economy, jobs are "rigid solutions to an elastic problem."[2] Blue-collar jobs have been halved, and the managerial class has recently taken its hit. Although only nine percent of the American work force is now self-employed, people created one out of five new jobs in the first three quarters of 1993 by putting themselves to work, and job growth in the self-employment category increased at twice the rate of overall job growth during that year, according to *Inc.* magazine. A related phenomenon is the "open collar" worker, those consultants, entrepreneurs, moonlighters and telecommuters who operate their businesses from home. According to Paul and Sarah Edwards, gurus of the home office movement, the six million home offices of 1980 soared to 36 million by the end of 1993.

"Corporations are going to a place where they will be chronically slightly under-staffed," contends David Lord, editor of *Executive Recruiter News*.[3] Charles Handy predicts in *The Age of Unreason* that by the turn of the century, less than half the work force in the industrial world will have "proper" full-time jobs in organizations. Everyone else will be self-employed, have a part-time job or be a temporary worker; it will no longer make sense to think of a full-time job as the norm.

William M. Lewis and Nancy H. Molloy describe their view of the staffing of the future in their book, *How to Choose & Use Temporary Services:*

> *The typical model . . . includes a stable core of permanent workers*
> *surrounded by rings of temporary, part-time, contract, and other "no*
> *strings attached" workers. These peripheral rings compose a work force*
> *that can be expanded, contracted, or redeployed according to the*

---

1. Today, farmers make up less than five percent of the work force in any developed country, and servants as a class have pretty much disappeared. Peter F. Drucker, "The Age of Social Transformation," *The Atlantic Monthly*, November 1994.

2. William Bridges, "The End of the Job," *Fortune*, September 19, 1994.

3. Mark Silver, "The Truth About Temping," *U.S. News & World Report*, November 1, 1993.

*shifting needs of the company. Not unlike the much-heralded
"just in time" inventory management, contingent-staffing arrangements
let employers respond quickly to short-term changes in product or
service demand. This elastic outer ring also buffers regular
workers against the shocks of downturn or recession, mergers
or acquisitions.*

Much of what has occurred in the corporate world has been accompanied by resistance and anger. At this point, though, it's clear there's no turning back. Even if we were to accept that it would be a good thing for our entire work force to have jobs, that is simply not the direction in which the business world is heading.

THE RISE OF THE FIRM

Like corporate America, the legal profession has changed structurally in the last 100 years. In the old days, solo practitioners dominated the profession—in influence as well as numbers. In fact, before the Civil War, groups of more than three partners were rare. Although by the turn of the century such firms were common (especially on Wall Street), as recently as the mid-1950s only two percent of lawyers practiced in firms of nine or more lawyers.

The "firm" emerged on Wall Street at the end of the 19th Century to support proponents of economic expansion—industry, commerce and finance. The clear trend from 1970 through the early 1990s was not only to larger firms, but to the disproportionate influence of those firms. By 1988, 28 percent of all lawyers in private practice were in firms of over ten lawyers (versus only two percent in the mid-1950s); nine percent were in the largest firms of over 100 lawyers.

By the late 1970s and well into the 1980s, lawyers came to believe that "growth is what we do and leverage is how we make money," says William C. Cobb, a management consultant in Houston.[4] To keep profits on an upward curve, firms increased the ratio of associates to partners. In 1991 most of the firms near the top of *The American Lawyer's* profits-per-partner ranking maintained between three and 4.5 associates per partner. This practice of "leveraging" encouraged the hiring of young associates and succeeded as long as demand remained strong.

According to a July 18, 1992 survey in *The Economist*, "Large firms devoted to serving business clients have always been an Anglo-American oddity." Their

4.   Don J. DeBenedictis, "Growing Pains," *ABA Journal*, March 1993.

spectacular growth in the 1980s eclipsed the old solo-practitioner model—even though in 1988 solos still made up 46 percent of lawyers in private practice. The furious hiring pace of the large and even medium-sized firms from the mid-1970s until the early 1990s supported both the growth of law schools and the ideal of apprenticeship as a big-firm associate.

During the go-go 1980s, the fortunes of the big firms devoted to business clients "soared as never before. The furious pace of corporate restructuring, financing and litigation created a voracious appetite for upmarket lawyering."[5] Hourly rates rose to as much as $500.

Many observers credit the billable hour with contributing to—if not causing—some of the most far-reaching changes in the profession. In the old days, state and local bar associations published minimum fee schedules that lawyers were required to follow in billing clients for their services. For example, some schedules set the fee for a simple will at $50, a $300 fee for drafting a partnership agreement, and a rate of $350 per day for trials.[6] With schedules like these, lawyers did not need to account for their time.

A 1967 study showed, however, that lawyers who tracked their time for internal purposes made 20 percent more money than lawyers who did not. Then, in 1975, the U.S. Supreme Court in *Goldfarb v. Virginia State Bar*, 421 U.S. 773 (1975), held that the minimum fee schedules violated antitrust laws. Thus was born the billable hour, which began as a servant to the profession and became its master.

The reign of the billable hour has meant many things for lawyers and their clients. It has glorified the working of killer hours. It has devalued efficiency. It has, arguably, encouraged exaggeration, if not downright lying, in record keeping. According to *The American Lawyer*, a partner in a major Chicago law firm billed more than 6,000 hours annually from 1990 through 1993. He claimed to have worked every day of the year and to have put in at least one 24-hour day every week on average. The remaining hours calculated to over 15 *every single day* of the year on top of the 52 days he worked around the clock. Somehow, in the remaining nine hours—six days per week—this lawyer slept, bathed, dressed, ate, commuted, kept up his CLE requirements, performed law firm administrative duties like preparing the bills themselves, and also acted as husband and father to his large family. The lawyer was outraged when the veracity of his account was challenged.[7]

Since at least the early 1980s, billable hour "goals" promulgated by law firms have become more and more common—and increasingly unrealistic. For example,

---

5. "On Trial—A Survey of the Legal Profession," *The Economist*, July 18, 1992 (cited as "On Trial").

6. Joseph T. Karcher, *How to Build a $100,000 Law Practice* (Institute for Business Planning, Inc. 1976).

7. Karen Dillon, "6,022 Hours," *The American Lawyer*, July/August 1994.

average hours billed by associates in large New York City law firms increased from 1780 annually in 1982 to 2290 in 1987. The easy translation of hours worked to dollars earned skewed the lawyer's professional mandate away from doing the best job possible for the client and toward billing as many hours as possible to keep money flowing into the firm.

The billable hour on its own might not have had much power, but its influence was magnified by journalistic interest in the legal profession. *The American Lawyer*, founded in 1979, took the lead in making law firm economics public. Before long the "AmLaw 100" told the world about per-lawyer revenues and per-partner profits at the largest firms in the country. Such disclosure, healthy though it may have been after decades of silence on the subject, was bound to trigger lawyers' competitive spirit and encourage high salaries as *the* sign of success.

The service savvy that enabled the lawyer population to grow much faster than the population as a whole, the boom in business-related practice that nurtured big firm growth, and the billable hour that helped lawyers enhance the bottom line, converged in the 1980s to produce a culture seriously unlike the old "gentlemanly" practice of pre-War years. The 1980s lawyer, in image if not in fact, was driven by a maniacal insistence on the value of overwork and by an attention to profits that could be mistaken for simple avarice.

It's not clear exactly when trouble struck the legal community. One possible point was the October 1987 stock market crash, after which property values in East Coast metropolitan areas began to fall. By 1990 the West Coast real estate boom was over, and real estate lawyers all over the country were hurting. The pace of mergers and acquisitions slowed after 1987 as well. The profession was "battered by a transatlantic triple blow of recession, collapsed property markets and a slump in corporate dealmaking."[8]

In terms of hard numbers, the slowdown did not look so bad. According to *The American Lawyer*, average profits per partner at the AmLaw 100 firms peaked in 1989 at $433,000 and "bottomed out" in 1991 at $400,000. They climbed steadily through the early 1990s and by 1996 had reached an all-time high of $492,000. Even the "low" figures in the early 1990s, however, were well ahead of profits for 1986 ($305,000) and 1987 ($341,000).

The sense that the era of boundless (and mindless) growth was at an end had a psychological impact far more serious than the numbers would suggest. In 1991, Latham & Watkins, one of California's and the nation's most prominent and profitable firms, shook the legal community with its decision to "downsize" by firing

---

8. "On Trial."

43 associates. The panic spread, and soon actions that would have been unthinkable in 1987 were commonplace.

In 1992, with the country deep in recession, major firms all over the country fired associates, cut back on hiring, and asked "less productive" partners to leave. In March 1992, New York's Milbank, Tweed (18th in profits per partner at $555,000 per the 1991 AmLaw 100) announced that 29 senior-level associates and seven partners had been asked to leave; Milbank had fired 39 associates the year before. In May 1992 Chicago's Winston & Strawn (34th in profits per partner at $400,000) gave 19 partners their walking papers. The shock in the legal profession was at least equal to that caused by the corporate "downsizings" that had flooded the job market with dazed middle-aged middle-managers.

But it wasn't only the recession that hit lawyers hard. The business clients that had fed the phenomenal big-firm growth were wising up. In-house counsel scrutinized legal bills with an educated eye. Bills were challenged, and more and more work was brought in-house. In 1991, John F. Walker, Jr., then managing partner of Latham & Watkins, attributed their large staff reduction to clients no longer willing to tolerate a highly-leveraged firm fraught with inefficiencies. "We see the market changing back to the '70s," he said, "where the structure of the work will require a higher partner involvement. We have to present ourselves as adding value, as being in the position to solve a problem."[9]

Technology also had an impact. Where management consultants used to estimate a reasonable overhead figure as 40 percent of gross receipts, their estimates increased to 60 percent, primarily as a result of the costs of purchasing and upgrading such office necessities as fax machines and cellular phones, notebook computers, laser printers and software. Technology also undercut the concept of the billable hour. With the help of computers, complex documents could be generated in a fraction of the time it would have taken without them, making them less expensive to clients billed on an hourly basis, and therefore less lucrative for the firms.

Those technological advances are now threatening the dominance of the megafirms. A 1995 *American Lawyer* feature reported that smaller firms are working more quickly than big firms to find creative uses for new technology. By conducting complex litigation with the help of computers rather than troops of associates and paralegals, small firms and solo practitioners can produce equally high-quality documents quickly and cheaply, thereby undermining the big-firm advantage. The *New York Times* reported on July 22, 1994, "Legal consultants nationwide agree . . . the competitive marketplace—with firms dissolving and merging, cutting back hiring,

---

9. Nancy Rutter, "Shaken to the Core," *California Lawyer*, November 1991.

becoming more corporate and less collegial places to work—is driving more lawyers to set up solo or very small practices."

DEMOGRAPHIC INFLUENCES

Starting in the late 1960s, women entered law schools and the profession in increasing numbers. From 1951 to 1967 the proportion of women admitted to the bar each year stayed steady at around three percent. Then, in 1968, the number grew to four percent and continued growing. In 1982-83, 34 percent of new admittees were women; that figure rose to over 40 percent in 1990-91. Women as a percentage of the profession as a whole increased from 2.5 percent in 1950 to 22 percent in 1990. Women lawyers were distinguished not only by their sex but by their youth. In 1988, 74 percent of women lawyers were under the age of 40, in contrast to only 41 percent of male lawyers.

As women lawyers became more common, they influenced not only substantive areas of law (rape, pregnancy, and domestic violence, for example) but law practice management issues as well. Their collective need to develop a practice model that didn't require a wife at home, and allowed time for family, loosened the rigid hold of the old models. Parental leave and part-time or flexible schedules found acceptance— or at least lip-service—in the law firm world.[10] As women lawyers began to articulate their discontent with their professional world, many male lawyers agreed, legitimizing the notion of lawyer discontent.[11]

It is ironic, but had numbers of women been allowed to enter the profession before the profit-driven 1970s and 1980s, they might have had less to complain about. As it was, their numerical influence coincided with the influence of economic

---

10. In *Breaking Traditions* (ABA 1993), the Law Practice Management Section of the ABA collected 47 articles on nontraditional work alternatives as well as such subjects as lawyer burnout and the need for balance.

11. Literature on lawyer discontent is extensive. *Running from the Law* by Deborah Arron, first published in 1989, chronicles a relatively early phase of the phenomenon. A 1991 ABA study entitled "At the Breaking Point" found overall lawyer dissatisfaction had increased dramatically between 1984 and 1990, with many lawyers complaining of a "time famine." 1994 may prove to have been the peak year for commentary on the subject of dissatisfaction among lawyers and with the legal profession. *See* Sol Linowitz, *The Betrayed Profession* (Scribner 1994); Mary Ann Glendon, *A Nation Under Lawyers* (Farrar Strauss Giroux 1994), and Mona Harrington, *Women Lawyers: Rewriting the Rules* (Alfred A. Knopf 1994).

boom times, increasing firm revenues, and increasingly inappropriate focus on billable hours. Their rebellion was inevitable. In 1990, the ABA reported that dissatisfaction among all lawyers increased by 27 percent; among women—especially women partners—the increase was more than 50 percent higher.[12]

Now, as the influence of large corporations and megafirms is waning and women are making their mark, shifting generational values are also beginning to be felt. According to William Strauss and Neil Howe, the generation that walked lock-step into the organizations of the 1950s and 1960s (the "Silent Generation") valued conformity and climbing the ladder of success. The Baby Boomers espoused the same values as they settled into careers and families, but as they enter mid-life they are returning to their earlier revolutionary attitudes. "The Boom elite will assiduously maintain individual identities apart from institutions," contend Strauss and Howe in *Generations: The History of America's Future, 1584 to 2069.* "Many a Boomer will work for a corporation and have a business (or profit-making hobby) on the side. Feeling in control of their choices, midlifers will make career switches easily. Turnover will rise in top-level jobs."

It's not surprising, then, that many lawyers in their 40s have chosen self-employment as a better way to achieve satisfaction. At the same time, more and more two-career couples are frustrated with the balancing act required by two jobs, neither of which encourages (or even allows) spending time with family. The frustration can lead one or both partners to try designing a solo career. As Baby Boomers age, the trend is likely to accelerate.

Charles Handy predicts in *The Age of Unreason* that most workers will put together a "portfolio" career that enables them to use their talents in many places rather than in one full-time job. He believes that as the aging population devises new ways to stay active, the word "retirement" will become as obsolete as the word "servant" is today.

And what about the next generation? Unlike the "Silent" and "Boom" generations, the next generation—called the 13th by Strauss and Howe, and popularly referred to as Generation X—has none of the old loyalties. "Their self-esteem rests heavily on their hopes for economic success—a fact confirmed by countless youth polls over the past decade," say Strauss and Howe. "For many, the clearest path to success may be to leave elder-led institutions and strike out on their own." "Generation X is definitely not going to be workaholic," says Bob Filipczak, who wrote about this phenomenon for *Training* magazine. "They're not going to marry a job."

---

12. The overall increase among women was 41 percent. Among women partners, however, dissatisfaction jumped 280 percent, from 15 percent in 1984 to 42 percent in 1990!

Lawyers of this generation have only recently entered the profession, but their presence is already noticeable. We've heard Baby Boomer partners complain that young associates lack a "work ethic." When probed, they explain the "work ethic" as a willingness to sacrifice one's personal life for the good of the firm.[13] These partners want their associates to work enormous numbers of hours on the chance they will eventually share the largesse by being invited to partnership. If the associates don't perform to expectations, they're let go, then often rehired on an hourly basis by another law firm. It's no loss for many Generation X associates. They appreciate their high salaries but don't mind earning less money in exchange for more free-time and less pressure. This clash in values has also contributed to the rise of contract lawyer arrangements.

RETOOLING FOR THE FUTURE

As with the industrial and commercial markets it serves, the law firm must change if it is to thrive. This is a shock to many lawyers who consider the prosperous years of the 1980s their birthright, and the uncertainty of current times a temporary and unfair aberration.

Only a few years ago, some commentators were predicting that the megafirms would take over the profession. They would continue to grow in numbers of lawyers and geographic coverage, squeezing out mid-sized and even large firms, at least in urban markets. In 1989, for example, an article in a symposium on large firms predicted "an accelerating trend toward larger and more diverse law firms," modeled on the Big Eight accounting firms.[14]

This is no longer a course experts can see. Rather, many big law firms have abandoned aggressive expansion—and some are actually getting smaller. On the other hand, specialty boutiques, mostly spin-offs from the large firms, are proliferating. As a 1995 *American Lawyer* report on "The Big Firm - Small Firm Debate" asserted, big firms can no longer take their leadership role for granted.

---

13. One third-year associate was criticized in her annual review for not showing enough commitment to the firm. A few months earlier she had let the firm know that she might have to work part-time during the end of a difficult pregnancy—even though she actually billed more hours that period than anyone else in her department. The firm explained its disappointment by saying that work should be her first priority.

14. James F. Fitzpatrick, "Legal Future Shock: The Role of Large Firms by the End of the Century," 64 *Ind. L.J.* 461, 462-63 (1989).

Law firms thought they were thinking like businesses when, during the 1980s, they became obsessed with the bottom line. But astute observers say they were not acting enough like businesses. Overcharging clients, engaging in short-term thinking, rewarding inefficiency—what business based on such principles will survive?

In the next few years, with a saturated market and sophisticated consumers, the firms and lawyers that succeed will have to—surprise!—be more entrepreneurial and service-oriented. The opportunities will be there, but mostly for those who can focus on client needs, spot market openings and change rapidly. Lawyers will be paid for their wisdom and counseling rather than their ability to produce stacks of documents. Firms will thrive by minimizing overhead and entering into partnerships with other professionals to form flexible service teams. More than one observer has suggested that contract lawyers are a key to the competitive future of the law firm.

Part II

WHAT
EVERY
CONTRACT
LAWYER
SHOULD
KNOW

3

THE CASE FOR WORKING AS A CONTRACT LAWYER

Thousands of lawyers across the country turn to contract lawyering to express workstyle preferences, to enhance job satisfaction and to support transitions within the profession or to other careers.

Lawyers do contract work for different reasons. Some prefer it to other ways of practicing law; others would rather be doing something else, but see contract work as a temporary solution to their cash flow needs, confusion or other transition problems. These five lawyers typify the lawyers who practice on a contract basis:

- *Katherine Foldes has completed over 350 projects in the areas of real estate, personal injury, debtor-creditor, family law and more since she started doing contract work in Portland, Oregon, in 1984. When she began her contract career, she had no law firm experience and was starting a family. First, she headed to the law library to check ads for legal research and writing services. Then she posted her own, making certain it looked better than the others. Word of mouth soon took over. She works around her children's schedules, stopping daily when they return from school. Although she has broadened her expertise into trial consulting, she still loves contract research and writing and has no plans to move on to a different career.*
- *Tom Singman was married with two children when he quit working as an associate for a solo practitioner who treated law as a series of emergencies. Singman advertised his availability to work on a project basis for other lawyers, thinking he could find enough research, writing and legal analysis assignments to support his family if he didn't have to invest in conventional office overhead. An attorney in a three-person law*

firm handling a huge patent case opposed by three other firms responded to his ad. The firm was facing a stack of summary judgment motions and interrogatories and needed help fast. Singman worked on a provisional basis, writing responses to the summary judgment motions. The other lawyers respected his work and asked him to join the firm.

- *Cindy Vranizan, a Seattle lawyer, used contract work to get started in the profession when she found herself still unemployed two years after graduation from law school. She had to beg for her first assignment from a family friend, but that one led to others. Much of her success can be attributed to her not being afraid to ask other lawyers for work, and her willingness to adjust her fee schedule to reflect her lack of experience. As a result of her pricing strategy, the first year she earned far less than her classmates with law firm jobs. Two years later, though, Vranizan was doing better financially than most of her peers, while enjoying her career more.*

- *San Francisco lawyer Steve Weinstein had contract work thrust upon him in 1988. After working five years for the federal government and eight years for Safeway as in-house counsel, he found himself the victim of a leveraged buy-out. With the help of a temporary placement agency, he has supported himself ever since with contract assignments. Weinstein estimates that half his assignments have come through the temporary agency; the rest he has found on his own without investing much time in marketing. He charges between $55 and $78 per hour. Due to what he describes as "professional dissatisfaction, a market glut, and declining ethics of law practice," Weinstein plans to leave the practice of law eventually.*

- *Peter Zerilli of New York City is another "transitional" contract lawyer. He left his associate position at Skadden Arps in 1991 to attend graduate school, thinking he was leaving the law altogether. When he found his advanced degree in Soviet studies less useful than his law background, he turned to contract work. "It pays better than most of my available alternatives," he explains, and it supports him while he's launching a writing career. He has worked mostly in long-term, on-site assignments with medium-sized New York law firms, making about $45 per hour and finding time for his personal writing.*

In general, lawyers choose contract work for one of three reasons: workstyle preference, career satisfaction or transition support.

WORKSTYLE PREFERENCES

Increased acceptance of the contract work option—as well as other alternative work arrangements—has enabled many lawyers to practice their profession in a way that is more compatible with their personalities, preferences and lifestyle concerns.

AUTONOMY

Working on a contract basis allows lawyers to be in charge of their own careers rather than prisoners to law firm or client expectations. They can decide when and how much they want to work, what kinds of projects they want to accept and with whom they work.

The ability to say "no"—whether or not they ever exercise it—gives them a feeling of control. Seattle lawyer Susan Shulenberger likes "the independence of being able to pick and choose" clients and projects, and to extricate herself when she realizes she's in a bad situation. Hindi Greenberg reports turning down a three-month assignment because it overlapped with a previously scheduled backpacking trip. They have the freedom to take a day off just because they feel like it—even if it means working late the night before.

The sense that they are in charge of their own careers can more than compensate for the fear that they won't make it. "I just love being my own boss," says Lee Archer of New Orleans, expressing the feelings of many contract lawyers.

FLEXIBILITY

"I am not someone who is gung ho to spend seven days a week on law," says Sue Samuelson of Seattle, who has worked as a contract lawyer for four years. "Contract work gives me so many options. It's a lot easier to like what you do when it's two days a week rather than your entire life." Former contract lawyer Robert Thomas describes contract lawyers as "people who don't want to lose their souls to the law." San Francisco solo practitioner Richard Kaplan sees them as people who want to "remove the chains from their ankles."

Most contract lawyers learn to expect flood times as well as dry spells. Although the unpredictable flow of work can cause cash flow worries, those who choose contract lawyering consider the anxiety the price of having time to do other things with life. Lawyers with ambitions in the arts appreciate the flexibility of contract work. Contract assignments can support them while they work on a novel, pursue an acting career or spend time with a jazz trio that may never make a record but is much in demand at local clubs.

Others have time-consuming hobbies and use their legal talent to support their passion. Skiers disappear in the winter, sailors disappear in the summer. One formerly high-powered lawyer bought a country home and switched to contract work so he could indulge his passion for gardening. Hindi Greenberg took up contract work in the 1980s because "it allowed me the time to go backpacking when I like, to garden when I like, to train horses for free when I like."

David Welch used long-term contract assignments from New York City firms to fund a series of adventures. In 1989, he spent ten months in the Caribbean reading, scuba diving and serving as a camera assistant on a documentary film shoot. Five years later, he visited 21 states on a 21,000 mile New York to Seattle car trip. He also worked as a location manager on independent film projects in New York, house-sat a film director's home in Beverly Hills, and lingered in Montana working in a bookstore. By mid-1995, he was again employed as a contract lawyer for a well-respected Seattle law firm, based on a hunch that he'd found the place he'd like to settle.

VARIETY

Lawyers who appreciate the variety of contract work thrive on dealing with different personalities and work styles. Many also need the stimulation of learning different areas of the law. "I worked on a newspaper before I went to law school," says Elizabeth Bottman. "I really love the variety of issues that come up in my contract work. To me, this is really exciting."

TIME FOR FAMILY

Linda Gill Taylor, founder of the contract lawyer agency Of Counsel in Kansas City, Missouri, places many young mothers as contract lawyers:

> *They're usually in their mid-30s, highly regarded and very skilled former associates or partners of mid-sized to large law firms who were essentially driven out of their firms because they couldn't work out a meaningful part-time arrangement. "I was a star and now I'm being viewed as a problem," they say. They eventually realize that they aren't problems; they're still stars. So I work with them to reorganize their practices so they can work their own hours.*

Laura Masurovsky, a 1984 Harvard Law School graduate, quit a part-time position with a prestigious Washington, D.C., law firm when her third child was born. She accepts occasional assignments through Baltimore-based placement agency Special Counsel. "I don't have to look over my shoulder when I have three pediatrician appointments in a row," says Masurovsky. "And I don't have to answer to anyone if I have only three billable hours one day." She believes that doing contract work is preferable to being on the mommy track in a large law firm. "It's very professional. People are grateful for my help. I come in to do battle, or to uncover a brilliant option for counsel. Then I leave it on his desk and go home." [1]

New York lawyer Michelle Englander also appreciates the benefits of contract work. She accepted a two-day-per-week, two-month assignment with a solo practitioner when she had a toddler. As she prepared for the birth of her second child, she stayed closer to home and handled closings of cooperative sales for a real estate management company. "It's very enjoyable to get out of the house and put on my lawyer clothes," she explains.[2]

CAREER SATISFACTION

Many lawyers think an alternative job or career is the only cure for dissatisfaction with their current professional situation. But leaving the law may be too drastic a solution. More and more contract lawyers renew their career satisfaction by concentrating on tasks they *do* enjoy to benefit hiring lawyers who *don't* enjoy those tasks.

THE ABILITY TO CONCENTRATE ON THE RIGHT WORK

Fierce competition for clients and the intricacies of modern law firm management have alienated many formerly contented practitioners, especially those who relish the intellectual and creative challenges of the law. Contract work can be a solution for lawyers who enjoy the pure practice of law—legal analysis, research, writing, and problem solving, court appearances and depositions, for example—rather than the business of law—dealing with law firm expectations, courting and keeping clients, shepherding a case through the court system for months or years at a time and managing other lawyers and clerical staff.

Chris Green, a small-firm Michigan lawyer who works with contract lawyers, notes that the interpersonal aspects of law are nearly incompatible with legal analysis and writing. "The up-front work moves at such a fast pace that it's tough to slow down for the kind of methodical analysis that can make or break a case," she says.

---

1. Jaclyn Fierman, "The Contingency Work Force," *Fortune,* January 24, 1994.
2. Pamela Mendels, "They'll Make It Brief: Temp Lawyers Seek Limited Duty," *New York Newsday,* February 29, 1988.

"The more active one gets in trial work, it seems, the less able one is to write a persuasive brief."

Green often asks a contract lawyer to handle the background work—and indeed, this is what many contract lawyers most enjoy. Sue Samuelson loves to ghostwrite briefs, figure things out, bounce ideas around with the partner who spends all his time talking on the phone or running to meetings. Tom Singman likes research, writing, legal analysis and strategizing, and his stint as a contract lawyer allowed him to concentrate on those tasks. Cindy Vranizan, who's adept at preparation and negotiation, works in tandem with a skilled trial lawyer. Other contract lawyers prefer the "up front" work. One booming area of contract practice in California is "appearance" work; lawyers advertise their services to handle routine court appearances for a flat fee.

LIMITED CLIENT CONTACT

Many lawyers feel, deep in their hearts, that "client contact" is much overrated as a source of professional satisfaction. Some clients just never seem to sleep—and their problems can keep you from sleeping too. Sue Samuelson says:

> One of the reasons I withdrew from my partnership to work on a contract basis is that I was really tired of whiny clients. Whenever a former client would phone with a new problem, I'd automatically think to myself, "Oh God, now what's the matter?" I should have been happy clients were calling me—that's the whole name of the game—but I prefer it when I don't have to deal with them.

Former Colorado contract lawyer Peter Ludwig echoes Samuelson's sentiments. He loved "being remote," that is, never having to answer the phone or fight with clients and other lawyers. "Me and the books and the problems and the computer was fun!"

AVOIDING OFFICE POLITICS

Ludwig also found he could avoid office politics by taking temporary assignments. "I didn't like the scheduling demands and bickering, games being played and one-upsmanship of handling cases. I saw myself as a Super Adjuster—a more sophisticated and highly paid claims adjuster who wasn't very valued by either the law firm or the client." Elizabeth Bottman notes that "law firms tend to chew up associates and spit them out. There's also the conformity that's required, like driving the right car. I don't want to be a part of that." Sue Samuelson sends the same message in different words. "I end up liking everybody in the office because I don't know what their faults are. It's one of the advantages of contract work: not having to deal with the everyday politics."

TRANSITION ASSISTANCE

More lawyers than ever are "in transition." New graduates can't find jobs; veterans lose their positions in layoffs, mergers and closures. Dissatisfied lawyers want to escape the pressures of their law jobs for more rewarding work outside the law or as solo practitioners. Contract work can help smooth all kinds of transitions.

A BRIDGE INTO THE PROFESSION

New admittees unable to find jobs in a saturated market turn to contract work to gain experience and exposure to potential employers. In fact, contract work is fast becoming—like summer clerkships during law school and judicial clerkships after graduation—an accepted way to find a first-year associate position. Wiebke Breuer, fresh out of law school, approached small firms in her area, expressing her willingness to work hard and her eagerness to learn. One firm hired her on a contract basis. When it had enough business to support another full-time associate, she was offered the position.

TO REENTER THE PROFESSION

Lawyers also use contract work as a means to reenter the profession after interrupting their careers for childrearing or trying out another line of work. Contract work can help them decide whether they really want to come back while providing the opportunity to showcase their skills in the legal marketplace. Janine Iverson left her public defense career in 1988 to try a career in sales. Four years later, she decided she missed the intellectual challenge of law and found a contract position. This year, she was promoted to "of counsel" status with the firm.

TO SUSTAIN A NEW SOLO PRACTICE

Lawyers starting solo practices can augment their incomes with contract work while developing a full clientele. John Costa backed into contract work when he left a large firm with a business client that couldn't sustain his practice then but probably would in the future. He tried to market himself to other law firms as "of counsel" but found no takers. What he did find was interest in having him come in as a contract lawyer. Now he shares office space with a mid-sized commercial firm; he can serve his existing client, develop more business, and cover his overhead and expenses with the commercial litigation projects he handles on an hourly basis for the law firm.

TO FIND ANOTHER JOB IN THE PROFESSION

Many contract lawyers use contract work to broaden their experience and improve their chance of finding a next job in the legal profession. New York placement agency Special Counsel estimates that 25 percent of its temporary placements turn permanent every year. Robert Wilson used a temporary assignment through Special Counsel to find a permanent position after he lost his job at a Wall Street firm. In 1990, he responded to a blind ad placed by Special Counsel to work for another Manhattan firm on what was expected to be a short-term assignment. After starting with glorified paralegal work, he wrote the responses to a series of complex summary judgment motions. Several months later, Wilson's job search paid off with an offer from a firm in Philadelphia. Realizing it did not want to lose him, the New York firm made him a permanent job offer he could not refuse.

TO MAINTAIN SKILL LEVEL AND ENTHUSIASM WHILE UNEMPLOYED

Wilson's contract assignment gave him more than the opportunity to find a permanent job: it also enabled him to get out of the house and keep his mind active:

> *I noticed in the first couple of days back at work that I had to rediscover my thinking and analytical processes and I was grateful that because of the temporary assignment my skills didn't "rust." After a couple of months without a job I also got bored. Unemployment wasn't fun any more. The contract position got my mind off my nervousness.*

TO GENERATE INCOME WHEN BETWEEN JOBS

The lawyers in this category typically lost their jobs through layoffs, mergers or closures. Chris Maiocchi had 20 years of in-house real estate experience before her job as vice-president of real estate at Paine Webber disappeared. In 1994, she worked on a temporary half-time assignment at IBM while hunting for a full-time job. "Continuing on a temporary basis could be enticing," she said, "if there were some way to work out a good health care package." At the time, though, she was grateful to have the work in a depressed real estate market; her experience as a contract lawyer was, in her words, "definitely a plus."

Zoe Topsfield was laid off, along with most of the other lawyers in the corporate department of her Los Angeles firm. Rather than looking for another job, she tried contract work. She found one long-term assignment through an agency, then connected with a friend in San Francisco who asked her to handle court appearances in Los Angeles. At that point she decided to establish her own practice rather than return to the insecurity of someone else's practice. She continues to accept contract assignments because "contract work pays money quickly, and real clients don't."

TO SUPPORT A TRANSITION OUT OF THE LEGAL PROFESSION

Contract work can also help with transitions out of the law and into other careers. A flexible work schedule gives lawyers in transition time to study, write, or start a business.

Steve Weinstein's contract assignments allow him to pursue his goal of becoming a financial planner by taking classes and obtaining the necessary licenses. Peter Zerilli uses contract work to pay the bills while he tries to establish himself as a writer. "It's not a permanent job, which is a very important psychological factor for me," he says about his current long-term assignment at a New York firm. "I can still feel I'm doing something leading toward the goal of supporting myself by writing full time."

For Dorothy Streutker, contract work started as a source of income while attending seminary so she could begin a new career as a minister. But a long-term contract assignment on a death penalty appeal helped her see that she could apply her religious convictions to her law practice. Now, in part because of the work she has done as a contract lawyer, she has decided to remain in law but to change direction and practice in a way that's more in accord with her spiritual interests.

TO CONFIRM A CHOICE TO LEAVE THE PROFESSION

Many lawyers test their suitability to the practice of law by hopping from job to job—a year here, a year there, trying out large firms and small, government practice and in-house corporate roles—until their résumés demonstrate both their skill at finding jobs and their lack of loyalty and commitment. Contract work is a far less painful and damaging way to learn the same lesson. By accepting assignments in different environments and handling a variety of projects for wide-ranging personality types, lawyers experiment without going through the trauma of a series of job changes.

Lawyers who want to leave the profession, but accept contract assignments to tide them over until they find another job, can also use contract work to test their decisions. Both Michael Krantz and Rob Schoenmaker were supporting wives and children when they decided to leave their secure positions—Krantz as in-house counsel with an insurance company, Schoenmaker as an associate with an insurance defense firm. Both solicited contract assignments while they searched for their next jobs. Escaping the long hours, contentious opponents and pressures of litigation did not restore their sense of satisfaction. Rather, their freelance experiences confirmed the wisdom of their original decisions to abandon the practice of law altogether.

CONCLUSION

The message of this chapter boils down to one word: versatility. Contract work is as valuable an option for lawyers trying to stay afloat financially as it for those seeking flexibility and control over the shape of their legal careers. It is not a good choice for every lawyer, though. The next two chapters explore some of the risks and provide a framework to help you decide whether this work option is right for you.

4

WEIGHING THE RISKS

Contract work is not the right solution for every unhappy lawyer. But it's not fraught with the horrors that some would have you believe. As with most choices in life, real benefits coexist with definite disadvantages.

Some say you'll ruin your career prospects because only lawyers who can't find permanent jobs would stoop to temporary employment. Others insist contract work is a great way to secure a permanent position in today's legal marketplace. We heard so many contradictory and misleading statements that we decided to devote a chapter to separating the myths from the realities.

MYTH: CONTRACT LAWYERING IS A RADICAL CONCEPT.

This comment might surprise Shirley Hufstedler, the retired Ninth Circuit Court of Appeals judge, now a partner with Morrison & Foerster in Los Angeles. She began her legal career over 40 years ago as a contract lawyer. She started by "ghost-writing" briefs for other lawyers, then was asked to argue the motions and assist at trials, and later became known as a litigation specialist. Although she eventually developed her own practice, she continued to be retained by other lawyers for work on complex litigation matters until she was appointed to the bench.[1]

Indeed, contract lawyers have a long and honorable history. Bob Webster of The Lawsmiths observes that lawyers have always hired other lawyers to help out temporarily when they were overworked, or needed expertise in another area. The megafirms of the 1980s replaced these informal relationships with hordes of associates; the shrinking of those firms has brought back contract lawyer arrangements.

---

1.   From an interview in Adele M. Scheele, *Skills for Success* (Wm. Morrow & Co. 1979).

MYTH: CONTRACT EMPLOYMENT IS NOT A PROFESSIONAL WAY TO WORK; IT DEGRADES THE PROFESSION.

Seattle lawyer Robert Thomas disagrees with the assertion, but understands its roots:

> *Lawyers are beginning to see contract lawyers as a more important and significant part of the profession, but they're still largely regarded as second-class citizens. Maybe that's because lawyers value stability so much. People who choose contract lawyering as a way of life are people who lack, or don't need, stability. They're not really building anything, especially if they're bopping from firm to firm.*
>
> *It may help to compare the situation to society's attitude toward working women before the equal rights movement: most employers believed that women didn't need to make as much money as men because their husbands were the primary providers. As a result, those who worked in traditionally female professions were paid much less and accorded much less status. Lawyers tend to view contract lawyers the same way. If they needed the money, they'd take stable jobs. If they can't find one, they're not worth paying for. We're fighting prejudices that will take years to overcome.*

Others relate the attitude to the notion that truly "professional" lawyers are continuously available to their clients. This objection has also been voiced against permanent part-time arrangements with law firms. The strongest counter argument is identical: *No lawyer in private practice is continuously available to any client.* If they were, failure to return telephone calls and stay in communication would not be the client population's main criticism of their lawyers.[2]

In any event, increasingly sophisticated communications technology has lessened the need to be in the office daily. "Our contract counsel only wants to work a limited number of hours each week and oftentimes her clients, who are at work 40-hours plus per week, need to get a hold of her," says Michelle Petrilli, chief marketing counsel of PNC Bank. "She has a beeper and a fax machine in her home. Even though she is only in the office on a 20-hour maximum basis per week, she's available for questions at all times."[3]

Another lawyer objects to contract lawyering as a force that "commoditizes the

---

2. "Disciplinary Notes," *Washington Lawyer*, September/October 1994.

3. "Temp Time: Are You Ready?," *Corporate Legal Times*, September 1994.

legal profession in a way that is damaging." He worries that the distinctions between lawyer and client are blurred, especially when an agency is involved. Who is the contract lawyer's client? The agency? The hiring lawyer? The hiring lawyer's client? All three? To whom does the contract lawyer owe first loyalty? The Rules of Professional Conduct, as well as industry practice and understanding, all point to the hiring lawyer's client. But discomfort with changing practices—as well as change itself—causes more tradition-bound practitioners to object to contract lawyer arrangements.

MYTH: YOU'LL RUIN YOUR CAREER PROSPECTS.

According to U.S. Department of Labor statistics, contingent workers—including part-timers, temporary, per-diem workers, leased employees, extra workers, supplementals, freelancers, independent contractors, and consultants—comprised 25 percent of the work force in 1988. The *Wall Street Journal* reported that one-quarter of all new positions in the early 1990s were assigned on a temporary, contract or consulting basis. Some labor experts estimate that eventually three out of every seven workers will be hired on a temporary basis.[4]

Time magazine writer Lance Morrow observed in 1993 that:

> *America has entered the age of the contingent or temporary worker, of the consultant and subcontractor, of the just-in-time work force—fluid, flexible disposable. . . . Its message is this: You are on your own. [T]he workers of the future will constantly have to sell their skills, invent new relationships with employers who must, themselves, change and adapt constantly in order to survive in a ruthless global market.[5]*

Would-be employees, therefore, must repackage themselves as purveyors of skills, interchangeable to a wide variety of employers. "People have got to look at employment as a temporary assignment," concluded Kirk Johnson in the *New York Times.* "Where people used to be loyal to a company, now they're loyal to a profession." [6] Thus, the choice to work on a contract basis, rather than being a career breaker, may assure your longevity.

Career counselor and former practicing lawyer Kathy Meija Morris of Chicago believes "the jury is still out" on what impact a history of freelance assignments will

---

4. Lance Morrow, "The Temping of America," *Time,* March 29, 1993.

5. Id.

6. Kirk Johnson, "Workplace Evolution Alters Office Relationships," *New York Times,* October 5, 1994.

have on a lawyer's career. In the short term, you certainly won't find the prestige that partnership in a well-respected law firm confers. But prominent former contract lawyers like Shirley Hufstedler would disagree that a period of contract employment is synonymous with failure. So would Robert Thomas, who was debating a permanent exit from the profession when he accepted a contract assignment that led to a partnership offer. Michael Anderson served as a contract lawyer for several small companies before being invited inside as general counsel for a nationally-traded corporation. Many other experienced lawyers and new admittees featured in this book would also take issue; they developed thriving solo practices, the contacts that led to their next full-time employment or a lucrative specialty practice by first taking on piecework from other lawyers.

It is true that some members of the legal community see contract work as the refuge of the second-rate lawyer. Because of this, you risk being considered someone who couldn't make it in the "real" world by those who are ignorant about the realities of contract lawyering. But the versatility of this career option, as well as its prominent place in the future of the profession, make its lack of any well-defined career path a real blessing.

MYTH: YOU CAN'T CREATE A SECURE FUTURE BY BEING A CONTRACT LAWYER.

Most would agree that modern conventional employment guarantees neither security nor success. "The so-called security of a regular paycheck is an illusion," claims political consultant Jody Severson.[7]

Finding true security requires developing one's own expertise. Tom Peters, best known for writing *In Search of Excellence*, tells of an independent house painter whose reputation for reliability, care and creativity makes him much in demand. His fabulous reputation, Peters argues, gives him *real* stability—more reliable in today's business environment than "a corporate logo on a paycheck."

Similarly, lawyers today must rely on their own resources, not the whims (and fortunes) of their employers, if they want job security. We talked to many lawyers who were laid off from large law firms or downsized out of in-house legal departments, but developed long-term security through a series of contract assignments.

MYTH: YOU WON'T BE ABLE TO GET THE EMPLOYMENT BENEFITS YOU NEED.

When it comes to insurance, a contract lawyer resembles a solo practitioner or partner in a small law firm. It's up to the contract lawyer to obtain an individual policy. The good news is that practically every bar association in the country,

---

7. Anne Murphy, "Do-It-Yourself Job Creation," *Inc.*, January 1994.

including the ABA, now offers attractively priced comprehensive group insurance policies for members.

"It's hard to take a vacation if you aren't getting paid while you're away," says contract lawyer Susan Shulenberger. "In that way it's much like having your own law practice." Indeed, all self-employed practitioners—whether working alone or in a firm—sacrifice income when on vacation unless associates or contract lawyers can handle the work in their absence. Aside from the income loss, however, contract lawyers may do better than solo and small firm lawyers, many of whom can't leave the office behind. "I went into partnership with another lawyer with the idea that we would cover each other's absences, but it hasn't worked," says Doug Christopher, a partner in a small law firm. "The problem is that my cases are under control when I'm away but when my partner leaves, there's always a big crisis." Solo practitioner Daniel Edwards brings his computer on every vacation and calls his office daily.

Contract lawyers usually don't experience these problems. As long as they notify their regular customers of upcoming absence, their time away is truly their own. No client emergencies or office crises follow them. They can even arrange their time off so that no assignments await them when they return.

MYTH: YOU'LL FEEL LIKE A "LOSER LAWYER."

In the last 15 years or so, "successful" (and therefore good) lawyers have come to be defined as the ones with the highest incomes or most prominent media profiles. As a result, many able lawyers feel unsuccessful. At the same time, the rewards of law firm life have diminished. Surviving to partnership consideration can mean fulfilling criteria you didn't know existed until you learned you didn't meet them. Having your legal abilities judged by your billable hours can be frustrating and disillusioning.

If you listen to those who are caught up in conventional definitions of success, you might feel less than competent. But for most contract lawyers, the experience of working for themselves brings renewed faith in their abilities.

After working in a law firm where everyone was considered brilliant and an expert, with lawyers who could and did teach the law, Denise Kuhlman was demoralized by always being told she didn't know enough. Only a few assignments into her contract practice, she developed a new appreciation for the level of expertise she had honed in five years with a major firm: she knew a lot more than she thought she did. For Kuhlman, becoming a contract lawyer has removed, not reinforced, her sense of being a "loser."

SOME MYTH; SOME REALITY: YOU'LL BE PERCEIVED AS A "LOSER LAWYER."

Eugene Hardy, who chose contract work after nearly 20 years of government legal experience, has noticed that conventional practitioners still look down on contract lawyers. Their unspoken words are: *Why couldn't you get a real job? Should I trust someone who can't get a real job?*

Lawyers who have actually hired contract lawyers, however, have nothing but praise for their colleagues who choose this work. (To learn how contract lawyers are perceived by hiring lawyers, read Chapter 10.) Pick your audience well and you'll avoid this potential drawback of contract work!

SOME MYTH; SOME REALITY: YOU'LL NEVER HAVE CLIENT CONTACT.

For lawyers who love rainmaking and one-on-one communication with clients, contract work is probably not the way to go. Most contract lawyers work behind the scenes, and deal with clients, if at all, as a peripheral or secondary figure rather than as chief problem-solver and hand-holder. But not always. Trisha Mathers—who introduces Chapter 10—routinely assigns a contract lawyer to handle all client contact except the initial intake interview, the client's deposition and final settlement negotiations.

SOME MYTH; SOME REALITY: THE WORK YOU HANDLE WILL BE LESS CHALLENGING.

It's true that hiring lawyers don't want to do the work you're being assigned. That may mean it's tedious and unpleasant; it can also mean they don't have time for the thoughtful analysis you enjoy. Rochelle Kosnitsky loves the routine of her debt collection practice; the more times she handles the same type of matter, the more comfortable she feels about her life. Having to figure out a complex legal issue or apply facts to an unclear area of law increases her stress level beyond her tolerance. She therefore calls an experienced contract lawyer every time a novel situation arises. Would you rather do Kosnitsky's work or that of the contract lawyer she consults?

REALITY: YOU HAVE TO GET COMFORTABLE WITH AN UNCERTAIN WORK SCHEDULE.

"You never know from one hour to the next how long your services are going to be needed," says Steve Weinstein. He was asked once to set aside several months for depositions in a huge commercial case; a few weeks later the case settled. "Now I won't tell you I wasn't forewarned," he says. "But what do you do? Do you say 'Okay, I'll take my chances,' and wait to see if you get a three-month assignment? Or do you find another, less attractive assignment and say 'sayonara'?"

A contract assignment is temporary; that's the nature of the beast. You never know whether more work is right over the horizon or whether you should be hustling the next assignment. The erratic work schedule can prove wearing even to free spirits who thrive on a lack of structure in their lives. It's no different, though, from the life of any other private practitioner who bites his nails whenever business (inevitably) slows.

REALITY: YOU HAVE TO GET USED TO THE STRESS OF CONSTANT CHANGE.

Beth Cohen Besner tried freelance contract work in Miami, but returned to her old firm when she decided she preferred both the predictability and the types of assignments she received there. She found it stressful to have to impress each new hiring lawyer, and to adjust to different personalities and areas of law. To be happy as a contract lawyer, she learned, "you ought to be particularly easygoing."

REALITY: YOU MAY FEEL ISOLATED.

If you're used to an office environment, contract work can be lonely. An in-house contract assignment may bring you into daily contact with other human beings, but you can still feel lonely if you're treated like an outsider. You're even more likely to have trouble with isolation if you work out of your home. You can't just walk into the office down the hall when you feel like complaining; there's no secretary or receptionist to schmooze with when you need a break from the brief you're trying to finish. You have to make a real effort to find other lawyers for brain-storming strategy. It can be hard to find a mentor if you're a new lawyer. "For me it's a bit lonely," Elizabeth Bottman confesses. Unless you cherish every minute of solitude, you'll have to be deliberate about making human contact part of your routine, rather than getting it naturally through an office setting.

REALITY: CONTRACT WORK WILL NOT MAKE YOU RICH.

Our informal survey of contract lawyers across the country reveals typical annual incomes between $25,000 and $35,000, with some lawyers earning $100,000 or more in long-term in-house placements and others scraping by with occasional $250 projects. Although contract lawyers receive a respectable fee for almost every hour they bill, the slow times—and significant periods without work—do depress their incomes significantly compared with those of other practitioners. Most lawyers who choose contract work, however, downplay the importance of money in their lives. Many are seeking reasonably well-paid part-time employment and don't expect to earn hefty annual incomes. Others use their contract experience to build solid solo practices; their contract work leaves them in better shape their first year or two than if they hadn't accepted the assignments.

5

IS CONTRACT WORK RIGHT FOR YOU?

Just as all lawyers are not cut out to be top partners at high-pressure big city law firms, not all are suited to the free-spirited but unpredictable life of a contract lawyer. Preferences, personality, and life circumstances should all enter into your decision about whether to seek contract work.

William Bridges, an expert on the subjects of transition and employment and author of *JobShift*, identifies four qualifications for any kind of employment: (1) you really want to do the work (desire), (2) you are good at what the work requires (ability), (3) you are productive and happy in the work (temperament), and (4) you have whatever other resources the work requires (assets).

If you've graduated from law school, you have the ability and the assets to handle contract legal work. But while any lawyer can do contract work, certain traits and sources of satisfaction distinguish successful contract lawyers from those who try this option and decide to move on.

Do you want to work as a contract lawyer? Is contract work a reasonable option for you now? The self-evaluation process outlined on the following pages will help you decide whether you have the desire, the temperament and the personal and financial readiness for success.

EVALUATING DESIRE

Being a successful contract lawyer, like being a successful solo practitioner, requires a love of autonomy and independence, comfort with uncertainty, and the ability to take things as they come. When you read in Chapter 3 about lawyers' reasons for choosing contract work, did you feel a thrill of recognition? Did you think, yes, that's what I want? Or did the enumeration of the delights of contract lawyering make your skin crawl? Were you left cold—or worse, feeling anxious and uncomfortable? If you're not sure how you feel about it, the following should help.

A LOVE OF INDEPENDENCE

It is no coincidence that at the same time law firms have been redefining their missions and reengineering their structures, more and more lawyers have been deciding it's time to strike out on their own. Some are the victims of downsizings, but large numbers have simply had it with being employees. Even many casualties of cost-cutting end up viewing their termination as liberation.

One of the main appeals of contract work is feeling in control of your life—being able to do what you want to do rather than what the job description specifies, to work where and when you want, to escape office politics and other outside pressures. The most important question, therefore, is: do you want to be your own boss? Remember that with freedom comes responsibility, and if your income is the one on which you and your family rely, that responsibility is all the greater. Because the life and income level of the self-employed tend to be unpredictable, you'll do better if you have either a high tolerance for uncertainty or a strong desire to be on your own, or both. Take the quiz below to determine whether you have the appropriate spirit for self-employment.

NATURAL INCLINATIONS

The values clarification exercise on page 42 may help you decide whether

---

ARE YOU INDEPENDENT AT HEART?

1. Do you work best when you're in control of the project?
2. Do you tend to question authority?
3. Do you consider yourself a nonconformist or outsider?
4. Do you enjoy making your own rules?
5. Do you resent office politics and power games?
6. Is having control over the hours you work very important?
7. Do you work well by yourself?
8. Do you like spending time alone?
9. Are you motivated more by your own desire to do the job well than by the expectations of others?
10. Do you like variety and dealing with new challenges?

If you answer "yes" to most of these questions, you probably want to be on your own badly enough to overcome the inevitable problems and setbacks.

contract work suits your desires. Any lawyer who's moderately satisfied with the profession values achievement, intellectual challenge, justice, knowledge, power and influence, service to others, skill and work productivity. The values of people who love contract work also include adventure, autonomy, family, flexibility and variety. In contrast, if loyalty, recognition, safety and wealth make it into your top six, you will probably find more satisfaction in a permanent position.

LONG-RANGE PLANS

Think about where you're going in life. What are your goals? Does the free-lance lifestyle fit your vision of the future? If you want to raise self-sufficient, happy children, build a thriving solo practice or buy time to figure out your goals, contract work may suit you. On the other hand, you'd be better off pursuing other options if your goal is to save money for retirement, develop a reputation as the finest lawyer in your city or have a predictable schedule and income.

EVALUATING TEMPERAMENT

The successful contract lawyers we interviewed shared many traits. You have what it takes to succeed as a contract lawyer if you are:

Adaptable: cooperative, flexible; able to communicate and get along with all kinds of people; able to start and stop quickly; have good interpersonal skills and a sense of humor; work well under pressure.

Dorothy Streutker can "mold myself to the high-tension type A partners and at the same time I can get along with the secretaries."

Enterprising: ambitious and possessed of initiative; good at spotting and taking advantage of opportunities; adventurous about new situations and people.

Agency owner Werner Lewin placed an older lawyer with great credentials to handle a short project. Athough the law firm was located right across the street from his office, the contract lawyer mailed his finished work product and didn't enclose a cover letter or note inquiring whether the firm needed further help. "The guy was out of touch with reality," says Lewin. Contract lawyers are in business for themselves and must approach their work with an enterprising spirit.

Independent: able to work without supervision; a self-starter and self-motivated; enjoy working alone.

"I enjoy working alone, and I'm very motivated," says Cindy Vranizan. "I like being able to take a project, come back to my home office, and devote as many hours as I want until I get it done."

A Quick Study: able to absorb facts and new areas of law quickly.

"I'm the last of the generalists," says Susan Shulenberger. "I can learn new areas quickly," says Sue Samuelson. "With 15 years of experience, I can handle assignments without much start-up."

Humble: willing to take instructions and ask questions; to take direction from people less knowledgeable, skilled or experienced; to deal with criticism and pettiness without taking it personally.

New York City lawyer Bradley Rosenblatt couldn't stand being assigned to work for a first-year associate. "I'd say something shouldn't be in a contract and she'd insist that it must stay in. Then she'd check with the partner-in-charge who'd tell her I was right." Simon Jarvis was frustrated by his secondary role on a high-profile case. Although his research and analysis won the case, the partner wouldn't let him sign the pleadings or argue before the court. Neither Rosenblatt nor Jarvis understood the supporting role of a contract lawyer: a contract lawyer is there to get the job done, not to take the credit.

Conscientious: reliable, punctual and responsible, with high standards.

Laurie Craghead says, "I try to be conscientious and get the work done as fast as possible." George Hindin takes pride in his work even when doing something he doesn't enjoy.

Communicative: a good listener; not afraid to ask questions or seek clarification.

"I'm easy to reach and quick to communicate information to others," says Cindy Vranizan. "I'm good at keeping in touch with other lawyers."

Resourceful: good at managing time and money; organized and efficient; good at finding answers.

Chris Maiocchi attributes her success to her ability "to be a one-person operation."

If these traits do not apply to you, and if you really don't want to be your own boss, invest your time and energy in locating assignments that may lead to a permanent position. (See "Using Contract Work to Find a Job" at page 43.)

EVALUATING YOUR FINANCIAL READINESS

You don't always have the luxury of preparing financially for change. If you find yourself thrust without warning into the world of contract lawyering, skim this short section and do what you can after the fact. If you haven't yet left your job, or if you're planning to enter or return to the work force, consider both your financial and your personal readiness for this next step of your life.

VALUES CLARIFICATION EXERCISE

Read quickly through the following list of values, crossing out those that are least important to you. Then review the ones that are left, checking off those that are most important to you. When you have finished this second review, allocate an imaginary $1,000 to purchase the values you would most like to have, spending more for the qualities most essential to your sense of fulfillment. Assume you have none of those values now. Spend the entire $1,000, no more or less.

_____ Achievement (accomplishment; results brought about by persistence)

_____ Adventure/Excitement (action, risk and a fast pace)

_____ Autonomy (independence; personal freedom; control over decision-making)

_____ Creativity/Self-Expression (innovating new ideas, designs, solutions)

_____ Flexibility (a ready capability to adapt to changing requirements)

_____ Honesty/Authenticity (being frank and genuinely yourself with others)

_____ Humor/Wit (a sense of humor; holding things in perspective)

_____ Intellectual Challenge (learning new things; stimulating the mind)

_____ Justice/Fairness (treating others impartially; wanting equity for others)

_____ Knowledge (seeking truth, information, or principles out of curiosity)

_____ Love/Family (affection, intimacy, caring; attachment to a family)

_____ Loyalty (maintaining allegiance to a person, group or cause)

_____ Morality/Personal Integrity (maintaining ethical standards or honor)

_____ Power/Influence (having authority; power to change or get things done)

_____ Recognition (acknowledged as important or significant; respected)

_____ Safety/Security (protection from threat or danger)

_____ Service/Helping Others (devotion to others' interests; serving a cause)

_____ Skill/Competence (being good at something)

_____ Tangible Results (see, touch, hear, smell, or taste the results of effort)

_____ Variety (regular contact with a broad number and type of experiences)

_____ Wealth/Possession (owning things; ample money for things you want)

_____ Work Productivity (being actively productive)

When you have spent the entire $1,000, list the six items for which you spent the most money. These are the qualities you most value and ought to emphasize in your work.

1.

2.

3.

4.

5.

6.

USING CONTRACT WORK TO FIND A JOB

Contract work can be an effective way to secure a full-time job if you use the following strategy:

1. Target small to mid-sized law firms rather than solo practitioners. Although solo practitioners are an excellent source of contract work, they tend to prize their independence and have little desire to add to their payrolls.
2. Scour the classified ads, going beyond the "Positions Available" columns. Lawyers seeking office share arrangements or those who want to bring a successor on board in anticipation of retirement can be good prospects. A stint as a contract lawyer may convince either lawyer that you're the right person to fill a permanent slot.
3. Be flexible, and communicate your flexibility to prospective employers. When you write to firms, whether in response to their ads or as part of a targeted mailing, state in your cover letter that although you seek a full-time position, you are willing to prove your suitability by starting with contract assignments.
4. Remember that nowadays having a job is not a guarantee of anything. Your security depends as much on your own ability to develop and market your skills and reputation as on your employer's balance sheet and client development prowess. Whether you choose to be employed by others or by yourself, you must shift to entrepreneurial thinking. Working as a contract lawyer will sensitize you to others' needs and teach you how to appraise and take advantage of opportunity.

APPRAISE YOUR CURRENT FINANCIAL SITUATION.

Create a balance sheet—a summary of your assets and liabilities—and calculate your monthly expenditures. Do not guess at either total. From this information, calculate the cash reserves and income you'll need to maintain your spending patterns.

IDENTIFY CURRENT EXPENSES.

Pay particular attention to those directly related to your current employment situation (for example, commuting, parking, clothing, dry-cleaning, lunches, and entertaining clients). You might find that by working out of your home or by working fewer hours you will eliminate some expenses. You could also have time for household chores that you now pay others to handle for you.

CALCULATE THE FUNDS YOU'LL NEED.

Estimate the cost of setting up a home office and marketing your contract services. Don't be afraid to provide liberal sums here. It may take a while to recoup this up-front investment, but it is necessary. (See Appendix 2.) Include sums as well to cover living expenses for the several months it can take to become profitable. If you've already saved this amount, skip the rest of this discussion. If not, your next step is to accumulate the money you need to get started.

EVALUATE WHERE YOUR SPENDING CAN BE TRIMMED.

Then, begin cutting back. Watch out for "impulse buying," stop indulging in nonessentials like that daily latte or lunch out, and forego or postpone major purchases, vacations or expensive entertainment. Put your credit cards away and pay off any revolving debt you've incurred. Make a pact with your family to discuss and agree on every purchase above a specified price *before* it is made.

THINK ABOUT SUPPLEMENTING YOUR EARNINGS.

If there's not much fat in your budget or you want to save the necessary reserve fund faster, you can:

- *Take a second job, such as teaching a course in a continuing education program, accepting contract paralegal work through a temporary placement agency or serving as live-in manager of an apartment building.*
- *Rent extra space in your house or apartment for residence or storage. Take a close look at the possibilities—a spare bedroom, an unused recreation room, your garage or other off-street parking.*
- *Borrow from a relative, or from your retirement plan or life insurance policy. Draw upon credit card or home equity lines of credit only as a last resort.*
- *Use (or make sure you are compensated for) all your accrued vacation and sick leave; take advantage of any law firm sabbatical policy.*
- *Loot the kids' college account. If college is years away, you'll have time to recover the money; if college is fast approaching, the drop in your income could help your child qualify for financial aid and government loans.*
- *Sell items that you aren't using or that you are willing to trade for a more fulfilling work life. But don't sell your house if you can avoid it. The cost of replacement housing could exceed what you're paying now. You'll also aggravate the stress of job transition by imposing another major change upon yourself.*

EVALUATING PERSONAL READINESS

You need the cooperation and support of your family, spouse or partner, and children to succeed in any self-employment venture, including work as a contract lawyer. Find out in advance how much support you can count on.

EMOTIONAL SUPPORT

Question your spouse or partner closely about the feelings generated by your new course in life. If they're not comfortable with uncertainty, you may end up squabbling even if your spouse or partner earns a regular paycheck. If you are married to a lawyer who puts in killer hours at a law firm and is frustrated and unhappy, you could find yourself the target of envy or resentment. Try to anticipate emotional issues and explore them before you make the change.

CHILD CARE

Think about your children as well. Maybe you've chosen contract work so you can spend more time with your kids—but have you arranged child care from the moment you start marketing? Katherine Foldes strongly recommends that every parent attend to this detail *before* soliciting assignments. She learned through experience that it's better to postpone your start-up a few weeks than to have to turn work away because you can't get child care—or, worse, accept the project and do a second-rate job because your mind was on keeping your youngster out of the kitchen.

Full-time day care can be expensive, though, and you may feel you can't afford the expense before you have a steady income. Contract lawyer Hazel Lewis-Brown has these suggestions. Start with a part-time arrangement (and if possible trade time with friends or enlist a willing relative), but make sure any arrangement is regular and predictable, so that you can make appointments with potential clients. "It's fine not to be available on Tuesday," says Lewis-Brown, "if you can say with complete confidence, 'Let's have lunch on Wednesday.'" Be aware that, unless there's a grand-mother next door who can drop everything to help out, big fast-turnaround projects will not be suited to your schedule. Finally, you'll want to be sure you can command high enough hourly rates to compensate for time spent away from your family. (See Chapter 7.)

WORKING FROM HOME

Maintaining a functional home office presents special concerns if you have a family. Chapter 19 of Paul and Sarah Edwards' *Working From Home* explores some of the problems a home-based business can create in a long-term relationship. If you have children and use the home telephone line for your business, you'll need to pay attention to telephone etiquette issues. (Appendix 2 contains tips for equipping and running a home office.) If you plan to work while other family members are at home, you'll also have to establish physical and psychic boundaries. See Chapter 10 of Lionel L. Fisher's *On Your Own* for a thorough discussion of this concern.

6

A FOUNDATION FOR MARKETING YOUR SERVICES

Many contract lawyers make the mistake of not specifying what they have to offer, assuming they'll attract more business if they say they can handle any problem. We help you narrow your personal profile so you can reach your market more effectively.

If your idea of what you have to offer is unclear, you won't be able to convince other lawyers to pay for your services. Before you make your first marketing contact, spend time figuring out what will distinguish your résumé or brochure from those of your competitors.

The preparatory steps are these: Create a personal profile. Position your services as novice, experienced, specialist or niche lawyer. Then research your potential markets.

CREATE A PERSONAL PROFILE

It goes against logic but it's been proved time and again: *narrow your focus and you broaden your appeal.* Before tackling the usual résumé-type information, develop a self-portrait that focuses on your personal qualities and preferences, considering the attributes of personality traits, availability and skills.[1] The more

---

1. To develop a complete picture of what you have and want to offer, work through the self-assessment exercises in Deborah Arron's career planning book, *What Can You Do with a Law Degree?* (Niche Press 1999), or career books geared to the general population, such as Richard Bolles, *What Color Is Your Parachute?* (Ten Speed Press annually updated), Laurence G. Boldt, *Zen and the Art of Making a Living* (Penguin Arkana 1993), or Nancy Anderson, *Work with Passion* (Carroll & Graff 1995).

specifically you describe the assistance you can give, and the more confident you are that you will excel in that type of work, the more likely you are to find hiring lawyers to use your services.

PERSONALITY

Review the list of traits in Chapter 5 on pages 40 and 41, and pick the three that describe you best.

AVAILABILITY

What time commitment and schedule do you want: full-time projects of limited duration, a relatively steady 15 hours a week of work you can do at your convenience, or something in between? Can you work on site or must you maintain your own office? Are you willing to travel outside your neighborhood, region or even the country? How about telecommuting?

SKILLS

Read the lists of skills and tasks on page 49 and check those that best describe your abilities.

SUMMARY

Now incorporate the results of the previous exercises into a 25- to 50-word pro-file. Do not focus exclusively on your legal experience. Instead, describe yourself and what you do in an unexpected way, something like the mission statement of a business plan. For example, instead of a self-portrait like: "I'm a bankruptcy lawyer with seven years of experience," you might say:

> *I'm a "techie" with detailed knowledge of the bankruptcy code. I love high pressure and hand-to-hand combat.*

or

> *I'm independent and intellectual—I love analysis and strategy. I'd rather work behind the scenes, planning or writing the perfect brief, than negotiating or trying the case myself.*

or

> *I have a family and a working spouse, so I'd prefer to devote a steady four hours per day to legal research and writing and spend the rest of my time with my children. When my kids are older I'd like to develop a practice of my own, maybe in partnership with a lawyer who loves courtroom work.*

SKILLS CHECKLIST

GENERAL ABILITIES:

- act decisively in emergencies
- act on new information immediately
- assimilate new data quickly
- bring projects in on time and within budget
- deal well with the unexpected or critical event
- establish systems
- flourish in a highly competitive environment
- follow through
- handle many tasks and responsibilities efficiently
- quickly size up situations
- take responsibility for projects
- work well without supervision

DATA-RELATED SKILLS:

- analyze
- anticipate problems or needs
- apply what others have developed to new situations
- brainstorm
- clarify information
- classify expertly
- conceive new interpretations, concepts and approaches
- consolidate
- coordinate operations and details
- critique
- edit
- file to facilitate retrieval
- find practical applications for ideas
- gather information
- generate solutions
- interview individuals to obtain information
- keep others informed
- keep track of details
- organize
- persuade
- proofread
- read quickly and comprehensively
- recognize the need for, and locate, outside experts
- strategize
- summarize
- synthesize and organize volumes of material
- troubleshoot
- update
- write persuasively

PEOPLE-RELATED SKILLS:

- allay fears
- clarify values and goals of others
- communicate technical concepts
- confront others with difficult personal matters
- counsel
- deal with difficult people
- develop rapport and trust
- disseminate information accurately
- empathize
- employ "active listening"
- explain complicated theories or procedures in simple terms
- gain cooperation among diverse interests
- give professional advice
- handle emotional outbursts
- hone and use powers of observation
- identify problems, needs and solutions
- listen critically and intently
- negotiate
- perceive and assess the potential of others
- persuade
- resolve conflicts
- sell a program or course of action to decision-makers
- speak clearly, articulately and engagingly
- speak cogently and persuasively
- think quickly

POSITION YOUR SERVICES

The next step is to evaluate your experience, in terms of both years of practice and areas of expertise, and define your market position as (1) novice, ranging from recent graduates to those with up to two years of experience, (2) experienced lawyer, having worked in private practice, government or a corporate environment for more than a couple of years, (3) specialist in a particular subject matter or practice, or (4) niche lawyer, distinguished by background or knowledge base rather than years of experience.

Some hiring lawyers will prefer new admittees to whom they can pay lower hourly rates even if it means they must spend time on supervision and training. Others will want practitioners with enough experience to work on their own, or even to take over a case entirely. There's room for all experience levels. Let's look at them more closely.

THE NOVICE

Unless you have developed a special subject matter or skills expertise that places you in the niche category, you belong here if you're a new admittee, first- or second-year associate, or someone who's been developing a solo practice since graduation a couple years ago. Evaluate what distinguishes you from your classmates. Get away from the message you learned in law school that the only meaningful markers are your law school's reputation, your grades and whether or not you belonged to law review.

Instead, list both law-related and non-law experiences that give you a knowledge base or orientation different from that of your peers. Do you have clerking or externship experience you can emphasize, or did you study an unusual area in law school? Did your college construction jobs help you understand how sub-contractor disputes arise? Did your retail sales experience teach you the art of persuasion or how to deal with difficult people? Are you adept at interviewing clients because you volunteered at your law school's legal clinic? Illustrate your background in a way that reflects both the breadth and the depth of your "life credits."

THE EXPERIENCED LAWYER

If you've worked as a lawyer for more than a couple of years, you've probably developed skills that can be worth a lot to hiring lawyers—e.g., facility in spotting legal issues, efficient work habits, the ability to think creatively about problems and to learn new areas of the law quickly, and familiarity with court procedures. But what distinguishes you from your equally accomplished peers? To define yourself,

YOUR HISTORY OF ACHIEVEMENTS

List your accomplishments in the practice of law. These achievements need not have been acknowledged by others, nor be remarkable in any way.

Begin with the areas you checked in the exercise at page 49. You can also review your calendars, diaries, work product examples and case or client files. Go back no more than ten years.

For each, describe in writing the work you did. Include both the nature of the project and the results you achieved, being specific about dollars involved, time consumed, and other objective measures. If possible, find examples of your work product for each project—e.g., correspondence, pleadings, agreements, or briefs.

Look for similarities or patterns among these accomplishments. Are most of them in one subject matter or practice area? Does one kind of work—e.g., legal research and writing, transactions, negotiations, trial preparation or organization, oral arguments or client relations—dominate the list? Do your accomplishments reflect your versatility?

Save this list to use in designing your marketing materials (Chapter 8).

complete "Your History of Achievements" above. This exercise will help you distill your years of experience, areas of proficiency and occasions of triumph for use in a brochure, résumé, or project list.

Many years of experience may also mean you have more expertise than the lawyers who want to hire you. This creates special problems. Less-experienced hiring lawyers may be uncomfortable giving instructions to lawyers senior in age or experience. Likewise, older contract lawyers may resent being supervised by a lawyer who knows less about the subject matter. Such an arrangement can work if both contract and hiring lawyers remain flexible and open-minded. But if you've reached mid-life and are considering contract work, you'll need to anticipate the situation. The best solution, if it applies to you, would be to position yourself as a specialist or niche lawyer.

THE SPECIALIST

While we may think of the specialist as a lawyer with an LLM in tax or one who has concentrated for 20 years on a narrow area of law, this is not necessarily the case. A lawyer with five to ten years' experience in a particular subject matter—such as bankruptcy, environmental law or intellectual property—may also qualify. Others position themselves as trial preparation specialists after working as litigation associates.

Some specialties go in and out of vogue or are in demand in some parts of the country but not in others. Steve Weinstein notes that he's one of the few contract lawyers in the San Francisco Bay Area with "serious antitrust" experience—but he hasn't had to use it for several years. In contrast, Laura Black, founder of Attorneys Per Diem, could keep a good antitrust lawyer busy every day in the Washington, D.C., area.

NICHE LAWYER

This is the lawyer who offers unique expertise derived from pre-law experience in a field such as accounting, engineering or medicine. Richard Kaplan hired a former engineer to help in a case involving defective construction plans. The lawyer's expertise not only helped Kaplan to decipher the plans, but enabled him to determine through deposition testimony where fault for the plans actually lay.

Many contract lawyers—including new admittees—find that the work they did before law school can now be put to use. For example, lawyers who do personal injury, workers' compensation, or medical malpractice work should find it helpful to consult with contract lawyers with nursing backgrounds. An engineering or building design background would make you a good choice for lawyers involved in either litigating or negotiating construction contracts. An MBA degree or CPA certification, signifying the ability to deal with sophisticated financial information, could enable you to assist a lawyer in general practice confronting complicated data in divorce, probate, business or litigation matters. A background in psychology or social work could come in handy in an office specializing in domestic relations.

There are many examples of successful niche lawyers. Nanci Klinger knew in law school that she wanted to work in environmental policy-making. As a new graduate, she targeted a governmental agency and negotiated a series of contracts on the application of complex environmental regulations to the agency's operations. Werner Lewin tells of a very senior lawyer he had despaired of placing until an assignment came up that required his expertise—in oil and gas leasing. Several lawyers in the Los Angeles area limit their practice to arguing motions for relief from stay in bankruptcy cases. There are also lawyers who specialize in drafting qualified domestic relations orders for division of pension plans in divorce cases.

Review the lists of practice areas, duties and responsibilities, and esoteric specialties on the next page. Check every one in which you have experience. Circle those you'd like to make part of your contract career.

Once you've completed your review of practice areas, skills and specialties, expand the "mission statement" you wrote at page 48 to incorporate your level of experience and areas of expertise. For example, you might add:

EXPERIENCE CHECKLIST

IDENTIFY PRACTICE AREAS
- ___ administrative law
- ___ adoption
- ___ agricultural
- ___ alternative dispute resolution
- ___ antitrust
- ___ banking
- ___ bankruptcy
- ___ biomedical issues
- ___ bonds
- ___ business organizations
- ___ civil appeals
- ___ criminal appeals
- ___ commercial finance
- ___ commercial litigation
- ___ commercial banking
- ___ communications
- ___ computer
- ___ constitutional law
- ___ construction
- ___ consumer rights
- ___ copyright
- ___ corporate
- ___ corporate reorganization
- ___ criminal law
- ___ debtor-creditor
- ___ discrimination
- ___ domestic relations
- ___ elder law
- ___ employment
- ___ employment relations
- ___ energy
- ___ entertainment
- ___ environmental
- ___ estate planning
- ___ family
- ___ federal courts
- ___ federal tax
- ___ franchising
- ___ general civil litigation
- ___ general practice
- ___ governmental relations
- ___ guardianship
- ___ health care
- ___ immigration
- ___ insurance
- ___ insurance defense
- ___ intellectual property
- ___ international finance
- ___ international
- ___ labor
- ___ land use
- ___ leasing
- ___ lobbying

- ___ mergers & acquisitions
- ___ natural resources
- ___ oil and gas
- ___ patent
- ___ pensions
- ___ personal injury
- ___ probate
- ___ product liability
- ___ public contracts
- ___ public utility
- ___ real estate
- ___ securities regulation
- ___ secured transactions
- ___ social security disability
- ___ sports
- ___ taxation
- ___ trademark
- ___ transportation
- ___ trusts
- ___ workers' compensation

IDENTIFY PAST DUTIES AND RESPONSIBILITIES
- ___ Case initiation
  - ___ meet with client
  - ___ prepare a complaint
  - ___ review file for issues and action
- ___ Civil discovery
  - ___ answer interrogatories
  - ___ attend a deposition
  - ___ document review and retrieval
  - ___ draft interrogatories
  - ___ draft requests for production
  - ___ prepare memoranda in support of motions
  - ___ prepare responding memoranda
  - ___ respond to requests for production
  - ___ review and analyze medical records
  - ___ take a deposition
- ___ Court appearances
  - ___ argue appeals
  - ___ argue routine motions
  - ___ argue summary judgment and other complex motions
  - ___ ex parte appearances
  - ___ handle jury trials
  - ___ handle trials before the court
  - ___ handle evidentiary hearings
- ___ Legal research and writing

- ___ cite check
- ___ edit
- ___ prepare settlement notebook
- ___ Shepardize
- ___ research to develop theory of case or strategy
- ___ write memoranda of points and authorities
- ___ write appellate briefs
- ___ Transactional work
  - ___ advise a corporate department manager
  - ___ partnership and corporate documentation
  - ___ loan and credit agreements
  - ___ security agreements and other documentation
  - ___ equipment leases
  - ___ construction contracts
  - ___ prospectuses etc. (stock offerings)
  - ___ bond documentation
  - ___ drafting, interpretation, negotiation
  - ___ research and write opinion letters
  - ___ review for conformance with applicable laws and regulations
- ___ Trial preparation
  - ___ compile the trial notebook
  - ___ draft jury instructions
  - ___ prepare the trial brief
  - ___ prepare witnesses

IDENTIFY SPECIALTIES:
- ___ acquainted with the ADA
- ___ cater to large law firm domestic relations clients
- ___ computerized legal research
- ___ technical language, e.g., engineering, computer
- ___ medical records and terminology
- ___ intricacies of commercial construction industry
- ___ jurisdictional analysis expertise
- ___ medical research
- ___ rush projects
- ___ specialties within specialties like ERISA compliance
- ___ other_____
- _____
- _____
- _____

> *I practiced for ten years in the real estate area and am comfortable with both transactional work and litigation.*

On the other hand, you may now see your breadth of experience and adaptability as being your greatest asset. If so, model your statement after Susan Shulenberger's self-description:

> *I'm good at contract lawyering because I have a general business litigation background and have worked in a wide variety of areas. With all my experience, I'm quick to figure out how legal concepts apply to new fact patterns and I'm comfortable handling a broad range of assignments.*

A new graduate who wants to position himself as a niche lawyer might create something like this:

> *I can assist you with technical issues in the health law area. I'm an RN, and worked for five years in the trauma center of a teaching hospital before attending law school. In law school I completed every course related to health law as well as two externships to obtain trial practice experience.*

A recent graduate with a less focused history could write, for example:

> *Most of my summer jobs since high school have been in retail sales. I've learned how to deal with cranky customers and to find the right solutions for a diverse population. I can transfer this experience into a general practice by gathering information from your clients to answer interrogatories or prepare affidavits, and by handling telephone calls from difficult clients.*

Another way to describe yourself is to state a problem and then show how you can solve it. For example:

> *You know how some lawyers are great at getting and keeping clients, but hate to churn out paperwork. Well, I love office work and help other lawyers with it on a project basis.*

RESEARCH THE MARKET FOR YOUR SERVICES

The self-assessment you've just completed is the first step in targeting a market. The second step is to research demand for the combination of personality, experience and expertise you offer. Use the questions below to create a list of lawyers and firms, corporate legal departments and government agencies that might be able to use your services.

DEFINING YOUR MARKET

Start with the *substantive areas of law* you checked on page 53. Is there a market for lawyers with your expertise? If so, think about the kind of help you want to provide. For example, if your area is bankruptcy, do you anticipate getting work from firms with a bankruptcy practice and too much work, or from lawyers with no bankruptcy expertise who will hire you to provide that expertise? Identify lawyers and firms you think could use your help.

If your area of expertise is not in demand, or if you have no law-related experience, think about developing a niche with a ready market. Explore current demand and distinguish yourself from others seeking the same kind of work. Right now, American Disabilities Act (ADA) litigation is exploding; if you learn the statutes and regulations, you can narrow your focus and still find plenty of opportunities. New admittees can review their non-legal experience and identify subject matters or industries—such as retailing, sports, or government—with which they are familiar. Your practice area will influence the lawyers you contact, the kind of ad you write, the organizations you join, and your decisions about malpractice insurance and office equipment.

Next, identify the *types of projects* you'd like to handle, and learn which hiring lawyers are most likely to offer that kind of work. Busy solo practitioners are more likely than firms with an army of associates to need the staples of contract work: legal research and writing, and litigation assistance. If you'd rather focus on transactional work—reviewing and drafting contracts, participating in the negotiation of agreements or supervising the closing of a deal—your best bet may be vacation or leave coverage for boutique firms with that specialty. You could also target companies with understaffed in-house legal departments.

You may find you are more versatile than you suspected. Zoe Topsfield was an experienced corporate lawyer before she decided to work freelance, but much of her early contract work involved deposition and motion appearances. "I had a really steep learning curve in those first twelve months," she admits. "I had no idea what a motion was." She's been supporting herself with a mix of contract assignments and work for her own clients ever since.

Consider also the range of *potential hiring lawyers.* The best markets for contract lawyers with no practice experience are small firms and solo practitioners who need help with research and writing or who need a second chair at trial. Lawyers with some experience might investigate the possibility of helping out recent graduates who have paying clients but aren't sure how to handle their cases. Many contract lawyers begin the contractor's life by giving notice at their law firm and then negotiating an hourly rate to complete matters they were handling. If you've cultivated good relations with opposing counsel you have a distinct advantage: they can be one of your best sources of future work.

Don't neglect corporations. In-house counsel provide the lion's share of assignments secured by contract lawyer placement agencies. To target the corporate market, locate small companies with only one in-house lawyer.[2] Then take the lawyer to lunch and talk about projects that would overburden him but are not large or complex enough to warrant hiring an outside firm.

Lawyers have also found temporary positions with government agencies at every level. Many new permanent positions are funded first as temporary slots; the lawyer who accepts the short-term assignment is in a good position to secure the permanent post. Travis McKenzie filled in for a government employee on maternity leave; when the new mother decided not to return to work, he was offered the permanent position. Government agencies also bring in "permanent temps," lawyers trained to substitute for permanent employees with specialized functions when they are on vacation or other leave. Sarah Knowles has been working for almost two years as a replacement hearing examiner for two different state agencies; the arrangement provides an adequate annual income and allows her to take time off to ski and backpack.

Think about the *number of hiring lawyers* with whom you'd prefer to work. Most contract lawyers accept a variety of assignments from a variety of practitioners. Katherine Foldes has found she can stay busy by working with three or four hiring lawyers at a time and that the mix changes about once a year. Some lawyers find full- or part-time on-site positions for one lawyer or firm that may last six months or longer. Agencies specialize in locating these assignments, but you don't have to work through an agency to get this type of work. Peter Zeughauser, senior vice-president and general counsel of California's The Irvine Company, hired his first contract lawyer when she told him she'd worked in her last job on an issue similar to one his company was facing. The problem developed into litigation, and

---

2. Directories of in-house counsel exist for many geographic areas and for certain specialized bar groups.

she's still working on the project several years later.

Finally, decide whether or not to limit the *geographic area* in which you offer your services. If you're willing to travel—whether to the next county or out of the country—you can increase your chances of finding work. But it's not always necessary to be physically present to widen your geographic arena. Advances in computer and communications technology have made working for distant clients more feasible than ever.

Farsighted contract lawyers should think about how technology can extend their marketing sphere. At the most basic "telecommuting" level, a contract lawyer in a city with good law libraries can provide research for lawyers in towns without such resources and transmit the results by fax or modem. For example, Eric Ebel in Ann Arbor, Michigan, where the law library is exceptional, does contract work for small-town lawyers who have access only to basic resources. A contract lawyer doing mostly research and writing—if he's equipped with a CD-ROM library and access to Lexis or Westlaw—can live and work anywhere and send his finished product by fax or e-mail to hiring lawyers wherever they may be.

RESEARCHING THE NEED FOR YOUR SERVICES

Once you've identified your ideal market(s), engage in some research on the realities of contract lawyering in your geographic region, and the demand for your particular experience and abilities. Arrange interviews and ask a lot of questions. Record the results of your research in a notebook or computer file, and keep the facts accessible. Information is your ally; the more you gather and retain, the better prepared you'll be to find assignments and customers.

Other contract lawyers. Ask colleagues for the names of lawyers in your area who do contract work. Telephone those lawyers and ask them what kind of work they do; their background and experience; what they charge for their services; how they find work; who they work for; who else they know who might need help. You can also call lawyers who advertise their contract services in your local bar journal or other legal publications to learn whether they have found work by advertising. Some may be reluctant to share information with you, but asking for advice is a good way to disarm those who might be reluctant to talk to a potential competitor.

Potential customers. Concentrate on lawyers practicing in the substantive areas in which you expect to work. If the process intimidates you, talk first to lawyers with whom you have a good relationship whatever their practice backgrounds. Depending on the circumstances, you may want to interview them by telephone, asking for only ten or 15 minutes of their time, rather than scheduling a personal meeting. Keep notes of these interviews as well.

Before your first interview, write a list of questions. These could include:

- *Have you ever hired a contract lawyer? If not, what are your concerns about using contract legal services? If so, was the experience satisfactory? What kinds of projects did you assign?*
- *Can you imagine assigning a project to a contract lawyer? If so, what kind(s)?*
- *Do you know colleagues who have worked with contract lawyers? If so, what did they tell you about the experience? What are their names?*
- *What experience and credentials would you look for in a contract lawyer?*
- *Would you prefer to use an agency or personal recommendations to locate a contract lawyer?*
- *Have you ever answered an ad placed by a contract lawyer? If not, why not? If so, what information in the ad attracted you? Did you hire the advertising lawyer?*
- *What hourly rate would you expect to pay a contract lawyer (at my level of experience and expertise)? How do you feel about flat rates and contingent fees?*

At the end of each interview, request names of two or three other lawyers who might be willing to talk to you. (Ask for permission to use the lawyer's name in introduction.) When you thank each lawyer at the end of the interview, ask if you might send a résumé or brochure along when you've finished your research.

Although the purpose of this exercise is not to solicit work, it would be disingenuous to pretend you would refuse work offered on the spot by one of the lawyers you were questioning. Therefore don't be too coy. When you begin the conversation, make it clear that your primary purpose is information gathering, but that the research is in aid of the successful marketing of your services.

With information and a list of potential customers in hand, you have a good starting point for pricing your services and finding work. The next two chapters assist you with those aspects of business.

7

SETTING YOUR RATES

What billing rates are fair and reasonable? How much can you get? This chapter tells you what lawyers across the country charge, how they set their rates, and how you can determine what rate to charge for your services.

"How much should I charge?" is the first question most contract lawyers ask. And with good reason. Setting the rate too low could turn off hiring lawyers who equate price with quality. Setting it too high might scare them away. Finding the right balance for plenty of business and a comfortable income can be an art. Here's what some of the contract lawyers we talked to charge for their services.

- *Steve Weinstein, a San Francisco Bay Area contract lawyer with over 15 years experience, eight of them in-house, earns between $55 and $78 per hour.*
- *Susan Shulenberger, a 1982 law school graduate who practiced with several respected Seattle firms before turning to contract work in 1993, charges from $35 per hour (for one friend) to $90 for specialty assignments.*
- *Molly Tami, a Cincinnati lawyer expert in legal research and writing, charges $70 per hour to private practitioners and works on a flat-fee basis with a legal publisher. A 1983 Boalt Hall graduate, she previously worked for two big Bay Area law firms and for the city attorney in Norfolk, Virginia.*
- *Ellen Singer practiced law for 13 years in California before moving to Eugene, Oregon, where she charges $35 per hour for her services.*
- *Lee Archer, with ten years of experience exclusively in appellate advocacy, charges $65 per hour for her work in New Orleans.*
- *Peter Ludwig is able to get only $25 to $30 per hour in Denver despite his*

seven years of labor law and civil litigation experience with Holland &
Hart and Cooper & Kelley.

- *His colleague Wallace Chakerian, a "sophisticated generalist" with an LLM*
  in taxation, charges $50 per hour for projects ranging from estate planning
  to business and related litigation.

- *Chris Maiocchi had 20 years of in-house real estate experience before*
  accepting a part-time contract assignment at IBM in Westchester County,
  New York. She receives $50 per hour for her work through The Wallace
  Law Registry.

- *Eric Ebel, a legal research and writing specialist in Ann Arbor, Michigan,*
  with 18 years of experience, has charged $50 per hour since 1988.

We learn from this overview that the rates for contract lawyers across the
country vary much less than do the rates charged by lawyers to clients.

Some contract lawyers resolve the pricing dilemma by starting low and raising
their rates after they've gained confidence. This strategy can backfire, though, if
your customers become convinced they can't afford to pay you a penny more than
they already are. In addition, the tendency of many contract lawyers to ask for too
little has led many hiring lawyers to expect unrealistically low rates.

When Deborah Guyol was coordinating the Oregon Women Lawyers Contract
Lawyer Referral Service, a law firm asked for names of experienced contract lawyers
to handle three months of full-time work on several employment cases. She referred
three lawyers with appropriate backgrounds to the firm; they all turned down the
assignment because the firm offered only $35 per hour. Guyol then referred a less
experienced lawyer who was willing to work for $25 per hour. The firm turned her
down as unqualified. Sometimes you just can't win!

DETERMINE YOUR LOWEST RATE

Your first step is to decide on the lowest rate you are willing to accept. This
"what-you-can-live-with-rate" will not necessarily be your rate, but it's helpful to
begin negotiations with a firm sense of the point beyond which a rate becomes
unacceptably low so you'll be able to say "no" without hesitating.

PROJECTED ANNUAL EXPENDITURES

First, project your estimated annual costs of being self-employed, maintaining
your license to practice law, and the amount you need to cover reasonable living

expenses. Add 25 percent to the last figure to cover Social Security and federal income taxes, and an additional percentage for any state income tax. You'll find forms to calculate these expenses on pages 62 and 63.

PROJECTED BILLABLE HOURS

Next, determine the number of hours you hope to bill annually. For a reasonably accurate estimate, follow these steps and complete the form on page 64:

1. Determine the number of hours you want to devote to work each week. Note that there are 168 hours in a week. Subtract the time you spend eating, sleeping and running errands, then subtract ten more hours for good measure, and you'll have a sense of how much time is left for work and play. Most important, decide how many hours a week you really *want* to spend working.

2. Estimate the time you'll spend weekly on office administration, transition time between projects, billing, telephone interruptions and legal research dead ends, and deduct those hours from your weekly total. As former San Francisco contract lawyer Hindi Greenberg says, there's "spinning wheels" time, "getting-familiar-with-it" time and "transportation-between-things" time. Bear in mind that if you work as a contract lawyer for several hiring lawyers, you are practicing law part-time no matter what your intention; the rest of your time is spent running a business. Lee Archer describes herself as "secretary, receptionist, accountant, computer technician and gofer," as well as a lawyer. You will find it impossible to bill the number of hours a typical law firm associate is expected to bill even if you work full time, evenings and weekends. In fact, lawyers who work on discrete projects rather than long-term on-site assignments typically report that a full-time practice yields 15 to 20 billable hours per week.

3. Add up the number of days off you expect to take for sick and mental health leave, holidays and vacations, as well as days you will be unable to bill any hours because of lack of business, attendance at CLE programs or attention to marketing efforts. Keep in mind that July, August and December tend to be slow for contract lawyers. For every five days you anticipate not working, subtract one week from the 52 weeks in the year.

4. Multiply the net hours per week you calculated in step 2 by the number of weeks you calculated in step 3. This is the number of hours you expect to bill in a year. Subtract ten percent for collection and other unforeseen problems.

MINIMUM HOURLY RATE

Divide the net annual billable hour figure into your annual expenses. This is your minimum hourly rate. For example, if you project your total annual expenditures at $40,000, and estimate that you can bill 1,000 hours in a year, your minimum hourly rate is $40.

Another way to determine your hourly minimum is to select a tentative rate and divide it into your annual expense figure. Then decide whether the resulting number of billable hours is reasonable. Our research indicates that the most common assignments are five-hour research projects and 10 to 15-hour research and writing projects. Figure out how many of these you will need to meet your monthly expenditures; then ask contract lawyers in your area whether your goal is attainable.

RATE-SETTING FORMULAS

Once you know how little you can charge and still cover your expenses, it's time to figure out how *much* you can charge and still attract business.

Rate setting is a subjective process, so we can't tell you exactly what your rates should be. We can, however, give you formulas that others use, as well as this advice: Be flexible; be prepared to charge different rates in different situations. And be brave. Don't be afraid to ask for what you're really worth.

WHAT DO OTHER CONTRACT LAWYERS CHARGE?

Most lawyers we talked to charge between $35 and $75 per hour, but we've

---

ESTIMATED COSTS OF DOING BUSINESS

	PER MONTH	PER YEAR
office rent, if applicable	_____	_____
telephone lines (business, fax, modem)	_____	_____
malpractice insurance	_____	_____
disability or income replacement insurance	_____	_____
bar association and other licensing fees	_____	_____
elective bar association dues	_____	_____
other elective membership fees	_____	_____
advertising	_____	_____
office supplies	_____	_____
office equipment upkeep and repair	_____	_____
books and subscriptions	_____	_____
on-line services	_____	_____
CLE and other programs	_____	_____
parking	_____	_____
TOTAL	_____	_____

ESTIMATED LIVING EXPENSES

	PER MONTH	PER YEAR
mortgage payment or rent		
real estate taxes and insurance (if not included in above figure)		
utilities		
household upkeep and repair		
medical insurance		
dental insurance		
uninsured medical/dental expense (including deductible)		
life insurance		
automobile expense:		
payment		
insurance		
gasoline		
upkeep and repair		
registration/tax		
other transportation expense		
student loans		
credit card or other revolving debt payment		
IRA/pension contribution		
food		
daycare/tuition		
personal expenses (haircuts, manicures, cosmetics, etc.)		
clothing		
gifts and donations		
entertainment & athletic expense		
travel		
other_____		
other_____		
other_____		
SUBTOTAL		
federal taxes (multiply subtotal by 25%)		
state taxes (multiply subtotal by applicable percentage)		
TOTAL		
add estimated costs of doing business		
TOTAL EXPENDITURES		

PROJECTED ANNUAL BILLABLE HOURS

1. Hours I want to devote to work each week   _____
2. Hours I expect to spend weekly on:
   - office administration, billing   _____
   - transition time between projects   _____
   - telephone interruptions   _____
   - written-off time   _____
   - marketing calls or meetings   _____
   - bar association activities   _____

total nonbillable hours   _____

3. Subtract the total of #2 from the figure in #1   _____
4. Weeks I expect to take annually for:
   - sick and mental health leave   _____
   - holidays   _____
   - vacations   _____
   - lack of business   _____
   - attendance at educational programs   _____
   - concentrated marketing efforts   _____
   - total number of weeks   _____

subtracted from 52 =   _____

5. Multiply the net hours per day from #3 by the net number of weeks from #4 to equal your total estimated annual billable hours:

   _____ x _____ = _____

6. Multiply the annual billable hour estimate by 10% and deduct this figure to reach your estimated collectible hours:

   _____ x 10% = _____
   annual billable hours   uncollectible hours

   _____ − _____ = _____
   annual billable hours   uncollectible hours   net annual billable hours

7. Divide the figure from #6 into your total annual expenditures to get your minimum hourly rate:

   _____ ÷ _____ = _____
   annual expenditures   net billable hours   minimum hourly rate

heard of rates as low as $12.50 per hour and as high as $150. We don't recommend rates below $20, even for inexperienced lawyers, except on a one-time introductory basis. Asking for less than $20 per hour indicates more desperation than talent. Experienced lawyers might test their clientele by starting in the $40 to $50 per hour range, with an understanding that this introductory rate will be raised after the first assignment. Highly experienced specialists, selected because of their expertise, may be able to command rates of close to $100 per hour to start.

The contract lawyer phenomenon is new enough that the upper range of rates is still being explored. Do some research in your area to learn what contract lawyers at your experience level charge. Then experiment. You'll know you've moved too high when new customers flinch or don't call back. And, you'll know you're charging too little when you have plenty of business but aren't netting enough to support yourself. As Elizabeth Bottman says, "I figure if everybody is happy but me, my rate is too low."

WHAT DO YOUR POTENTIAL CUSTOMERS CHARGE CLIENTS FOR THEIR LEGAL SERVICES?

Many contract lawyers, as well as hiring lawyers, feel that a fair rule is to make the contract lawyer's hourly rate a percentage of the rate billed to the client. Law firm rates accommodate law office overhead (space, support staff, equipment and supplies), employee benefits (health insurance, sick leave, vacations, membership in such voluntary legal organizations as the ABA) and professional necessities such as malpractice insurance, bar membership fees and tuition for CLEs. There are also dollars allocated to administration, pro bono work, business development and, at least in theory, profit. The law firm using a contract lawyer who works out of her own office doesn't have these expenses loaded into the hourly rate; anything it charges above what it pays for contract services is profit (unless the lawyer supervising the work is not charging the client for oversight). The lawyer or firm can either keep the profit, or pass along a discount to the client. Bear this in mind when negotiating your rates.

If you work from your own office, ask for half of the rate at which the hiring lawyer *can* bill the client for your time. This rate provides recompense for your home office expenses and rewards you fairly for your expertise. If you're working on-site or will be paid as an employee (see Chapter 18), you should ask for about one-third of the firm's billable rate, to account for such overhead items as "reasonable rental" of the equipment, clerical assistance and the office you use. For example, if your time can be billed to the client at $120 per hour, you can ask for $60 per hour if you work from your own office, $40 per hour if you work on site and use the hiring lawyer's equipment and support staff and perhaps $35 per hour if you are paid as a non-benefitted employee.

This system works better in areas where billing rates are modest (say, in Billings, Montana) than in areas with high hourly rates. We have yet to hear of a contract lawyer who is paid $150 per hour because the firm can bill his time out at $300 (a typical New York City hourly rate)—although in San Francisco, Richard Kaplan pays $100 per hour and bills $200 per hour for the services of one top contract lawyer. In any case, it's important to know how much your hiring lawyers will charge their clients for your work.

In 1995, average law firm billing rates for a third- or fourth-year associate were less than $100 per hour in some low-end markets, around $135 per hour in Chicago, Dallas and Houston, and $190 per hour in Manhattan.[1] Based on these figures, associate-level contract lawyers should receive between $67.50 and $90 per hour in major markets; partnership level work should command upwards of $160 per hour. At press time, the associate-level figures are what *agencies* charge for partnership-level work, but more than most contract lawyers at any level charge directly.

If you contract work from a firm in which you used to be an associate or partner, or if you work on the firm's premises, you'll know your billable rate. Other firms may have different rate structures, however, so you'll need to do research. If you're just out of law school or new in town, make questions about rates part of your initial market research.

There are risks to basing your rate on what the hiring lawyer charges clients. Dan Terry learned this when he failed to distinguish between what the hiring lawyer *could* bill the client and what she *actually* billed. The first thing he told Ashley Lagenback when she called to ask about his availability was that he "was not cheap"; he usually charged between $55 and $65 per hour. Terry then made the mistake of suggesting that since they were equally experienced, Lagenback could pay him half the rate she charged clients for her time. Lagenback's hourly rate was $120, but she countered that she had billed out her last contract lawyer at $110. Without confirming the agreement in writing at $55—but assuming they'd agreed on that rate—Terry spent several hours on the project. Lagenback then told Terry that she'd gotten approval from her client to bill Terry's time at $85; she suggested Terry work for $42.50 per hour. They ultimately settled at $50 and Lagenback never called him again. Terry learned from that experience to put everything in writing. (He has also decided that hiring lawyers "who are the biggest hassle up front are often the least worth it!")

---

1. Partner rates may be as low as $125 per hour in small markets. They average $210 in Miami, and are $320 or more in New York City.

WHAT ARE FIRM LAWYERS WHO HANDLE THE SAME KIND OF WORK PAID?

If you are a former employee or otherwise have access to salary information, you can ask for an hourly rate comparable to the salary plus benefits divided by average billable hours of an associate or partner in the firm with the necessary level of expertise to handle the job; you might have to settle for a rate that does not take the benefit package into account. (See calculation in Chapter 11 at page 133.)

A partner at a large firm, accustomed to delegating the work she considers "routine" to junior associates, may want to vary the hourly rate according to the complexity of the assignment. Many contract lawyers are over-experienced for the work they are assigned. The law firm need not pay "of counsel" or partnership-level compensation to an experienced contract lawyer if the work could be handled by a junior associate. The theory doesn't apply to solo and small firm practitioners accustomed to doing everything themselves. They bill the client at the same hourly rate no matter what the task and are unlikely to think they should pay a higher rate for sophisticated or complex work—or a lower rate for routine assignments.

WHAT DO CONTRACT LAWYER PLACEMENT AGENCIES CHARGE FOR SOMEONE AT YOUR LEVEL OF EXPERIENCE?

Ask a local placement agency what it would charge for a lawyer with the necessary background and experience to handle your job. Offer to handle the work for $5 to $15 less per hour, assuming you have the same level of experience and credentials as the lawyers the agency is placing.

CALCULATE A REASONABLE PROFIT LEVEL FOR THE HIRING LAWYER.

Ask for an hourly rate that allows the firm to retain as profit from 15 to 33 percent of the fee charged to the client, after taking into account the cost of law firm office space and support services you will be using. The higher percentage is based on the outdated notion that rates charged clients generally go one-third to associate salary, one-third to overhead and one-third to profit. The lower percentage reflects today's actual profit margins of more like ten to 15 percent.[2]

VARIATIONS FROM THE FORMULAS

There are no strict rules about contract lawyer compensation. No matter what

---

2.　Robin Hegvik, "Profitability Models for Part-Time Lawyers," *Breaking Traditions* (ABA Section of Law Practice Management 1993).

formula you use and no matter what the standard rates are for services in your area, you can make arguments to increase that rate—or to consider reducing it—if any of the following variables apply.

THE AMOUNT OF RELEVANT EXPERIENCE YOU POSSESS

Experience is reflected in the rates law firms charge their clients, and it should be in yours too. The more experience you have in a particular specialty, the more efficiently and competently you will work, and the more the hiring lawyer can charge his clients for your time. If you are soliciting low-level assignments like reviewing documents, drafting interrogatories or responding to requests for production, however, you may not be able to command a high hourly rate, no matter how extensive your experience.

As an experienced lawyer, you can charge more for your work, although if you start off with high rates you may have to do some persuading. If you feel threatened by less experienced lawyers charging lower rates, you may be tempted to lower your rates to compete. On the other hand, lawyers who do exceptional work can pretty much set their rates as they choose. Richard Kaplan tells of a San Francisco contract lawyer, much in demand, whose rates are among the highest: "This man recognizes his competence and very high skill, and for his services I pay more than I have for others. To me it's worth it."

Earl Carulli, a St. Louis contract lawyer, handled a rush project for $65 per hour, his usual rate. The partner who hired him was so happy with his work that he wanted to assign him additional projects—but at a reduced rate of $55 per hour. Carulli was in a quandary; was he willing to risk losing a customer in order to get his price? Uncertain how to proceed, he showed his résumé to the hiring lawyer. When the lawyer saw that Carulli had over ten years' experience, including five with a well-known Wall Street firm, he agreed to the higher rate.

YOUR SPECIAL EXPERTISE

Do you have significant experience in a substantive area of the law? You may not be able to limit your practice to this kind of work in a small legal market, but you could charge a higher rate for work in your area of expertise than for general assignments. For example, if you've spent the last ten years immersed in the tax code, you can charge more to work on a tax issue than for research on a real estate transaction.

Be wary of accepting a lower hourly rate in your area of expertise when you have sole responsibility for the matter. Even if the assignment appears routine, its nature can change in mid-course. Steve Weinstein agreed to work for $55 per hour rather the $78 he usually commands because the two-week assignment was represented as a routine business closing for a partner who was going on vacation. In short order, the work became radically more complex and intense than he had expected. Since it was a short assignment, Weinstein didn't feel comfortable trying to renegotiate his fee; instead, he developed a raging case of resentment for underselling his services.

You may also be able to charge more if your time is passed directly through to the client without write-off. On the other hand, if the firm frequently trims your hours, they'll probably want to keep you at the low end of the scale.

THE REQUIREMENTS OF THE PROJECT

Many contract lawyers charge higher rates for rush projects—typically those requiring a 24-hour turnaround. (If it's a big project, a week could be considered a "rush.") Some contract lawyers charge higher rates for courtroom or deposition appearances than for research and writing. Some charge more for appellate work than for work at the trial court level. With experience, you can decide which projects command premium rates.

You may be willing to charge *less* per hour if you are guaranteed payment for a minimum number of hours weekly whether or not the firm has work for you, or if the assignment is for 35 hours or more weekly for several months. (Before you accept this type of assignment, however, consider whether handling a lengthy project for one hiring lawyer will hurt your relationships with others.) The hourly rate may be lower, but your total compensation will likely be higher than usual because you will lose little or no time to marketing, transitions from home to office and back, and other inefficiencies of small, home-based projects.

MALPRACTICE INSURANCE COVERAGE

Whether this is a factor depends on what is generally accepted where you practice. Being insured is less of an issue in California (where as many as 40 percent of the profession practices without liability insurance) than in Oregon (where malpractice insurance is mandatory except for lawyers whose work is supervised by other attorneys and who never represent clients directly). If your hiring lawyers require you to purchase your own coverage, or if they rely on you as a consulting expert, you should charge more for the added security.

THE WORK SITE

If you work on-site for a lawyer, firm or in-house counsel, there will be overhead attributable to you and your rate should be lower. On the other hand, if you work from your own office, the lawyer you work for has no overhead; you can either charge for the time you spend on administrative tasks or raise your rates to reflect the inefficiencies of this type of practice. Katherine Foldes admits that she charges for "transaction" time—the hours it takes to pick up, deliver and discuss assignments—but she attributes time spent talking about her clients' children to marketing. Deborah Guyol does not charge for "transaction" time. She figures that her high hourly rate should include some services and she often receives more work when she delivers a completed assignment in person.

YOUR PRIOR RELATIONSHIP WITH THE HIRING LAWYER

Contract lawyers who work with former co-workers or employers tend to earn more per hour than those who work for strangers. Beth Besner, who resigned from a well-respected Miami law firm to devote more time to political campaigns, was invited to return to the firm on a contract basis two years later. The partner-in-charge offered to pay her $35 per hour. She knew that, as a fifth-year associate, $50 was more appropriate—especially since the firm would be charging her out at $175. When she responded with a simple, "I'm leaving," the firm met her price.

Be careful also of reducing your hourly rate for a struggling colleague. Catherine Bitterman, a West Coast contract lawyer with 12 years of general practice experience, typically charges between $50 and $80 per hour for her time. She agreed to bill only $35 per hour to a solo practitioner friend who needed help but claimed to be in poor financial health. Three years later, he's the only hiring lawyer who calls her late at night to plead for help or to talk about case strategy. And her hourly rate has stayed the same; it's hard to raise rates on a financially-strapped friend who seems to be working so hard.

PAYMENT TERMS

Your rate may also vary depending upon when payment is made. One way to deal with slow-paying hiring lawyers is either to offer a lower rate for quick payment, or to charge more for delayed payment. For example, you could charge $50 per hour if you are paid within ten days of invoice; $55 per hour for payment more than ten but within 30 days of invoice, and $65 per hour for later payment. This could be a good arrangement if you're working on a contingent fee case that is expected to settle. A different approach would be to set your rate somewhat higher (especially for a hiring lawyer with a history of slow payment) and offer a discount for payment within ten days. You could quote $65 per hour, but offer a ten percent discount if payment is made within ten days and five percent if within 30 days. Be certain to make any such agreement when you are hired, so your bill reflects the appropriate rates.

ALTERNATIVE BILLING ARRANGEMENTS

The foregoing discussions assume you are being paid per hour. There *are* other compensation arrangements. Commentators have been predicting (and advocating) the end of the billable hour system for years, and in some legal markets the process is well under way. To keep up with the times, consider the following alternative billing systems.

FLAT FEES

Flat fees can be an attractive option, because they offer hiring lawyers the advantage of predictability. Any flat fee you offer is based on your sense of how long the project will take. If you offer a flat fee, you are in essence betting that you will be able to complete the project in fewer hours than the total fee divided by your usual hourly rate. Offer flat fees only when you've had enough experience with a certain kind of project to predict accurately the time it will take, or when you're trying to attract repeat business. Molly Tami accepted a flat-fee consulting contract with a legal publisher that works out to less than half her usual hourly rate of $70. The monthly retainer creates steady income, though, and she hopes that as she becomes more efficient her effective rate will increase.

Flat fees can be offered in hybrid form as well. For example, you could quote a fee based on an estimate that the project will take 25 to 35 hours. If in fact the project takes fewer than 20 hours, you charge your usual hourly rate rather than the flat fee; if it requires more than 35 hours, you charge the flat fee plus a charge for hours in excess of 35 at a lower than usual hourly rate.

CONTINGENT FEES

Good contingent fee assignments are hard to find. In our research, we discovered only one contract lawyer working on a contingent fee basis on a case that promised to be lucrative. Most hiring lawyers who do both contingent fee and hourly work manage their caseloads by handling the contingent fee cases themselves, and assigning work on hourly matters to contract lawyers. This way, the contract lawyer generates a profit for the practitioner and all the work gets done. And personal injury lawyers with thriving practices are usually willing to pay hourly rates to contract lawyers as costs advanced—like expert witness and deposition fees.

Therefore the lawyer who asks you to work on a straight contingent fee basis may have a marginal practice—or may want to hand off a case that does not look promising. Some contract lawyers who run regular advertisements report calls from personal injury lawyers who ask them to take over a particular case on a totally contingent basis. These hiring lawyers work on volume and figure they'll increase their odds of turning a profit if someone else handles the small cases and long shots. Be cautious about accepting a case on a strictly contingent fee basis.

If you decide to try contingent fee work, follow the example of Sylvia Linscott, who handles most of her contract assignments for a contingent fee. She does not accept the assignment unless she believes there is a 99 percent chance of recovery. "I don't do it unless I've sat down with the attorney, assessed the relative merits of the case and confirmed a settlement plan, or a reasonable range of verdicts. I don't just go in cold." Her approach makes sense for contract lawyers without much hourly work. If you're willing to invest another five to ten hours a week in a case that may not pay, you'll gain experience and exposure, develop leads and expand your market.

A straight contingent fee arrangement might provide that if the client prevails, you will receive 25 percent of the fee the hiring lawyer receives. (The percentage will depend on how much work you perform. It should be decided in advance. The Rules of Professional Conduct require disclosure and client consent for division of fees. See Chapter 17 at page 202.) One way to reduce the risk is to agree on a hybrid fee structure. You could charge an hourly rate much lower than your usual rate, payable immediately, and receive more only if the client prevails. For example, if your usual rate is $50 per hour, you might agree to do the work for immediate payment of $30 per hour. If your client lost you would receive nothing more, but if he prevailed you would receive an additional $45 for each hour you had billed on the case, so that you ultimately received a total of $75 per hour (50 percent over your usual rate).

If you agree to any payment that is contingent on receipt of a settlement or verdict, file the papers necessary to associate yourself on the matter and assure that your name is included on any settlement check. Elizabeth Bottman took this precaution when she assisted at a medical malpractice trial, representing the husband in a claim for loss of consortium. "I drew up a contract in which I was to receive a low hourly rate for my time and if the husband was awarded anything for loss of consortium, I would also get a percentage fee for that," she says. "We didn't win the loss of consortium but I did end up billing about $2,000 for my time." Unfortunately, the hiring lawyer regretted the agreement when it came time to cut the check. Elizabeth had to co-sign the settlement checks, so she agreed to meet him at the bank and exchange her signature on the settlement check for a $2,000 check in her name. The hiring lawyer was outraged but acceded to her demand. "Afterwards, I felt kind of rotten," she admits. "But if I hadn't been paid I would really have stewed."

MINIMUMS

Some contract lawyers establish per project or per week minimums. You may want to do this if you find you are handling so many small projects that, taking transaction time into account, your effective hourly compensation is far below your stated rate. To solve the problem, charge a higher hourly rate for projects under, say, five hours, or tell your customers that you have a project minimum of three or four hours.

In the alternative, imitate lawyers who charge minimum fees for depositions and court appearances—say, a floor of $100, or a minimum of two hours at their usual rate. If the appearance takes more than two hours, they charge the time at their standard rate, but they're paid for two hours of work no matter what. Bundling several matters into one trip to the courthouse can produce a generous rate of return for the hours invested.

The issue may also arise if a law firm has asked you to keep yourself available to help them but has little or no work for weeks at a time. For such a firm, request a deal for a guarantee of, say, ten hours per week at a discounted rate. Hours over that minimum in any one week would be billed at your higher regular hourly rate. If one hiring lawyer comes to rely on your services to handle a number of very small research projects each month or quarter without ever assigning you more complex matters, you could ask for a monthly retainer based on a range of hours rather than charging per project.

Some contract lawyers shy away from project minimums, on the theory that a small assignment well done may lead to larger projects or regular work from that hiring lawyer. Other contract lawyers consider those small projects a service that keeps their regular customers coming back.

RETAINERS

Contract lawyers have also discovered that retainers, especially when dealing with new hiring lawyers or for small projects, greatly help with cash flow. One contract lawyer asks for a retainer equal to the expected fee plus expenses and deposits it into a trust account. Another asks for a substantial retainer on long projects, applies half to the initial billing and states that the other half will apply to the final bill. Then, she submits weekly statements. This way, she learns whether she has a slow-pay or no-pay customer before she invests too much uncompensated time in the case.

CONCLUSION

The more work you do as a contract lawyer, the less troublesome you are likely to find questions of rates. You will gain confidence in your abilities and a sense of how valuable you are to hiring lawyers. You'll feel more comfortable negotiating and you may develop new arrangements. Please let us know if you do.

8

FINDING WORK

Will a well-drafted résumé attract the work you want? Should you advertise? Do you have to network? What are the best ways to scout for assignments? Here we tell you what marketing tools work and how to tap the demand for contract legal services.

When Ellen Singer moved to Eugene, Oregon, after practicing law for 13 years in California, her first step was to call three or four women lawyers whose names she selected at random from the telephone directory. She asked if each would meet with her to discuss practicing law in a legal community much smaller and more isolated than the one she had left. "They agreed to have lunch with me," Singer reports, "and were really nice. I asked each for the names of other lawyers I could talk to, and took it from there." This was Singer's version of cold-calling.

Singer also tried advertising, and found that the announcement of the opening of her law practice she placed in the local bar news generated more responses than any of her subsequent ads for contract services. She has also done mass mailings to lawyers and firms in the area; she attends every bar lunch and CLE program she can; and she makes an effort to talk to the people she meets there. As a result of her very active marketing efforts, she's now well known in her community and has plenty of contract work.

Developing a clientele can be challenging for contract lawyers given the current market oversupply. Further, contract lawyers are selling a service that has not yet been completely accepted in all parts of the country. This is less of an issue if you practice in New York City and have a glowing résumé than if you've just moved to Nebraska after graduating from law school in Arizona. Between these two extremes are lawyers like Singer, who have some experience but work in towns or cities with no contract lawyer placement agencies, only a moderate-sized legal community, and many other lawyers hoping to find contract work.

In spite of the problems, there is plenty of work for contract lawyers of all types and in all markets. But you must take the initiative to find or create your own opportunities. The suggestions in this chapter are only a beginning.

WILL AN AGENCY HELP YOU?

Because temporary placement agencies have been so active in publicizing contract lawyer arrangements in recent years, you might believe that most contract lawyers find assignments through agencies. You might also assume that lawyers who do find steady work through agencies never need to establish their own offices, never have to market their services, and can depend on the agencies to negotiate rates and other terms of their engagements.

These assumptions are wrong for all but a few. This does not mean you should ignore agencies, however. Your first step is to learn whether there is a contract lawyer placement agency in your region. If there is, find out whether your experience and background fit the profile the agency is looking for, and consider whether working with an agency appeals to you. (See Chapter 21.) If it does, by all means sign up. Be aware, though, that most agencies consider the hiring lawyers their clients; they will not be trying to find assignments for *you*. You'll only get work if you match the specifications of a hiring lawyer, and if that lawyer picks your résumé out of those the agency submits.

Some agencies accept all applicants into their databases and can place new admittees in law clerk-level positions. Even if your background and experience wouldn't attract the typical hiring lawyer, it won't hurt to make your résumé one among thousands. It's always possible that a request will come in that matches what you have to offer—maybe for a graduate of the same law school as the hiring lawyer, or for someone who's worked on a railroad bankruptcy case, or for someone equipped with beeper, cell phone and notebook computer who is willing to make appearances in an out-of-the-way location. Just remember that your listing is a long shot, and that you cannot rely on the agency as your sole source of business.

To improve your chances with an agency, impress the placement personnel with your ability, good sense and dependability. Call in regularly to let the placement representative know of your continued interest and availability. Update your résumé and references as you receive other temporary assignments or expand your practice experience.

OVERCOMING RESISTANCE TO YOUR SERVICES

Unless an agency is smoothing the way for you, or you have an established network and a reputation to match, sooner or later you will meet resistance to the idea of contract lawyering. The legal profession is a conservative one, and some of the most successful lawyers are the most resistant to change.

At some point you'll hear such questions and comments as:

- *Why should I hire a contract lawyer when I can just work (or work my associates) harder?*
- *How can I be sure you'll be responsible, capable and conscientious?*
- *We wouldn't want it known that our firm had to resort to using contract lawyers.*
- *I can't afford to hire a contract lawyer.*
- *My clients want me to do all their work personally.*
- *I can't imagine what a contract lawyer could do for me.*

To counter these objections and persuade lawyers to use your services, read the discussion of myths and realities in Chapter 11, and develop such counterarguments as the following:

- *Using contract lawyers is not a disgrace; some of the most successful firms in the country regularly employ them.*
- *Fears that clients will not accept contract lawyers have proved unfounded. In fact, some companies demand that their outside counsel use contract lawyers.*
- *Contract lawyers can do the work you'd rather not do, leaving you free to concentrate on what you do best.*
- *Contract lawyers can do anything other lawyers can do.*
- *Many contract lawyers are first-rate practitioners.*
- *Contract lawyers are bound by the same rules of ethics as are other lawyers.*
- *Contract lawyers can produce profit for your office.*
- *Contract lawyers are flexible.*

These are just a few of the points you can make. But think through the issues ahead of time, so you can mount a spirited defense when the time comes.

TAKING ADVANTAGE OF PERSONAL CONTACTS

There's a reason why networking—making personal contacts—is first on every legal marketer's list. It really is one of the best ways to find new work. Staying in touch with others in the legal community and beyond also counteracts the potential isolation of contract work.

Although entire books expound on the concept,[1] networking for the contract lawyer boils down to a simple formula: Meet and stay in touch with as many other lawyers as possible. Make sure everyone knows you're looking for contract work of a specific type. Ask colleagues for the names of other lawyers you should meet. Expand your network of contacts while maintaining ties with the old. Keep doing it even if you don't see immediate results.

If you need a detailed road-map, follow this six-step program:

STEP ONE:

Take the advice of Terri Lonier, author of *Working Solo*, and prepare a "five minute brag." (Actually you shouldn't need more than 30 seconds.) Write out and practice a short script that describes what you do in a few positive, intriguing sentences. (We provide more suggestions for preparing such a statement in Chapter 6.) For example, don't say, "Well, I'm trying to find a little contract work while I look for a real job," or, "Um, I'm not really a lawyer. I mean I don't have real clients. I just, um, kind of do projects for other lawyers."

Instead, describe your talents and goals. "I do free-lance work for other lawyers. I'm a good writer, so I write their appellate briefs for them. I also consult with them on corporate tax issues." Practice with friends and family when you are asked the customary, "So what are you doing now?" It's important to avoid sounding apologetic, ashamed, or unhappy about what you're doing. Try to make what you do sound so interesting that your listener will want to follow up with questions.

Ellen Singer met one of her steady customers sitting side-by-side at a bar association luncheon. After she'd introduced herself as a contract lawyer, he asked, "What kind of contract lawyer are you?" "A good one," she promptly responded. Reflecting on that meeting, she says, "You have to be prepared to deliver on a statement like that!"

STEP TWO:

Get out and meet people. Since your customers will all be lawyers, bar activities

---

1. We recommend Cynthia Chin-Lee, *It's Who You Know: Career Strategies for Making Effective Personal Contacts* (Pfeiffer 1993).

are the best way to start. CLE seminars, especially in your practice areas, are great places to meet hiring lawyers. Committee work is another natural. Sign up for pro bono law work in a legal clinic setting and you will meet other volunteer lawyers, many of whom work in law firms, corporations and government agencies. Join and become active in the appropriate practice section of your bar and you will meet lawyers who might need your services. Your bar association activities will also keep you informed about goings-on in the legal community, including who is swamped with work or has just lost a valuable associate.

You must take the initiative in these settings; it's unlikely that someone will select your name from a list of several hundred and call on you to help. Don't just sign up for a committee; show up at the meetings and participate. One excellent prospect is continuing legal education committee work. If you help organize educational events, you will meet not only the other volunteers, but the speakers and lawyers who attend the event as well. You may even become a speaker yourself.

Writing articles for, or editing, the section newsletter is also a good way to meet people and get known. If you're shy or reserved, volunteer to handle behind-the-scenes organization for a social event, then attend as one of the in-crowd. Join local (e.g., city or county) or special interest (e.g., women's, trial, ethnic) associations of lawyers. No matter what group you choose, though, you must be active in it to get to know people.

New admittees can get up-to-date letters of recommendation by volunteering to complete legal research projects for non-profit groups or practitioners who accept pro bono or low-paid court appointments. You can also volunteer to provide legal analysis for special interest advocacy groups deciding whether to pursue litigation. Your volunteer experience will give you substantive knowledge that makes you more credible in an informal chat.

Don't overlook non-law activities. One contract lawyer's church contact led to a discovery project that kept five contract lawyers busy for nine months. Whether you spend your recreational time hiking, working out at the gym, playing bridge, singing in a chorus, or discussing the virtues of the mixed border at a garden club, don't leave your working life behind. For every extracurricular activity, there's a lawyer somewhere who found a new client—and a contract lawyer who found a new customer—while having fun with people with similar interests.

Since you never know what chance meeting will lead to a connection with another lawyer, you should mention your work to everyone. Maybe someone you met while walking your dog is married to an overworked lawyer. Maybe the last client in your accountant's office *is* an overworked lawyer, or maybe there's an overworked lawyer among the parents who drop off their kids at day-care when you do. Use your 30-second brag to convey what you do in simple and memorable terms.

We don't mean you should turn every encounter into a sales pitch. The point is to recognize that, just as you know very little about people you see often, they know very little about you. You may develop friendships or friendly acquaintances with some of them; maybe one will know someone who'll become one of your best customers. But nothing will develop if you keep your lip zipped.

STEP THREE:

Discipline yourself to reach out to lawyers who ought to be interested in your services. To assure yourself of a receptive audience, seek out practitioners who complain about being overloaded but don't have enough extra work to justify hiring an associate. Martindale-Hubbell will identify firms with fewer associates than partners. Overzealous downsizing or flight caused by dissatisfaction may have left them facing demand they cannot meet in some practice areas.

Make contact with lawyers or law firms that advertise openings for permanent positions. They probably need someone right now to handle the overload while they sort through the responses, interview candidates and make a final decision.

Study the local business papers for news of major lawsuits filed against local corporations. They—or their outside counsel—may need temporary assistance with document review, chronologies or other discovery work. In 1998, Preston, Gates & Ellis in Seattle hired a number of contract lawyers to help it respond to the Justice Department's well-publicized antitrust lawsuit against Microsoft.

Concentrate on solo and small firm practitioners, "the most solid and still-expanding employment base for new lawyers" according to Janet M. Jacobson, a legal search consultant in the Pacific Northwest. Confirmed solo practitioner Dick Maizels of Portland wishes he could find a contract lawyer willing to commit to spending four hours a day, three days a week in his office. He says that he and the other lawyers in his office could keep a lawyer that busy. Marjorie Leeds located a solo practitioner who was thinking about retirement. Once she convinced him she could do good work, he provided her with a steady supply of temporary assignments for over two years.

When work is slow for Ellen Singer, she calls all the lawyers she knows and asks whether they have anything for her. If not, she'll ask whether they know any other lawyers who are "so busy they're going out of their minds." Often they do. With the referring lawyer's permission, she calls the overworked lawyers and offers her services.

Finally, don't overlook the obvious. Cindy Vranizan developed a new client by researching good divorce lawyers for a friend whose marriage was falling apart. "I ended up talking to her about my practice," says Vranizan. "The first thing she said was, 'I could have used you last week.' I suggested that she keep me in mind." Since then, Vranizan has helped her out whenever she's overwhelmed before trial.

STEP FOUR:

Always carry a supply of business cards, and hand them out freely to anyone who seems interested. Write the names of people you've met this way in a small notebook you keep close at hand, or collect their business cards, noting on the back where you met each person and what kind of interest they expressed in your services. If the contact seems promising, follow it up with a telephone call, a short note, a letter and résumé or brochure, or an invitation to lunch.

STEP FIVE:

Follow up. Networking isn't something you do only once and then forget about. The minute you become self-employed, it should become part of your work day. When you meet someone you like, initiate further contact. Extend a lunch invitation. Call when there's an issue you need to hash over with another legal mind. If you meet someone who might have work for you, send a letter and information about how you work, or ask for an appointment to discuss the possibilities. Mail newspaper or magazine clippings on items of interest to lawyers you've met. The point is that you cannot wait for others to come to you. You need to take responsibility and take the initiative. Follow up and follow through.

STEP SIX:

Select networking methods that come naturally to you so that you don't have to grit your teeth to get through them. Review the Marketing Grid on page 82 to pinpoint the interactive activities—i.e., those in categories "B," "C," and "D"—that most appeal to you. Then initiate those types of contacts. Every bit of outreach helps. The only approach guaranteed not to work is to sit alone at home, away from the telephone and Internet.

ADVERTISING

Contract lawyer Deborah Guyol is partial to ads because they've consistently worked for her. She placed an advertisement in the *Oregon State Bar Bulletin* on a one-month trial basis. No one responded the month the ad appeared, or the next month, but almost three months later she received a response that yielded $5,000 in work. After that, she arranged to repeat the ad, but reworded it to give it broader

MARKETING GRID

A/ON YOUR OWN
Mail letters with résumés or brochures

Mail announcements of your contract
    practice

Leave your business cards or brochures in
    law libraries or bar associations, as
    permitted

Run a classified ad in the local bar
    publication

Place an announcement of the opening of
    your practice in the local bar
    publication

Post notices at local law libraries

B/ONE-ON-ONE
Person-to-person follow-up on mailings

Person-to-person follow-up on referrals

Initiate conversations with lawyers in the
    law library

Initiate conversations with lawyers at bar
    functions

Call on individual lawyers

Take a lawyer to lunch

Talk to friends and family

Do cold-calling

Converse through a lawyer forum on the
    Internet

C/IN A GROUP
Attend social functions

Take on committee work

Seek out a campaign volunteer position

Attend a bar association luncheon or
    meeting

Join a bar association committee

Attend seminars and lectures

Attend alumni association meetings

Attend sports events

Perform nonprofit volunteer work

D/AS A LEADER
Chair a bar association committee

Run for bar association elective office

Solicit public speaking opportunities

Write and publish articles

Chair a fundraising campaign

Chair a volunteer project or board

Direct a political campaign

Become a community activist

Found a home office support group

Edit a bar association publication

Write a column on contract lawyering

The most effective marketing takes an active rather than a passive role, occurs with
person-to-person interaction rather than the written word and is directed toward
lawyers you have already met, have been referred to or with whom you have
something in common. In other words, most of the activities in Categories B through
D will be more effective than any in Category A.

appeal. This time, she received several responses. Only one led to a continuing
relationship, but it, too, was a lucrative one. After the ad had been running a year,
Guyol was getting so many responses she had to turn work away! After comparing
what she had spent on the ads ($400 for the year) with the money they yielded (over
$15,000), she decided to keep hers running indefinitely.

Not every ad is so successful. Several lawyers we interviewed have never gotten business from their classified advertisements. Elizabeth Bottman's ads paid off for several years when she had little competition; in the last year though, they've elicited almost no response. Denise Kuhlman's first ad listed the types of work she could handle but failed to mention her impressive big firm credentials; it got attention, but mostly from other lawyers interested in becoming, not hiring, contract lawyers.

Guyol's method was to study the ads in the *Bar Bulletin* for months before placing hers. Noticing that they all sounded alike, she worded hers in a catchy style, and described herself in a way that distinguished her from other advertisers. The ad went like this:

> CONTRACT LAWYER—*Extensive experience, impressive credentials, top quality work. Quick study, easy writer, good judgment; malpractice insurance coverage, flexible rates. Call . . .*

If you decide to try advertising, give it time to work. And if it does work, run it regularly. Media professionals maintain that advertising for a long period of time generates a subtle credibility. The assumption is that if you've been around for a while you must be offering a good service. Another theory is that the ad may not attract new customers, but it will let your current customers—and lawyers you've worked for in the past—know that you're still active, still accepting work, and still in the market for new customers. Finally, running an ad is evidence that you're an independent contractor offering your services to the public. (See Chapter 18.)

Many bar associations allow current members to place one-time classified ads in their publications free of charge; the cost is generally under $100 if you have to pay. Thus you only have to attract one paying customer per insertion to justify the cost of the ad. Whether or not your ad brings you work, you won't have risked much money for the experiment. So go ahead and advertise—but remember that unless you combine it with other efforts it's not likely to be enough.

BROADCAST MAILINGS AND FOLLOW-UP CALLS

On its own, the mailing of a brochure, or cover letter and résumé, will yield disappointing results. Not one of the lawyers we interviewed who had simply sent out announcements of their services received any significant work as a result. Done right, however, broadcast mailings can be an effective—if costly and time consuming—way to market your services. To produce good results, follow these five steps.

ELEMENTS OF AN EFFECTIVE PROMOTIONAL LETTER

How many times have you received a letter with first-class postage from a stranger and, after opening it, realized it was a form letter sent to all lawyers in your area but totally irrelevant to you and your concerns? Don't make the same mistake. The first rule of effective letter writing is to personalize your correspondence. Include something that relates specifically to the recipient, whether naming the person who referred you or mentioning a practice area or affiliation.

Don't waste the reader's time with too much detail. Limit your letter to one page, perhaps enclosing a brochure or letter of recommendation from a satisfied customer. Lawyers are busy, so keep the letter short and pique their (self-) interest in the first paragraph. Emphasize your value to the recipient, not the features of your service or background. You can do that in many ways.

- Focus on what you perceive to be their need or desire. A marketing expert with the Davis Wright Tremaine firm suggests you answer the question, "What's in it for me?" in the first few lines. Here's one example:

  In these days of fierce competition and shifting client loyalties, it's hard to commit to a $50,000 to $80,000 salary for another permanent lawyer. When there's more work than you can handle alone, making use of my contract legal services can be a cost-effective solution.

- Start with a thought-provoking or unusual question. You might paraphrase one hiring lawyer's observation: "Would you rather be tortured than spend a day in the library?" Or: "Would you enjoy your work more if you didn't have to deal with difficult clients?" Follow up that question with a statement of what you can do for them: "With a degree in psychology followed by ten years of family law experience, I'm skilled in calming clients, helping them understand the system and fully cooperate with you."

- Open with a provocative statistic:

  Did you know that temporary professional help, including contract legal assistance, is the fastest growing employment category in the United States? Maybe it's time for you to join the growing number of lawyers who are embracing this service for its cost-savings and efficiency.

- Use an appropriate quotation:

  "As recently as two or three years ago," observed the Wall Street Journal in 1995, "temporary legal help was used mostly by small businesses and tiny law firms. But ever since the recession forced companies to cut costs and poured hundreds of top-notch attorneys into the market, the use of legal temps has gone mainstream."

- Introduce the reader to your services by describing a relevant client matter or case study. The sample promotional letter on page 85 uses this strategy.

- Offer a free service to introduce your work. Some new admittees prove their worth by accepting a two-hour assignment at no charge. Other contract lawyers offer a money-back guarantee for the first assignment.

SAMPLE PROMOTIONAL LETTER

Mr. Jose Rodriguez
12345 Wilshire Suite 4400
Los Angeles, CA 90024

Dear Mr. Rodriguez:

Your colleague, Peter Dobkin, suggested that I let you know about my contract legal services.

Last month, Peter was overwhelmed with ten depositions in one case when he was scheduled for trial in another. Rather than rescheduling the depositions and disappointing his anxious client, he asked me to cover them. Peter explained my participation to his client and reduced the client's hourly rate to a figure halfway between his billing rate and mine. Everyone was happy with the arrangement. The client paid less even though my background and experience are comparable to Peter's; Peter made a profit on the hours I worked; and I was able to handle an area of practice I love for a reasonable return.

Besides deposition coverage, I'm available for routine court appearances; I frequently handle all aspects of motion practice. I've enclosed a brochure that more fully explains my background and experience and provides other references.

I hope you'll consider using my services.

Sincerely,

Barbara D. Lowe

STEP ONE:

Identify lawyers and law firms likely to need your services and mail only to them. This is when it pays to have figured out who your market is so you won't waste energy (and test your tolerance for rejection) by approaching lawyers for whom you don't want to work or who are unlikely to want you to work for them. If, for example, you do tax work, you probably shouldn't solicit large law firms with their own tax departments, or firms that specialize in plaintiff's personal injury or insurance defense work. On the other hand, solo practitioners and small firms without tax expertise, especially domestic relations lawyers and general practitioners who handle estate planning and probate work, may be grateful for the opportunity to consult with you on tax problems, rather than referring that work out or risking malpractice by trying to do it themselves.

STEP TWO:

Write a marketing letter targeted to your ideal customer. (Note that even if the mailing is to an unknown recipient, it should *not* be to an unnamed recipient.) Make the letter concise; describe the services you offer and how you work. Offer to provide writing samples and references, but don't include them in the initial mailing. We've provided a sample marketing letter at page 85 and suggestions for creating a strong opening at page 84.

Some contract lawyers also enclose a résumé; be aware that if you do, your letter may be tagged as an application for full-time employment and discarded. This was the experience of San Francisco contract lawyer Steve Weinstein, whose mailing to Bay Area in-house counsel failed because it was mistaken for a job application. Joseph Anthony asserts in *Kiplinger's Working for Yourself* that résumés are for people who are looking for jobs; the self-employed should use brochures.

If you do use a résumé, make certain that it clearly identifies you as a contract lawyer. "Since most temporary work is project oriented, clients wants specialists," declares *U.S. News & World Report.* "Your résumé should be expanded to give details of projects you have completed, especially any assignments undertaken with no advance notice or an extremely tight deadline."[2] Sample résumés are shown on the next two pages.

A better option than a résumé, if you have some experience, is a project list or summary. Use your history of achievements from Chapter 6 to develop this marketing piece. Feature what you consider your most successful projects—preferably those involving written material you'd be willing to offer as writing samples—and provide the names of the lawyers for whom you did the work (with their permission). Try to give a sense of the range of assignments you can handle and the depth of your abilities. Our sample project list is at page 89.

If you plan to pursue contract work for the foreseeable future, you may want to create a brochure. You can design your own using WordPerfect or a brochure-creating software like Microsoft Publisher, a laser printer and one of the new specialty papers (available at most office supply stores) that have been pre-designed and pre-scored for easy folding. If you are not adept at writing promotional copy or develop a headache when confronted by a new computer program, find a good graphic designer to write and produce the brochure. Since this service, including production costs, can easily exceed $1,000, you might want to wait until you know you are in business for the long term.

---

2. Marc Silver, "The Truth about Temping," *U.S. News & World Report,* November 1, 1993.

SAMPLE RÉSUMÉ FOR EXPERIENCED LAWYER

Jane Doe, Esq. / Contract Legal Services

123 Main Street
Chicago, IL 60601
(312) 555-1212

SUMMARY OF EXPERTISE

15 years of progressive **commercial law** *(transactions and litigation),* **real estate** *(leases, financing and sales)* **franchise law** *and* **civil litigation** *experience (domestic relations, landlord/tenant, business and municipal law), including:*

- Negotiating and drafting complex commercial agreements.
- Designing and preparing contracts, including marketing, distribution and trademark licensing agreements.
- Case initiation through prior fact-finding and legal research.
- All aspects of motion practice including briefing, oral argument and negotiation.
- Preparing a complex case for trial including deposition attendance.
- Negotiating among various constituencies.

REPRESENTATIVE ACCOMPLISHMENTS

Resolved a real estate lawsuit pending 14 years involving over 700 claimants.

Arranged a comprehensive right-of-way agreement between a telecommunications utility and a municipality.

Structured the formation and termination of over 100 closely-held corporations and partnerships, which accommodated the needs of all parties.

Represented successfully a disabled father against two sons who had stolen and mismanaged his assets.

Analyzed issues and researched and wrote a persuasive paper on representing the best interests of mentally disabled parents in child abuse and neglect cases.

CHRONOLOGICAL EMPLOYMENT HISTORY

Contract Legal Services	1994-present
Partner, Jones & Smith, Chicago, IL	1985 - 1994
Instructor, University of Illinois Extension, Chicago, IL	1988 - 1994
Partner & Associate Attorney, Rich, Richer & Doe, Lansing, MI	1980 - 1985

PROFESSIONAL CREDENTIALS

Juris Doctor (Ranked 1st of 113), 1980
Thomas M. Cooley Law School, Lansing, Michigan

Bachelor of Arts (G.P.A. of 3.94), 1974
Central Michigan University, Mt. Pleasant, Michigan

Admitted to practice law in Michigan and Illinois

SAMPLE NEW ADMITTEE RÉSUMÉ

John Doe, Esq., Contract Legal Services

123 Main Street
Tacoma, WA 98201
(206) 555-1212

SUMMARY OF EXPERIENCE

A background in legal research and investigation in **credit, domestic relations, criminal defense, personal injury, landlord-tenant** *and* **estate planning** *matters, with special expertise to:*

- Research legal issues
- Comprehend and apply laws and regulations
- Gather information by interviewing individuals
- Organize and coordinate complex projects

REPRESENTATIVE ACCOMPLISHMENTS

Researched legal issues, investigated factual questions and interviewed individuals to gather information for over 100 different cases while employed by two different law firms as a law clerk.

Researched and resolved over 500 credit disputes while employed by a central accounting company.

Synthesized information gleaned from depositions for use during trial.

Investigated complaints by interviewing complainants and respondents as member of a law school Conduct Review Board. Conducted fact-finding hearings. Issued recommendations.

Coordinated the start-up of a project to connect first-year law students with third-year student mentors

Prepared over 200 couples for research project on marital interaction. Assisted them in completing questionnaires.

CHRONOLOGICAL EMPLOYMENT HISTORY

Law Clerk, J. David Rich, Seattle, WA	1998-1999
Summer Law Clerk, Jones & Smith, Seattle, WA	1998
Supervisor, ADP/Telephone Computing Service, Seattle, WA	1995-1996
Researcher, Department of Psychology, University of Washington	1994-1995

PROFESSIONAL CREDENTIALS

Seattle University School of Law, Tacoma, Washington, JD, 1999
University of Washington, Seattle, Washington, Honor Society, BA, Psychology, 1996

Admitted to practice law in the State of Washington

Extensive experience with personal computers and word processing

SAMPLE PROJECT LIST

EXAMPLES OF LEGAL RESEARCH PROJECTS

Contract Law

Application of arbitration provisions to joint venture book publishing contract; appropriate restitution remedy where there is an express contract; validity of option, promissory note and contract in purchase of medical practice

Real Property Law

Bona fide purchaser status where title insurance showed clear title but judicial lien was recorded; whether an implied promise to share maintenance costs accompanies an express easement; validity of lease/option where lessor seeks to repudiate contract while accepting rent on a month-to-month basis

Debtor/Creditor Law

Elements of fraudulent conveyances prior to the Uniform Act; future earnings from insurance renewals as part of the bankruptcy estate; perfection of security interest in shares of stock under the UCC

Employment Law

Computing fringe benefits as part of back-pay award; remedy for violation of reinstatement rights of union post-strike employees; what constitutes constructive rather than actual discharge in at-will employment

Personal Injury Law

Effect of sexual relationship between the parties on interference with economic relations claim; law of nuisance for interference with aesthetic sensibilities claim; malpractice liability of hospital and psychiatrist for minor who runs away while on leave from hospital

COMPLETED LITIGATION PROJECTS:

Draft Documents:

Answers; complaints; counterclaims and crossclaims; demand letters; discovery motions, affidavits and orders; guardianship and adoption petitions; interrogatories, requests for productions and requests for admissions; jurisdictional motions; jury instructions for state and federal court trials; motions in limine; notices; pre-hearing statements; pre-trial orders; settlement packages; summary judgment motions, affidavits and responses; trial memoranda; writ of execution

Help with Strategy:

Initial case evaluation

Prepare for Depositions and Trial:

Draft questions for witnesses; prepare witnesses to testify

Investigate Facts:

Documentation; witnesses to accident

COMPLETED TRANSACTIONAL DOCUMENTS:

Buy-sell agreement; commercial loan documents, pledge agreement, UCC Statement; continuing care contracts; joint venture agreement for domestic partnership

PROJECT REFERENCES

Doug Smith, Smith & Wesson, 4400 Bank of the West, Denver, CO 80204; (303) 555-1212

Marie Curie, Attorney at Law, 1650 Bronson Suite 404, Denver, CO 80206; (303) 556-1212

Earl Sanderson, The Epperson Group, 400 Broad Street Suite 900, Denver, CO 80204; (303) 554-1212

STEP THREE:

Locate your target market through state, local, and specialty bar (including the American Bar Association) practice sections. *Martindale-Hubbell, West's Legal Directory* and the Yellow Pages will help you identify local and regional practitioners who might need your services. You can also purchase a targeted mailing list.

If you are a generalist, proceed by geographical area. Lydia Minkoff targeted solo practitioners with offices near her suburban home, and succeeded early on with a lawyer whose long-time contract lawyer had recently decided to leave the business. Not only did this lawyer have plenty of work for Minkoff, but he raised her hourly rate from $30 to $40—on his own initiative—after she completed her first assignment.

STEP FOUR:

Follow up every letter or brochure with a telephone call a few days later. Don't expect your contact to call you; this happens rarely. And don't mail so many letters at once that, even if you are diligent, it will take you weeks to reach everyone on the list. Networking expert Cynthia Chin-Lee says you don't want to wait so long that the person could have read your letter and forgotten about it. Equally important, don't wait so long that you lose interest or convince yourself that if the recipients

MAKING YOUR ASSOCIATIONS COUNT

Marketing contacts are not created by simply joining organizations or attending meetings and seminars. To find new hiring lawyers or contacts that will lead to new hiring lawyers, you must actively participate. Here are some suggestions.

- Use your 30-second brag (page 78), and be prepared to follow it up by explaining how you can help the lawyer you're talking to. Get a sense of what the lawyer needs first. For example, if Henry the hiring lawyer, who has just left a firm to set up his own shop, says he misses having partners and associates to help him talk through problems, Corinne the contract lawyer can say: "I love strategy. You can always call me for those kinds of discussion." If

Henry says he's got so many depositions scheduled he doesn't know when he'll have time to respond to a big motion, Corinne can ask, "Which would you rather be doing?" Then she can offer to help with the other project.

- Keep a supply of your business cards easily accessible—in a coat pocket rather than your wallet or purse—and exchange cards with everyone you meet.
- Scan the room for people who are standing alone or who look uncomfortable. They'll be grateful for your company and conversation.
- When you return to your office, follow up by telephone or mail with the lawyers whose business cards you gathered.

really wanted to use your services they would have called *you* by now.

Don't be discouraged by a low rate of response. Based on the experience of other contract lawyers—and other businesses that depend on cold calls—you'll be doing well if you find one new hiring lawyer for every 100 targeted letters sent without follow-up and one for every ten letters you do follow up.

STEP FIVE:

Schedule a personal meeting with any lawyer who shows interest when you telephone. Ask the lawyer to lunch so you can explain more about your services. At lunch, ask direct questions about the lawyer's needs: Can this lawyer imagine your assisting with any specific types of projects? Is there an immediate project on which you could help? If the lawyer expresses doubts or misgivings about using contract services, ask what they are and try to allay them. If no work comes from this initial contact, but the customer seems interested, follow up with a telephone call in a week or two. If there is still no work available but you remain hopeful, put the lawyer on your "contact-every-three-to-six-months" list and stay in touch.

COLD CALLS

Cold-calling isn't anyone's favorite method of finding work, nor is it particularly effective. Although there are contract lawyers who find work by calling complete strangers, or by walking through the front door of a law firm and asking to speak with the managing partner or administrator, we believe such successes are rare. That's not to say you shouldn't try this method if it suits your style. It's always possible you'll connect with a busy practitioner who sees you as his savior.

Going door to door will not work, however, with mid-sized to large firms. Karen Summerville, a former law firm partner who is now a career counselor for lawyers, is certain you'd never get past the front desk. Small law firms and solo practitioners without extensive staff are a better bet. They tend to be busy with the minutiae of daily law practice and don't have the time to search for additional help. If you walk into the middle of a crisis with the right personality and credentials, you may be handed work on the spot.

If you venture forth in person, go equipped with several copies of your résumé, brochure or project list; samples of your written work product; the names of lawyers who will give you a good reference and a sample engagement letter. Ask enough questions to be able to explain how your contract services can help that lawyer. Be prepared to discuss your rates.

Remember that cold-calling pays off with only marginally better odds than the lottery. You might hit the jackpot, but you're better off using your energy to introduce yourself in "warmer" ways.

STAYING VISIBLE

All the aforementioned methods of finding work require endurance and patience. You have to keep doing them to get other lawyers to associate your name with contract work. Of course, some lawyers naturally attract attention; others have to work at it; many don't want it. But if you want to be successful in the contract market, you must remain visible, visible, visible.

Visit your hiring lawyers' offices frequently. If they see you there, they may be more likely to hand you an assignment than if they have to find time to call.

Speaking or writing about subjects in your area of expertise is an excellent way to stay visible. Maryland lawyer Mindy Farber attributes her rainmaking success to an energetic course of speaking and writing over a period of several years that helped her become known as an authority in her field.[3] Most lawyers are good at either speaking or writing (or they wouldn't have chosen to be lawyers); use your communication skills (wherever they lie) to develop a reputation as an authority.

Opportunities are everywhere. Sue Samuelson agreed to be interviewed and have her name used in an article on contract lawyering. As a result, she received steady work for over six months from two bankruptcy lawyers who read the article. Elizabeth Bottman donated five hours of legal research and writing services to two different auctions when she knew that a substantial number of attendees would be lawyers.

Even your experiences as a contract lawyer can translate into expertise. Lee Archer was invited to speak at the 1994 ABA convention in New Orleans on developing and keeping a successful appellate practice. Denise Kuhlman talked about starting her contract practice at a Seattle CLE program on "Hanging Out Your Shingle."

MAINTAINING A PROFESSIONAL IMAGE

Impressions are important, especially since many lawyers have an unjustifiably

---

3. Mindy G. Farber, "Women as Rainmakers—A Personal Perspective," *Law Practice Management,* July-August 1994.

poor view of contract lawyers in the first place. Everything about the way you present yourself contributes to your image, and it should be a professional one. Think about how you're perceived when you answer the telephone, when you dress for meetings with hiring lawyers, and when you hand in a finished memo.

But don't let your concern with a business-like image stifle your style and personality. All the best marketing advice emphasizes the importance of being yourself, whether your personality is flamboyant and talkative or bookish and reserved. Be true to your distinctive personal style and preferences and you will be memorable.

CONCLUSION

In today's professional environment, you should try just about any marketing idea to find the method that works best for you. Don't let conventional wisdom about what works and what doesn't discourage you from testing an unorthodox idea. We've aimed to cover all the possibilities, but there may be techniques we've never heard or thought of that will be right for you.

9

STAYING IN BUSINESS

You've targeted your market, established your rates, found a few customers and are hard at work. From now on your life as a contract lawyer will be smooth and predictable, right? Well, not quite. You'll also need to master the mechanics of staying in business, from nurturing relationships with hiring lawyers to managing your time, money and moods.

Elizabeth Bottman first tried contract work in 1986, assuming "it would just be until I found something more permanent." She had left four jobs since graduating from law school, and was not sure what to do next. To her surprise, she said, "Once I started contract work I found I liked it very much. I had the excitement of owning my own business without the stress of representing clients."

In the 12 plus years she's been working on a contract basis, Bottman has learned that the problems of the free-lance worker are different from those of the wage slave, but they are just as real: they keep coming at you, and they all seem to be related to communication, money and time. Many of the tips in this chapter derive from Bottman's hard-knocks advice.

HANDLING THE INTAKE INTERVIEW

When you are offered an assignment, it's up to you to determine whether the matter is within your expertise and ability, to assure you have no conflict of interest and to make certain the hiring lawyer understands your rates and payment terms. Most hiring lawyers call because they don't have time to handle the work themselves. As a result, the initial conversation may feel rushed and stressful as the hiring lawyer tries to tell you as little as possible as quickly as possible to get you on board without delay.

Despite the pressure to make a fast decision, ask questions and take detailed notes. "In the beginning I was afraid to ask a lot of questions," says Bottman. "Now I'm not. Sometimes I feel dumb, but at least I get the information I need." To control the interview, interrupt if necessary—especially if you fear breaches of confidentiality or a possible conflict of interest. Use this list to organize your discussion.

STEP ONE: CHECK FOR CONFLICTS OF INTEREST.

Ordinarily, a lawyer will telephone, explaining that a difficult case has a deadline coming up soon. Then, he'll start to give you the details. Stop him before he divulges confidential information. Ask the names of all individual and corporate clients, parties and potential parties, and other lawyers involved in the matter. Check for possible conflicts, and if you find one, discuss it with him. (Read the discussion of conflicts of interest in Chapter 17.) If there are no conflicts or potential conflicts, go to the second step.

STEP TWO: ASCERTAIN THE NATURE OF THE ASSIGNMENT.

You need to know not only the subject matter, but also the type of work to be completed. Does the hiring lawyer want basic research without analysis, or does he want a written memorandum as well? Are you helping him prepare for a motion or for trial? Do you even have an assignment? Former Denver contract lawyer Peter Ludwig thought he was having a preliminary discussion with a hiring lawyer; he was given no details or deadlines. Later the lawyer called him up demanding to know where the brief was.

If the assignment is straightforward but in an unfamiliar area of law, warn the hiring lawyer that you'll need time to learn the subject matter. The hiring lawyer can decide whether he wants to pay you for the additional time or find a contract lawyer with more relevant experience. You should always turn down an assignment if you doubt your ability to handle it. Bottman, for example, won't accept tax or securities assignments.

STEP THREE: AGREE ON DEADLINES AND HOURS TO BE SPENT.

Bottman notes that lawyers often don't tell her enough about what they need or the form they need it in. "I'll listen to what they say and then I have to ask questions. What do you need? What kind of motion? When do you need it? What's the maximum number of hours you think I should spend?"

It's also important to get a firm deadline—and don't settle for "as soon as possible." If the lawyer won't get specific, you should, as in, "Is Monday soon enough?" Ask about external events driving the deadline. Is a statute of limitations about to run, a firm date for filing a motion or response, a meeting scheduled with the client to decide on strategy? How far in advance of these dates must the lawyer have your finished product?

Some hiring lawyers will tell you how long they want you to spend on the project; if yours doesn't, take the initiative yourself. Ask straight out, "How long do you think this should take?" If the estimate seems reasonable, agree not to exceed it without prior approval. But tell the hiring lawyer if you think the estimate is low, and agree on a more realistic figure before you accept the assignment. Be sure to note deadlines in your engagement letter as well as any estimate of (or limit on) time to be spent. (See Chapter 20 for a detailed discussion of engagement letters and retention agreements.)

STEP FOUR: CONFIRM RATES AND PAYMENT TERMS.

State your rate; make it clear that you will be paid by the hiring lawyer, not the

---

INTAKE SHEET

Contact Name: _____

Firm Name: _____

Address:_____

_____

Telephone:_____ Fax:_____

Referred by: _____

Names of all parties and potential parties:_____

_____

Nature of assignment:_____

_____

Work product:_____

Deadlines: _____

Hourly rate: _____

Payment terms:_____

Retainer: _____

Malpractice insurance coverage & indemnity: _____

Requested: Follow-up:
___copy of entire file   ___checked bar for pending grievances
___all filed pleadings   ___credit check
___work samples   ___letter/agreement prepared and sent
___access to client   ___signed copy returned
___access to witnesses   ___retainer received
___contact with opposing counsel

client and that you will be paid whether or not the hiring lawyer is paid by the client. If the hiring lawyer has a problem with your rate, explain that he can charge your time to the client at a higher rate. Molly Tami of Cincinnati uses this simple argument when prospective customers balk at her $70 per hour rate. Or offer an alternative fee arrangement. (See Chapter 7.) Your rate and payment terms should be part of your engagement letter. (See Chapter 20.)

STEP FIVE: DISCUSS MALPRACTICE INSURANCE COVERAGE.

Let the lawyer know whether you have your own policy, and ask whether he is insured. If you do not have coverage, will his (or his firm's) policy cover your work? Discuss whether your written agreement should include "hold harmless" language. (See page 235.) Unless you act as a consulting expert, your work should be reviewed and approved by the hiring lawyer before being filed, and he should hold you harmless from any claims based on your contribution to the case. If you are acting as a consulting expert, it is reasonable for the hiring lawyer to obtain a hold harmless agreement from you.

STEP SIX: MAKE SURE YOU HAVE ADEQUATE INFORMATION.

You can't do a good job unless you have the facts. Many contract lawyers discover too late that they were given inadequate or inaccurate information by the hiring lawyer, and then learn, when they turn in the finished product, that they missed the most important issue. Bottman always schedules a face-to-face meeting for first-time customers, and for any large assignment. That way she can review as much of the file as necessary and get copies of documents she needs. Again, don't hesitate to ask questions (or call back later) if you need more information to do the job right.

STEP SEVEN: ASK HOW THE HIRING LAWYER FOUND OUT ABOUT YOU.

A hiring lawyer may begin by referring to your ad in the local bar journal. More often he'll simply introduce himself and launch into a description of the project. Ask every caller how he got your name. The answers will tell you whether your ad is paying for itself, how effective your networking efforts have been, and who to thank for any referral. Over time, you can use this information to improve your marketing efforts.

EVALUATING PROSPECTIVE EMPLOYERS

Deciding whether you can handle the assignment is only part of your job. You also have to think about whether you want to work with this lawyer or law firm. All hiring lawyers are not created equal, and once you accept an assignment you have a contractual obligation to see it through. Therefore, just as a prospective hiring lawyer will interview you, you should be interviewing him.

You can turn down any lawyer's projects for any reason—your lack of time, the hiring lawyer's working style or personality, or your aversion to the subject matter, client or nature of the work. For example if you are uncomfortable with last-minute, always-in-a-rush projects and the hiring lawyer knows of no other kind, it may be better to decline the projects than to suffer through them.

In the beginning you may feel that saying "no" is a luxury you can't afford. In fact, the reverse is true: sometimes saying "yes" is a luxury you can't afford. Moving from worst to best case, here are some occasions for saying "no."

PROFESSIONALISM PROBLEMS

You can certainly afford to say "no" to a lawyer who has been suspended from the practice of law or who is casual about his professional responsibilities—especially if you do not have malpractice coverage. Katherine Foldes once turned in a draft complaint to a lawyer two months before the statute of limitations ran, but the hiring lawyer failed to serve the defendant in a timely manner. Foldes later learned that he had been suspended at the time of the assignment. If you suspect a similar problem with a lawyer who has asked you to do a project, call the bar (or other licensing authority) to ask about his status.

CREDIT PROBLEMS

You can also afford to say "no" to a lawyer who's not going to pay you. There's no sure way to avoid this, but it helps to be alert to potential problems. Most of the payment problems we're aware of have been with contingent fee lawyers or solo practitioners—but don't let this scare you off either type of lawyer; they can also be your best source of work. If you're concerned about a lawyer's ability to pay, request a retainer. Or start with a small project and make sure you're paid on time before accepting a bigger one. With large projects, you can submit a bill weekly, or whenever you've accumulated $500 worth of time. Once a hiring lawyer fails to pay you, you can simply refuse to do further work for that lawyer. (There are no ethical restrictions on your ability to withdraw unless you are formally listed as lead counsel or have an agreement directly with the client.)

SLOW PAY

Whether you continue to accept work from a hiring lawyer who's a slow pay, but always pays eventually, is up to you. You can't afford to say "yes" to that lawyer if you need the money now. If immediate payment is not crucial, however, you can offer an alternative billing plan to encourage regular payment. (See Chapter 7 at page 70.)

LOW PAY

There will always be hiring lawyers who want to pay less than your usual rate. Unfortunately, many still feel that the perfect contract lawyer is out there some-where—editor-in-chief of the *Harvard Law Review*, ten years of experience at a top-flight firm, willing to work for $25 per hour and ready to start today. If you have customers who will pay you $50 per hour, it's easy to say "no" to someone who offers $25. It's a tougher call if you haven't had work for a month. Here's a tactic for that situation:

First try to negotiate a project fee. Sometimes a new hiring lawyer just wants to be sure that he won't have to spend more than, say, $500 for the project. Ask what the hiring lawyer was planning to spend; if you think you can do the job for that much, take it. If not, tell him you need to check first with your regular customers, then call everyone you've ever worked for and ask if they anticipate needing you in the next couple of weeks. If they do, your problem is solved. If not, and if you're truly desperate, you can still go back and take the low-paid project. But remember that you can't predict what the telephone will bring tomorrow; you'll kick yourself (and want to kick the hiring lawyer) if working on this project prevents you from accepting a better-paying one that comes along the next day.

CONFLICTS

Don't be timid about refusing to work on a case because of a potential conflict of interest, says Sandi Nichols, operator of a contract lawyer placement agency in the Bay Area. She cites the example of a San Francisco contract lawyer whose experience included work on environmental law cases for an East Bay firm. Her supervisor at a San Francisco firm later asked her to work on a personal injury case opposing the East Bay firm, telling her not to worry about her prior assignment. Even though the contract lawyer didn't know the East Bay attorney on the case, who had worked on a different floor, she refused. Her supervisor expressed dismay. To her, the supervisor's discomfort was irrelevant. It didn't matter that he couldn't see the conflict. It was her concern, and she didn't believe she could be too careful.[1]

This doesn't mean you must always turn down an assignment when you've done

---

1.　Sandi Nichols, "Tips for Hiring Contract Lawyers," *California Legal Registry*, April 11, 1991.

work for opposing counsel. (See Chapter 17 for an extensive discussion of real and possible conflicts of interest.) This is the sort of situation that calls for different responses depending on the personalities and work arrangements involved, and perhaps the size and collegiality of the local bar. Eric Ebel works out of Ann Arbor, Michigan, for lawyers around the state. He "will let the lawyer know immediately if opposing counsel happens to be someone I have a regular relationship with. Then I'll telephone opposing counsel to ask if they mind my researching the matter. They usually don't."

BUT BE REASONABLE

Of course, there's such a thing as being too particular, especially in a buyer's market. Laura Black of Special Counsel tells the story of a woman with extensive experience in leasing who stipulated that she would accept assignments only at a very high hourly rate within 20 miles of her home between the hours of 10:00 a.m. and 2:00 p.m. Laura's agency, surprisingly, found a leasing company that would pay her rate and didn't mind the restrictions on hours, but was located more than 20 miles from the woman's home. The woman declined the assignment. Of course, the agency never tried to find her another position. Part of the art of life is achieving a balance between what you want and what you can get; it's the same with contract lawyering.

SPECIAL ADVICE FOR NEW ADMITTEES

Doing contract work as a new graduate has its disadvantages:
1. You have to learn on your own time.
2. You have to start from scratch in marketing yourself.
3. You won't have ready access to role models and mentors.
4. You may be ignored by hiring lawyers who would rather work with lawyers who need little supervision and know their way around the courthouse.
5. You may be hired by lawyers who don't recognize that your low rate reflects your inexperience, and who will be disappointed if you can't work as quickly and proficiently as the veterans with higher billing rates.

If you are determined to make it as a contract lawyer, though, none of these obstacles are insurmountable.

Dady Blake is a good example of a young lawyer with the proper motivation and initiative. After graduating from UCLA School of Law, she moved to Portland, Oregon, hoping to find a tax associate position. While engaged in her job search, she volunteered her time generously, both on bar committees and for pro bono legal projects. Her networking didn't land her a permanent job, but did secure her first contract project.

The volunteer work also introduced her to elder law issues and led her to establish a solo practice — supplemented by contract work — in that growing field.

All contract lawyers have to prove themselves anew for each hiring lawyer, but it's especially important for inexperienced lawyers to realize this. You may not get a payback on your good work for months, but if you think contract work is just a way station toward a "real" job and you're tempted to slight a project for that reason, you'll never see any payback at all.

Proving yourself means writing off time if you think you've taken too long to finish a project. It means being patient; it may take more than one well-done project to convince a hiring lawyer you're up to the task. Think of your first year or so doing contract work as a period of apprenticeship or internship. You won't earn big bucks, but you'll learn a lot and, if you do it right, you'll establish credibility in the eyes of your customers.

To make yourself more marketable, develop a niche. The best choice is one that mixes your favorite subject with a kind of work that is much in demand. To find the right niche for you, spend time on the market research described in Chapter 5. Interview practitioners in subject matter areas that appeal to you; ask them about the issues that worry them most. Ask what kinds of work they are likely to refer out and what kind of experience they'd want the lawyer they hire to have. Then get that experience, whether from library research, CLE programs, or volunteer work. You can even ask to sit in on depositions or watch trials if you need that kind of experience.

It's also a good idea to find a mentor. At this stage of your career you need someone you can talk to when you don't know where to start on a project, when you think you may have gotten off track, when you'd like to brainstorm, or when you just need moral support. Sign up with any mentoring program sponsored by your state, local or specialty bar association. If there are no resources in your area, consider working with a bar group to start such a program yourself. You can also find a mentor on your own. Look for an experienced lawyer who isn't currently giving you work so you feel free to ask questions without being penalized for your ignorance or naiveté.

The networking you do to find work will help you locate a mentor. Another source of potential mentors is that old standby, volunteer work. If you meet someone you get along with who practices in an area of law that interests you, ask if he is willing to talk when you have questions. Then pursue the relationship by inviting the potential mentor to lunch. Ask if he knows people who might have other information you could use. Don't ask for work from your mentor though; assume he'll let you know if he has an assignment.

KEEPING CUSTOMERS HAPPY

Terri Lonier, author of *Working Solo*, estimates that as much as 80 percent of your work will come from repeat customers. Satisfying hiring lawyers, therefore, should be the primary focus of your business. This should go without saying, but apparently many lawyers are better at legal analysis than customer service. As an example, clients commonly complain that their lawyers fail to return telephone calls within 24 hours. Don't let this complaint apply to you.

With rare exceptions, contract lawyers are not such hot commodities that they can afford to let customer service slip from the forefront of their attention. You can keep hiring lawyers satisfied by following these rules.

RULE ONE: KEEP THE LINES OF COMMUNICATION WIDE OPEN.

Return all calls from current and potential hiring lawyers promptly, preferably within a few hours. This means calling in for messages once or twice a day if you are away from your office. It means notifying your existing customers when you intend to be out of your office for a day or more, whether for vacation or attendance at bar activities. It means arranging for a friend, relative or another contract lawyer to pick up your messages and return any urgent calls when you're out of town.

RULE TWO: HONOR YOUR COMMITMENTS.

The only complaint about contract lawyers we heard in our research is that some do not share either the hiring lawyer's sense of urgency or his level of commitment to the client and the case. Los Angeles placement specialist Liz Elliott had arranged for a contract lawyer to handle the business of a real estate lawyer who was flat on her back after surgery. The assignment had been confirmed two weeks before surgery. At the last minute, the contract lawyer called to say she didn't want to do it. Richard Kaplan's single bad experience with a contract lawyer came when the lawyer went off to a mountain top to experience a New Age event rather than finish a project. On the basis of one similar experience, Daniel Edwards concluded that "contract lawyers are not going to have the commitment to the case that I have."

You'll do best if you realize that the hiring lawyer probably has the same worries about you; your job is to prove him wrong. Be vigilant against over-booking assignments or taking on a large project that may interfere with serving your existing clientele. If meeting a deadline turns out to be impossible, let the hiring lawyer know immediately. If the summary judgment motion you said would take ten hours and be ready Friday turns out to have hidden issues that can't be finished until you've studied the deposition of the plaintiff's brother, tell the hiring lawyer what the problems are as soon as you become aware of them. If a court deadline is imminent, provide a memo listing what remains to be done to get the document filed on time.

RULE THREE: RELAX YOUR EGO.

Take criticism gracefully and compliments modestly. Accept that you may not get credit for work well done, and that you may be blamed for complications that are not your fault. If this is a problem for you, try to remember (or imagine) your days as a law firm associate! The contract lawyer relationship is not one in which you get to call a lot of shots. You are in a service business, and your job is to make the hiring lawyer happy.

Be sensitive to the hiring firm's needs and protocol as well. Liz Elliott was asked to find a lawyer who could complete a big writing assignment for a partner who had a major business trip planned. Elliott found a well-credentialed business lawyer with seven years of experience and a reputation for being extremely responsible to handle the assignment. The contract lawyer, who had never worked unsupervised, took over the hiring lawyer's office, spending time on the telephone for personal business and monopolizing the secretary, despite numerous protests by the hiring lawyer's partner. When the hiring lawyer returned to the country, he complained to the agency about the contract lawyer's lack of etiquette. Both the agency and the contract lawyer received a downward adjustment in fee.

The key is to be respectful and humble. If this rule annoys you, review Chapter 5 on whether you're cut out to be a contract lawyer in the first place!

RULE FOUR: RAISE ISSUES AND STRATEGIES OF WHICH THE HIRING LAWYER MIGHT NOT BE AWARE.

Rather than relying on the statement of the issues you've been given, think independently about the facts and the law. If you notice a missed issue, ask about it. But don't give advice gratuitously, or delve deeply into undesignated issues on your own. Maybe the lawyer didn't overlook it but has a reason to believe it's really not an issue. Maybe the issue has already been fully briefed. The goal is not to prove you're smarter than the hiring lawyer, but to instill confidence in your ability and make it clear that you take the project seriously.

RULE FIVE: ALWAYS DO YOUR BEST WORK.

Although we've left this almost for last, it is of prime importance. When you're an associate in a law firm and your work doesn't meet the expectations of the assigning partner, you will be told to revise it; when a hiring lawyer is dissatisfied with your work as a contract lawyer, chances are he simply won't call you again. Being a contract lawyer means constantly having to prove yourself. For that reason, it's important to get clear instructions up front, to provide absolutely current research even if that means checking advance sheets the day you turn in an assignment, and to offer the best product you can. If you accept an assignment in an unfamiliar area, either tell the hiring lawyer and ask for suggestions about where to begin, or be prepared to write off the time you spend getting oriented.

Former Florida contract lawyer Beth Besner recommends asking for work samples when you accept an assignment so you can adjust your style to that of the hiring lawyer, even if you think yours is more professional. For example, lawyers have different preferences for listing counts in complaints: some put the strongest one first, some put it last, some use no particular order. Discerning a preference before investing in the project will better assure satisfaction and efficiency.

Doing good work is absolutely the best advertisement you have for yourself. Since lawyers aren't usually generous with feedback—positive or negative—you can think that your work made no impression. Later, though, you'll hear through the grapevine that the lawyer for whom you handled a major summary judgment motion

MAINTAINING GOOD CUSTOMER RELATIONS

Your past and present customers are likely to become future customers — and to refer other hiring lawyers to you — if you follow these suggestions:

- Let them know you like working with them. A simple one-sentence thank-you at the bottom of the bill you submit is easy to write and builds goodwill. Send a congratulatory note when you see your hiring lawyers' names in print, or hear about personal events like weddings or anniversaries, or learn that they successfully concluded a case (especially if you worked on it). Send thank-you notes for referrals or other courtesies they extend to you.
- Provide "extra" value to hiring lawyers. Send them copies of articles in their areas of interest or practice forms you've devised that may make their work easier. Attach a post-it note or simple card with a handwritten "saw this and thought of you." Put yourself in your hiring lawyers' shoes. What extra service would make a difference to you if the roles were reversed?
- Stay in touch. Let them know when you plan to be out of town or busy with another long-term project, or otherwise unavailable to accept assignments. Try to call them before they call you, especially if you're going to be late with an assignment. Take responsibility for the delay, provide a simple and honest explanation for your tardiness and a realistic estimate of when the project will be completed. Or telephone without an agenda, just to let them know you're thinking about them.
- Keep them informed about your other customers and assignments. This will reinforce their good judgment in hiring you in the first place and may educate them about help you can provide on other kinds of tasks or subject matters.
- Get to know them personally. Look at the photographs in their offices and ask about their interests and families. Initiate conversations by telling them something personal about yourself.
- Demonstrate expertise in your practice area by assuming a leadership role in professional associations or writing and publishing in specialty newsletters and magazines. Ask your hiring lawyers to co-author articles with you, to speak at seminars you're coordinating or to join you at a professional group meeting.

was impressed with both your legal analysis and your writing. At that point you will realize that another lawyer just helped with your marketing plan. For ten years, Katherine Foldes has found almost all her work through word of mouth when satisfied hiring lawyers passed along her name to others. Eric Ebel, who claims he does "no marketing," manages to bill about 20 hours a week for repeat customers, some of whom he's been working with for ten years.

Doing a good job is not always recognized and rewarded at the time, but you can be sure that if you are casual about deadlines, or hand in shoddy work that needs significant revision before it can be used, or miss the recent case that changed the law, your reputation will suffer. Doing a terrific job won't get you your very first customer, but it will keep them coming back. And if you fail to do good work, your first customer could be your last.

RULE SIX: DEAL POSITIVELY WITH DISSATISFIED CUSTOMERS.

As Joseph Anthony explains in *Working for Yourself*, disgruntled customers can become your most loyal customers if you deal with their dissatisfaction properly. The trick, of course, is learning that they're dissatisfied. The lawyer who gave you a big project and then never called again may have decided to hire a full-time associate, or may have been unhappy with your work. If he's like most lawyers, he's too busy to talk to you about it. You won't learn what he thinks unless you ask. So make a habit of following up at least the first project you do for a new hiring lawyer within a week after you've turned it in. Ask if it was what was needed, and if there's anything more you can do.

If the hiring lawyer *was* unhappy, solicit details, listen carefully and take notes. Offer to correct the problem at no charge if this lawyer is someone you'd like to work with in the future. If correction will take a long time or the problem stemmed from the lawyer's faulty instructions, you can offer to complete the work at a reduced rate. Use your judgment.

MANAGING YOUR BUSINESS

TIMEKEEPING

It's amazing how painless timekeeping becomes when each hour you bill means a certain number of dollars in your pocket. Whatever old feelings you have about time sheets—and if you are a law firm refugee they may be bitter—the time sheet is your friend from now on. Not all hiring lawyers will require you to submit time sheets, but you should still keep track of all your time. Time slips help you track your monthly income. They test the profitability of any flat-fee agreement. They're also an essential record of your services in case of any fee dispute.

You need a method of time notation that you'll use faithfully. Some contract lawyers keep a notebook with a page for each project, and carry it with them at all times. When they finish a project, they transfer the time to their computer and bill the hiring lawyer. Others staple a sheet inside each file folder, and record time and functions as they work on the file. You may prefer a carbonless time sheet system on which you record your activity for each project each day on a different slip, then retain both an individual record to place in the project file and a running total of the time you spend on all your work each week or month. There are also computer programs that allow you to enter your time directly on the computer; the program will generate a bill.

Firms that require time sheets may give you a supply of theirs. Those that involve filling out a separate sheet for each day aren't really suited to contract work. A time sheet organized by project is a better idea. If you work ten hours on a project but the time is spread out over several days, you can provide the firm a single time sheet for the entire project.

BILLING

Exactly when you bill hiring lawyers will depend on how they are set up to pay you. Some firms pay only at the end of the month; some pay immediately upon presentation of the bill; some pay within a few weeks of being billed but only if they are prodded; a very few try to avoid paying at all.

Bill at the completion of very short projects. Projects lasting longer than a month should be billed at agreed intervals. For firms that pay only at the end of the month, ask what day they cut the checks and submit your bill a few days earlier. Susan Shulenberger discovered that mailing her statements gets them into the billing cycle faster and more reliably than dropping them off with the hiring lawyer.

The bill should always state payment terms—for example, "net ten days." If you have a faithful customer who's a habitual slow pay, it might help to hand-deliver the bill when you finish the project and ask for on-the-spot payment. Or offer a discount for prompt payment, or increase your rate for delayed payment. (See Chapter 7.)

One sticky issue is whether to bill for conversations with hiring lawyers that mix business and personal subjects. If you've ever worked in a firm, you're familiar with the client who invites you to lunch to talk about the case and then "can't believe you charged for that whole lunch" when he gets the bill. Similarly, you may have conversations with a hiring lawyer that begin as discussions of waiver and end up being about the kids' dance recitals. This is when you have to use your judgment about how much of the conversation to bill, keeping in mind that uncompensated telephone talks and meetings may lessen your income but provide valuable marketing points.

COLLECTING

Elizabeth Bottman has never had trouble with collections. She thinks it's "because lawyers are dealing with other lawyers and feel they need to be fair." But she's willing to be both flexible and firm when necessary. "A lawyer once told me that he had problems paying my bill right away and asked if I could wait a month. I said 'sure'; I figured he was doing as well as he could. He made two payments the next month and paid off the bill." She has also been firm when she smelled trouble, as with the contingent fee agreement described in Chapter 7 at page 72.

What can you do when a hiring lawyer simply does not pay the bill? First try polite telephone calls and repeat billings. Ask for partial payment immediately, with a date certain for payment in full. If these efforts fail, visit the lawyer in person: a live body is hard to ignore. If even this direct approach fails, there's not much you can do but continue to pester him or file a collection action in small claims court. Of course, you can decline additional projects until you've been paid, but most hiring lawyers will not call with assignments if you're actively trying to collect.

It's better to prevent the situation from coming up at all. Lawyers and firms with their own cash flow problems are the ones most likely to stiff you. Be alert for signs of trouble—a dirty or shabby office, or unusually surly staff (because they haven't been paid either). Katherine Foldes says she should have known she'd have trouble with one hiring lawyer when she arrived at his office and found the front yard grown thigh-high with grass and weeds.

If you have doubts about the solvency of a lawyer who has offered you a big project, discuss your misgivings and ask for reassurance. Better yet, request a substantial retainer, half of which will apply to the first billing and half to the last. Then submit regular bills and see if they are paid promptly. If they are not, you can apply the last half of the retainer to the bill. Or propose billing once a week, and tell the lawyer you will stop work on the project if payments get behind. Whatever tactic you choose, it is important to realize that *you* are the only person who can prevent yourself from giving away your services. Be as ruthless as you dare.

MANAGING CASH FLOW

As is the case with most businesses, it may be a few months before your contract work produces the income you need. You'll be more comfortable if you've taken the advice in Chapter 5 and accumulated some money for living expenses before you start. Even if you have, though, the erratic nature of your contract income will teach you the mysteries of cash flow. Accept at the beginning that your income stream will never be steady and predictable and you'll save yourself major worry. Whether you relax into the current or fight against it, though, you have to be careful in timing your expenditures.

CALCULATING RECURRING EXPENDITURES

Begin by making a schedule showing each monthly expense and when it needs to be paid. A form for this purpose is provided in Chapter 7 at page 63. (This discussion assumes you will depend on your work as a contract lawyer to pay your (share of) living expenses.) Make schedules showing payments that are due less often, such as bar association dues and insurance premiums. These schedules will tell you how much money you need to bring in each month to meet expenses.

Once you've estimated your annual expenses, make a schedule for the next several months, showing for each month the total amount of money you will need to pay expenses and reserve for taxes. Use this schedule to create your budget. If you are working on a long-term project, your income will be easy to predict and the schedule will tell you how much extra income (or shortfall) you will have. Given the uncertainties of contract work, it's always a good idea to accumulate enough money to see you through several months without work before you use savings to pay off an old credit card or buy a new mountain bike.

QUARTERLY TAX PAYMENTS

Unless you are working as an employee, you will need to reserve funds for your quarterly tax payments, which are not made precisely quarterly but on about the 15th of April, June, September and January.

One of the first rude shocks of working for yourself is the self-employment tax, a total of 15.3% of your net business income.[2] When you have a job, your employer pays half of your Social Security tax; the other half is deducted from your paycheck so you never see it. When you're self-employed, you have to pay the whole thing. It's much more painful to write that check to the IRS than to have money withheld from checks paid to you.

The pain is lessened somewhat when you take into account the advantages of being self-employed. Most of the expenses of running your business—including half your self-employment tax—are deductible for the purpose of calculating your income

---

2.   Actually, it's only paid on 92.35% of your net business income, but who's counting?

tax. If you work at home, you may also be eligible for the home office deduction. To qualify, your home office must both be your principal place of business and be used only for the conduct of your business. In other words, you won't qualify if you maintain a fully-equipped home office but work mostly on-site in hiring lawyers' offices. Similarly, if your desk is in a corner of the living room and your computer is stocked with games for your kids, the deduction is probably not available to you.

The Tax Code changes often and unpredictably, and court decisions affect its interpretation. All of the sources we've cited at page 312 on working for yourself contain more or less thorough treatment of tax issues.[3] The Internal Revenue Service, in cooperation with state and local taxing authorities, offers free day-long "Sole Proprietor Tax Seminars" in many cities across the country. Since lawyers have been identified by the IRS as potential audit targets, however, it's always wise to rely on the advice of a tax professional.

Once you've been self-employed for a while, you can estimate your quarterly tax payments based on experience. A rule of thumb for the single taxpayer with standard deductions and no dependents is to reserve for estimated taxes about a third of your net income each month. For example, if you bring in $3,500 and have $500 in business expenses, you should reserve $1,000 for taxes. If your net quarterly income is $9,000, your estimated tax payments will be around $3,000. Your tax liability will be smaller if you are head of household or married to a non-working spouse, or if you have significant deductions. Remember, though, that you can't avoid paying that first 15 percent.

INSURANCE COVERAGE

The second rude shock of self-employment is having to find your own insurance: malpractice, health, disability and life. Health insurance is a hot topic these days. If you're married and your spouse has a job with benefits, being added to his or her policy may be the best way to go. Continuation coverage (COBRA) is available for up to 18 months after you leave your job, no matter why you've left. It can be both costly and risky, though, since any illness you contract during that period may disqualify you from coverage under a new policy, and conversion policies are expensive. Many state and local bar groups, as well as the ABA, offer group rates on health insurance. Alumni associations may also offer this benefit of membership.

You may need life, property, business interruption, and disability insurance.

---

3. Bernard Kameroff, *Small Time Operator* (Bell Springs Publications 1994), is devoted almost entirely to tax and accounting issues for small businesses.

Again, learn what group plans are available through bar, alumni and other organizations. Consult your insurance agent. Then get yourself and your business as much insurance as your pocketbook will allow.

MEETING YOUR OBLIGATIONS

Now go back to the schedules showing the timing of expenses. You'll need to start planning well before the end of each month for payment of the next month's bills. Do you have enough—or will you be able to collect enough—to pay them as they come due? If you have statements outstanding, call with reminders so the checks will come in time for you to use them to pay your bills. Keep a line of credit (or credit card) to cover expenses when you don't get paid soon enough. And dream of the time when you'll have enough income to relax your vigilance.

MANAGING YOUR TIME

Besides being necessary for billing, keeping track of time has other benefits for the self-employed. Most contract lawyers—especially those who have never had to account for their time—start out wildly optimistic about how much they can accomplish in a day or week. Unless you get very busy with contract work right away, you may find that time seems to slip away from you unproductively and unnoticed. As one contract lawyer has said, you have to take hold of your schedule and wrestle it to the ground or it will control you.

If you find that you're busy all the time but somehow bill only three or four hours a day—and, as a result, don't have time for the other activities you were hoping contract work would allow you to enjoy—keep a daily time log for a month or so. This will show how long you take to eat breakfast, get dressed, get into your car and drive downtown. You may learn that the half hour you think you're spending on exercise is really more like 90 minutes. You may be surprised to discover that you've been spending an hour of non-billable time every day chatting with hiring lawyers about their personal lives.

The purpose of this exercise is not to make you a more rigid or self-conscious person. Rather it's to make you more realistic and sensible about how you use your time. You'll learn when you're most productive each day, so you can time your breaks, deliveries or networking calls during typically unproductive times. You may decide to start billing for those quick telephone calls you thought you'd toss in for free because they didn't amount to much, or to buy a fax or pay for a messenger service so you can cut out trips to pick up and deliver projects. You may even decide to raise your hourly rate.

OVERCOMING INTERNAL ROADBLOCKS

None of us, alas, is perfect. There probably isn't a lawyer alive who doesn't struggle with one or another unhealthy or unproductive tendency. When you're working in a firm, the externally imposed structure helps control such tendencies. When you're working for yourself, it's up to you to recognize them and do what you can to counter them.

There are times when you can't seem to get started and times when you can't seem to stop. Each has its merits—but only up to a point. It makes sense to put off writing a trial brief until the last possible moment if you truly believe the case will settle. And you need to keep working beyond the eight-hour day to produce good work against a tight deadline. But both procrastination and perfectionism become pathological when they interfere with your productivity.

PROCRASTINATION

If every time you have a brief to write you suddenly discover that your house needs cleaning and your office needs reorganizing, you have a procrastination problem. It's worse if every time you head for your office you find yourself (following a brief memory lapse) seated in front of the television or inexplicably immersed in a trashy best-seller.

Procrastination is usually a sign that the work is not something you want to do. It could be that you've completed similar assignments and found them boring or tedious, that you've never done this type of work before and have no interest in learning how, or that you're worried you won't be able to do a good enough job (see discussion of perfectionism below). If you suspect any of these reasons for your problem, head back to self-assessment and reevaluate the kind of work that suits you best. You may feel you have no choice at this time; you're doing contract work because you need the money and don't have any other skills that will yield the high hourly return of this kind of work. If this is the case, it is especially important to focus on what you like and do well in the practice of law, narrow your solicitations to that type of work, and get the jobs done competently and promptly so you'll be assured of the income you seek.

Sometimes, though, you procrastinate because you're not ready to tackle the project. You haven't thought it through well enough, you don't have a handle on the subject matter, or you're not certain what approach to take to solve the problem. If you have time, don't push yourself. But if you've promised the work by a date certain and that date is fast approaching, you'll need to arrange for external motivation to get yourself going. One trick is to act out the same routine you would if you had to commute to work. Awake to an alarm, take a shower, eat breakfast and be at your desk by a set time each day. Another solution is to give up working at home and find an office-share arrangement so that the activities of others motivate you. Yet another approach is to try to reason your procrastination away, following the program of Dr. David Burns in Chapter 5 of *Feeling Good.*

PERFECTIONISM

One manifestation of perfectionism is hard to distinguish from procrastination: feeling such severe anxiety about your ability to produce a "perfect" product that you avoid even starting to work on it. If the job you're facing means a lot to you and you're deeply invested in doing it well, you might experience a kind of "writer's block." The best way to overcome the resistance is to remind yourself that it's all right to write an imperfect first draft, or to make mistakes in the early stages of a project. The important thing is to begin.

The impulse to overwork an assignment is at the other end of the spectrum, and represents an unwillingness to let go rather than a reluctance to get started. A tendency toward perfectionism may actually be aggravated by being a lawyer, since in the law there are so many details that really do demand attention. Filing deadlines, for example, cannot be ignored, and Shepardizing significant cases up to the very last minute is part of doing a complete job. By perfectionism, we do not mean attending to these important details, but rather being so intent on freedom from error that you lose sight of what you need to accomplish. Such an attitude can hurt the contract lawyer who spends ten hours on a two-hour piece of research, or gets sidetracked from the main argument and spends hours polishing and perfecting a subsidiary one.

There is a practical way to deal with the competing interests of doing a thorough job and meeting the hiring lawyer's expectations. First, establish at the beginning of the project how long the hiring lawyer thinks it will take. If you disagree with the estimate, say so immediately. If he sticks with his estimate, offer a progress report after you've spent two-thirds of that time. If he continues to insist that you spend no longer than the estimate, do the best you can in that time and turn in the project with a memo detailing what steps you left out or gave less time than you think they merited. Explain why you believe more time was needed to do a good job. The lawyer's client may have strictly limited the amount of time to be billed; such a memo will give him fuel for persuading the client that more is needed. If the hiring lawyer is simply being unrealistic, the memo will show you were operating rationally and not driven by blind perfectionism.

If you find that you *always* spend more time on projects than hiring lawyers want or expect, your perfectionism may be interfering with your performance. Recognizing a problem is the first step toward dealing with it. Again, Dr. David Burns has concrete suggestions for overcoming counterproductive perfectionist behavior in Chapter 14 of *Feeling Good.*

FEELING UNTETHERED, UNDIRECTED, AND AT LOOSE ENDS

These feelings are natural responses to going from a highly structured environment (law school or law firm) to the unstructured world of irregular self-employment. If you chose contract work because law firm rules were driving you crazy, you probably believe you'll be happiest if every day is a blank sheet of paper on which you can write your life story as it comes. Wrong. Although we all have different levels of tolerance for externally imposed structure, almost no one is happy without structure of some kind. Even if you are reacting to or rebelling against the structure you left, the solution is not to reject structure altogether. Rather, the challenge is to create

HANDLING THE SLOW TIMES

Write an article on a law-related subject for:
- Your state or local bar publication
- A specialty bar section newsletter or journal
- Your local newspaper
- An ABA section's or other national specialty association's periodical

Give a talk at a CLE program

Volunteer your time for:
- Bar-related committee work
- Pro bono legal work
- Non-law interest group

Make lunch or coffee dates with other lawyers

Join a support group

Form your own support group

Spend time at the law library:
- Reading the latest issue of *The American Lawyer,* the *ABA Journal* or *National Law Journal*
- Chatting with lawyers you know
- Befriending a harried-looking practitioner
- Studying Martindale-Hubbell

Learn a new computer program

Revise your marketing plan

Read Dickens or Dostoevski—or John Grisham

Organize your office or your files

Take a class at a community college

your own. Think about yourself and the job you left behind. Identify the time of day you're most productive, when you'd rather be talking on the telephone or seeing people, and when you want to relax or get out of your head. Then, organize your day around your natural rhythms.

You can also use your short-term and long-term goals to create structure. To spend more time with your family, start by blocking out family time. When your work must be completed between 10:00 a.m. and 3:00 p.m., you'll feel more incentive to concentrate on it during those hours. Peter Zerilli finds the structure imposed on his life by his contract law assignments helps his productivity as a free-lance writer:

> *It's the old story of give something to a busy person and they'll get it done. With a computer on my desk, I can take half an hour in the morning, half an hour before I go home and the odd lunch hour and be a lot more productive than when I'm home, ostensibly writing while the phone is ringing and friends are dropping by. From the end of February until May, while working daily at a law firm, I've written seven chapters of a novel, finished one television screenplay, and outlined five more.*

ISOLATION

A last problem cited by contract lawyers who work from their homes is feeling isolated. You're less likely to feel that way if you follow the suggestions in Chapter 8 and develop your personal contacts. But it may be that what you miss is not simply human contact but contact with people in your own situation. Many bar associations have solo and small firm practice sections, and some have groups for lawyers who work out of home offices. Join one of those sections or, rather than waiting for someone else to take the initiative, get a program going yourself.

The Oregon Women Lawyers Contract Lawyer Referral Service was founded in 1990 by a contract lawyer who wanted to connect with others—to discuss common problems, share ideas, insights and often referrals, and ultimately to make friends. Elizabeth Bottman established a contract lawyer support group in Seattle through her state bar association's attorney assistance program. A benefit of taking a leadership role is that you will be identified in your community with contract lawyering, which can lead to interest in your services—or even another job. Bottman's presence at the Washington State Bar Association led to a steady three-day per week assignment helping disciplinary counsel process grievances.

Part III

WHAT
EVERY
HIRING
LAWYER
SHOULD
KNOW

10

THE CASE FOR HIRING
CONTRACT LAWYERS

If a new practice tool could increase your profits and give you more flexibility while improving client service and enhancing your job satisfaction, would you try it? It's no wonder that more and more lawyers across the country are hiring contract lawyers.

Trisha Mathers, a solo practitioner with 20 years of practice experience behind her, backed into the use of contract lawyers.

A 1974 law school graduate, Mathers founded her own law practice in 1981 after five years as a government lawyer and two years in a medium-sized law firm. Despite 15-hour work days and a healthy mix of real estate, probate and estate planning work for an upper middle-class, well-educated clientele, Mathers earned what she now calls a "low moderate" income during her first six years as a solo.

Her accountant repeatedly advised her that there were only three ways to increase her income: (1) to bill more hours, (2) to increase her hourly rate, or (3) to hire an associate who would generate billings in excess of salary and overhead expense. There weren't any more hours in the day to bill and market forces prevented her from raising her rates, but she resisted hiring an associate. She was certain there wasn't a lawyer around she could trust to do the job as well as she, and she never felt secure enough with her practice to contemplate adding a substantial salary to her overhead expense. Then, at age 41, she got pregnant. For a year after her son's birth, she struggled to run her practice in less time without reducing her income. The result was not only lowered income, but a severe case of pneumonia.

One day, a solution literally walked into her office. A friend of the two lawyers who shared office space with her asked if there was any work he could do for her. He had been an eighth-year associate at a major law firm, laid off when his firm lost a large chunk of business. By coincidence, Mathers had been procrastinating for several days on one case, not certain what course of action to take. She asked if he could research a specific point of law. Two days later, he provided her with a carefully drafted memorandum that resolved her quandary. Her response was to ask him what he wanted to be paid and hand him another file.

Now, she and the two lawyers with whom she shares space have established relationships with three additional contract lawyers, each with expertise in a different area. "I get to do what I like to do and they all get to do the same," Mathers says. All four contract lawyers maintain themselves as separate business entities, coming and going as they please. Mathers limits her practice to client relations, court appearances and strategy by delegating most paperwork and investigation to the contract lawyers, an unusual luxury for a solo practitioner. She's providing better service to her clients and earning a very respectable living while working an average of 30 hours per week.

Mathers' story—both her initial resistance to the notion of delegating her workload and her ultimate success in doing just that—is typical of the experiences reported by other users of contract lawyer services. She exemplifies the five reasons to hire other lawyers on a temporary or project-driven basis:

1. *To control costs and enhance profits (see this page);*
2. *To manage growth (see page 120);*
3. *To increase flexibility (see page 122);*
4. *To improve service to clients (see page 125); and*
5. *To enhance job satisfaction (see page 128).*

LAWYERS WHO WANT TO CONTROL COSTS AND ENHANCE PROFITS

Lawyers who hire contract lawyers can enhance their bottom line by avoiding the higher cost of adding a new permanent lawyer to the staff. Simple salary equivalents show how well a contract lawyer can pay off. A $70,000 per year associate billing the industry average of 1,800 hours per year,[1] 95 percent of which is collectible,

---

1. The median number of hours billed by associates nationwide in 1990 was 1820. Robin L. Hegvik, "Profitability Models for Part-Time Lawyers," *Breaking Traditions* (ABA 1993). Law firm partners in most fields bill clients between 1,600 and 2,200 hours a year, with averages per specialty ranging from a low of 1,460 for probate and estate lawyers to a high of 2,015 for insurance defense lawyers. Commercial lawyers average just under 1,800 per year, according to the 1993 Survey of Law Firm Economics, Altman Weil Pensa, as reported in the *Wall Street Journal* on June 17, 1994.

costs a firm approximately $46 per hour as an employee—before taking into consideration benefits, malpractice insurance and other direct employment costs. When those expenses are added, the hourly rate jumps to at least $52, and the annual commitment to $88,920. Adding overhead such as secretarial assistance, additional telephone lines and equipment and office furniture, and employment expenses like recruiting, training and tax reporting, can increase the hourly equivalent to as much as $85.15, and the annual investment to nearly $150,000.[2]

In comparison, contract lawyers handling associate-level matters typically receive $35 to $75 per hour for projects of 15 hours or less. Their time is generally passed on to the client at an hourly rate that includes profit for the hiring lawyer. "The whole point of being a contract lawyer," says Diane Rynerson, executive director of Oregon Women Lawyers, "is to be there when you're needed and then not be there when you're not needed."

The cost savings can be even more significant for the corporate and government legal departments that hire contract lawyers rather than paying outside counsel fees. Compare the $50 to $75 per hour paid to a top associate-level contract lawyer with the $130 to $190 per hour paid for an associate with an outside law firm. Compare the $60 to $90 hourly rate paid to a very experienced contract lawyer with hourly rates of $200 to $450 per hour for a partner at a major law firm.

Some law firms and corporations hire contract lawyers to avoid paying large headhunter fees before knowing whether a lawyer will work out. "The temporary attorney solution beats the problem with traditional search firms, where you're out 25 percent of your new hire's salary if you don't have a good fit," says Charles F. Preuss, partner of the San Francisco firm Preuss, Walker & Shanagher.[3] Others take the less stressful route of "try before you buy," when they must replace a key associate on the eve of trial or in the middle of a major transaction.

Even better, those who hire contract lawyers often avoid recruiting costs altogether. James A. Ounsworth, general counsel for Safeguard Scientifics, Inc., tells this story:

> I met a contract lawyer when he was looking for a job a year ago. At the time, we weren't sure we wanted to hire that level of person, but when a project came up, I asked him if he wanted to come with us for a time. I told him up front to win us over. He worked for us for about a month

2. This calculation adds surcharges of 56 percent for overhead and 25 percent for recruiting. Some sources estimate current overhead costs at even higher levels.

3. Samuel A. Frederick, "Temporary Attorneys: Here to Stay," unpublished manuscript, 1994.

and a half. The business people started coming to me and saying, "This guy is pretty good." It was terrific. We were able to skip the [time consuming] interviewing process we had gone through with other hires.[4]

Some practitioners increase revenues by bringing in a contract lawyer to handle a case they might have declined because of staffing shortages. "Hiring contract lawyers has had a very positive effect on my bottom line," says Seattle solo practitioner Daniel Edwards. "It has enabled me to keep a lot of cases going at the same time. I don't have to neglect some cases in order to get to others, nor turn good business away—and these are times in which I don't want to be turning *any* business away."

Contract lawyers can also help hiring lawyers produce more profit from their existing set-up. Unlike employees, contract lawyers seldom add anything to overhead, even when they work in-house. "It's a great way to generate more money from your existing overhead," says Robert Thomas, partner in Seattle's Stokes, Eitelbach & Lawrence. "You pay them for each hour they work, you bill your client what you would normally bill for work done by yourself or an associate, and the difference is your profit."

"Associates are viewed as profit centers by major law firms," observes contract lawyer placement agency owner Warren Hernand, "in that 'quotas' for billable hours are established to assure that each associate is responsible for generating a predictable amount of revenue to the firm."[5] The reality for smaller firms is that often an associate's salary plus overhead does not amount to much less than the income generated by his billable hours. In contrast, "assuming the contract lawyer does not involve any additional overhead for the firm and that you bill the client for the work at an associate-level rate, whatever you make off the contract lawyer is pure profit," says Thomas. "You're taking overhead that is already in place and finding ways to crank additional money out of it."

LAWYERS WHO WANT TO MANAGE GROWTH

One New York City firm accepted a huge tort litigation defense a year into discovery without the staff necessary to handle it. Its solution was to hire a number of contract lawyers to summarize stacks of depositions. Six weeks later, the firm was

---

4. "Temp Time: Are You Ready?," *Corporate Legal Times,* September 1994.

5. Warren Hernand, "Reinventing the Lawyer Workplace," *San Francisco Attorney,* February/March 1994.

swamped with summary judgment motions. One contract lawyer stayed on to help with the motions while interviewing for a full-time permanent position. When he obtained an offer in Philadelphia to start two months later, the New York City firm offered him a better-paying associate position even though it had not intended at the outset to hire any of the contract lawyers permanently. The months of temporary employment had convinced the firm that its heavy workload was likely to continue and justified another associate on staff.

Thus, law firms hire contract lawyers on a full-time temporary basis to determine whether there is enough work to warrant a permanent hire. The tactical use of a contract lawyer "provides a breathing period in which the firm can determine whether a long-term issue exists and if so, how it should be resolved," notes Samuel A. Frederick, co-founder of Assigned Counsel. "If the problem is long-term, temporary attorneys automatically constitute experienced and tested candidates for the new positions."

Some lawyers, like New Jersey practitioner Ralph Lowenbach, use a contract lawyer to avoid the hasty hire of a new associate to replace one who suddenly leaves the firm. Lowenbach lost a real estate associate at a busy time; the feelers he broadcast for a permanent replacement attracted a pool of unqualified applicants. Rather than settling for the wrong candidate, he hired a lawyer with twelve years' experience in a now-dissolved New York firm to work on a temporary basis. The timing couldn't have been better. With help from the contract lawyer, Lowenbach was able to defer choosing a permanent candidate until the market improved.[6]

In a comparable situation, a partner of a large and prestigious West Coast firm died suddenly while on vacation. The remaining partners asked a contract lawyer placement service to locate a temporary replacement. Attorney Assistance, the San Francisco Bay Area agency, found a former partner of another respected firm to handle the deceased partner's pending matters for four months while they searched for a new partner.

Another benefit of this type of growth management is the increased ability to nurture the potential of partnership-track associates. Walt Schlotterbeck, general counsel of General Electric explained the key to his high-quality legal department to Samuel Frederick: "Hire excellent people, and give them challenging work to do." Making use of contract lawyers to handle routine work has enabled department managers—in law firms or in-house legal departments—to increase the learning curve of their permanent lawyers by keeping them excited about their work.

---

6. Walter Lucas, "'Temping' Comes of Age," *New Jersey Law Journal,* October 10, 1991.

Some hiring lawyers have also learned that using contract lawyers to handle extraordinary workloads, rather than bringing on permanent employees, avoids damage to employee morale from downsizing while more effectively cutting costs. Fewer than half of the corporations that lay off substantial numbers of employees see operating profits improve or report increases in worker productivity. But eight out of ten have problems as a result of lowered employee morale.[7] Law firms recount the same negative experiences. According to the *ABA Journal*, it takes at least six months, and often as many as 18, to reduce costs in line with a firm's diminished size. Some studies indicate that profits may never recover. It also takes time to restore morale among the "survivors" of a downsizing, especially if the staff cuts are handled insensitively.[8] "This continuous downsizing—it's corporate anorexia," claims Gary Hamel, an expert on competitiveness who teaches at London Business School. "You can get thin, but it's no way to get healthy." [9]

LAWYERS WHO WANT TO INCREASE FLEXIBILITY

Today's law office economy demands leaner operations that still respond quickly and professionally to client needs. Law firms of all sizes, as well as corporate law departments, now use contract lawyers to handle normal fluctuations in workload without increasing fixed overhead. This notion of "just-in-time hiring" allows legal employers to adjust staffing so that they "hire for the valleys rather than the peaks," says Howard Bloom, a principal of Hernand & Partners in Dallas.[10] Or, in the words of Patricia E. Fleming, assistant secretary and administrative lawyer for the BOC Group, a medical and industrial gas company in New Jersey, companies can use temporaries to avoid "warm bodies and no work" when there's a lull.[11]

- *Harry Gill, retired general counsel of Arco Chemical, was faced with a*
  company-wide reorganization in which his office inherited more than
  15,000 small claims. "We didn't have the people to go through those

---

7. Ronald Henkoff, "Getting Beyond Downsizing," *Fortune,* January 10, 1994.

8. Don J. DeBenedictis, "Growing Pains," *ABA Journal,* March 1993.

9. "Getting Beyond Downsizing," supra n. 7.

10. Howard Bloom, "Just-in-Time Hiring: A Key to Profits and Cost Control," *Texas Lawyer,* February 28, 1994.

11. "Temporary Lawyers Allow Firms Greater Practice Flexibility," *Lawyer Hiring and Training Report,* November 1988.

claims," he said, "so I hired a contract lawyer who had been a general counsel to go through them."[12]

- A 28-lawyer firm in Portland, Oregon, hired five contract lawyers to review hundreds of thousands of documents for privilege and relevancy. The firm kept the lawyers on to create a database for information retrieval, create a privilege log and draft discovery motions. The assignment lasted nine months.

- A mid-sized commercial firm took on a huge lender liability case representing the debtor. Four or five lawyers were working on the case full-time—and neglecting other matters. The firm had never used contract lawyers before but in desperation called a local agency and were put in touch with Sue Samuelson, whose last case as a partner in a small law firm involved lender liability. It was a perfect fit. She worked from July until the case settled in December, then was asked to stay on for an additional six months to work on other sophisticated commercial law matters.

- A 14-lawyer corporate and litigation firm in a medium-sized city was offered substantial additional work from an existing client if it could immediately open an office in another city. "We needed a partner-level contract attorney candidate, available to open the office for us in three weeks. A contract attorney service found the ideal candidate, ready to accept our offer, in days."[13]

Law firms also gain flexibility by hiring contract lawyers in complex cases as a tactical move. Without telling the opposition that the lawyers assigned to a matter are not members of the firm, they use the contract lawyers to subject the other side to a blizzard of motions and depositions. All the opposing counsel knows is that the lawyer is "with the firm" and that the firm appears to have resources beyond what would be expected by its size. Although no lawyers we interviewed for this book would admit to this policy, several agency owners reported filling requests for precisely this reason.

Mid-sized and small firms have broadened the scope of their practices by using contract lawyers. Daniel Edwards hired a contract lawyer to help him with a construction case that was so time-consuming he would have had to neglect the rest of his practice to handle it. He looked specifically for a contract lawyer with a construction background—someone he could rely upon to review and organize the case

---

12. "Temp Time: Are You Ready?," supra n. 4.

13. "Temporary Attorneys: Here to Stay," supra n. 3.

and get him "on track with the issues." The lawyer he hired had 25 years of experience as a partner in a small law firm that had recently unraveled.

Tom Watters of Los Angeles' Hart & Watters first hired a contract lawyer in 1989 when a client brought in a big, complicated antitrust and unfair competition case to defend. A Los Angeles contract lawyer placement agency put him in touch with a securities and antitrust litigation attorney who ended up working virtually full-time in their offices for more than a year. Hart & Watters provided office space and supplies, a parking place and secretarial support and paid the lawyer $75 per hour, 50 percent of the rate billed to the client (a differential justified by the firm's hefty overhead investment).

Other groups hire contract lawyers to handle matters beyond their expertise or interest. For example, a large in-house legal department hired a senior contract lawyer fluent in Portuguese to work for three months in its Brazil office on a complicated corporate transaction.[14] Some general practitioners prefer to hire domestic relations specialists to handle contested divorce and custody matters brought in by their clients. And some inexperienced solo practitioners hire senior-level contract lawyers to advise them on strategy and procedure.

Hiring lawyers sometimes use contract lawyers to fill temporary service gaps. Service gaps may develop when a firm cannot guarantee a partnership slot to a discontented associate, or cannot recruit a permanent upper-level practitioner, because of its inability to offer an adequate salary. For other lawyers, the service gap occurs because of a simple lack of time to pursue a permanent hire. New Jersey corporation BOC was faced with such a situation when a lawyer handling a major deal suddenly announced his departure. The general counsel hired a contract lawyer to take over until a permanent employee could be found. The contract lawyer was so competent that the general counsel asked her to complete the entire transaction and then retained her to work on an as-needed basis. When a firm tries instead to fill the gap by rotating an under-utilized associate or partner into a different area of practice on a short-term basis, it exposes itself unnecessarily to liability claims and may anger the client with excessive bills resulting from the lawyer's lack of familiarity with the subject matter.

Contract lawyers become a realistic and valuable alternative to lateral hiring when a firm becomes thinly staffed at the senior-associate level because of defections or downsizing. Many contract lawyers are "master technicians" who were let go by law firms that didn't see them as client-getters or partnership material. "Now

---

14. Lesley Friedman, "What Firms Should Know Before Using a 'Temp' Attorney," *New York Law Journal*, November 18, 1991.

the firms need them," says Linda Gill Taylor of Kansas City, Missouri's Of Counsel. Taylor hears from her clients time and again, "Now that so and so is gone, the brains have left. Who's going to do this sophisticated work?" The answer, she says, is a qualified contract lawyer.

Finally, hiring lawyers have found contract lawyers to be one of the most efficient ways to manage scheduling conflicts. A small California law firm had depositions in two different cases scheduled at the same time. In one case, one plaintiff was suing a number of defendants. All the defendants needed to be represented, but lead counsel for another defendant would be doing most of the questioning at this deposition. The small-firm lawyer prepared a contract lawyer by pointing out a few obvious questions and information that needed to be brought out on his client's behalf. As a result of this positive experience, the firm used the contract lawyer several times to handle similar depositions and motions.

LAWYERS WHO WANT TO IMPROVE CLIENT SERVICE

One of the most valuable but least noted benefits of using contract lawyers is in the area of good client relations. Daniel Edwards says:

> I hire a lot of contract lawyers for research because they can get the job done for less cost to the client. I'm billing out over $100 per hour. If I go into the library and do ten hours of research, it costs the client $1,000. If I use one of these guys charging $25 per hour, it can cost 75 percent less. They might not draw the same conclusions from the citations they find, but as long as they find the cases and bring them to me, I can work out my own strategy. It's much more efficient to do it that way.

The multi-state, 25-lawyer firm of Kasowitz, Hoff, Benson & Torres used several contract attorneys from one placement agency, was able to negotiate lower hourly rates, and passed on the savings to the client. "Our clients have been happy from the beginning about getting high-quality work at considerably cheaper rates than elsewhere," says partner Marc E. Kasowitz. "We feel we have been able to do document-intensive work very successfully while addressing client concerns with cost." [15]

Inexpensive trial assistance is another benefit to the client. Edwards says:

---

15. "Temporary Attorneys: Here to Stay," supra n. 3.

*The first time I hired a contract lawyer was to assist me during a jury
trial three years ago. I made a checklist of points I wanted to be sure to
cover. The contract lawyer's mission was to watch the testimony and
check off each point I'd covered. As I went through the examination, I'd
occasionally swing by the desk and get reminded of the issues I hadn't
yet raised. The experience worked so well I've continued to hire
assistants whenever I'm in trial. You can take someone literally right out
of law school. You don't need a person with a great deal of background,
but lawyers are better than paralegals because of their research skills. If
a door opens, or a portion of the roof falls on your head mid-way
through the case, you can send them scurrying off to the law library.*

Another advantage to clients is making partner experience and oversight more
cost-effective. Paul Mishkin, a partner in the New York law firm of Mishkin, Kohler &
Imholz, says, "Clients want senior partners and they want experience, not troops
and associates for back up." Often partners ask associates or other partners to
brainstorm strategy on a case. This is not economical for the client not only because
of the high cost of their time, but because law firm colleagues may not have relevant
experience and background. Sue Samuelson, however, provides this service to one
of her peers on a contract basis:

*I'm the only one in the firm who does the same kind of work he does. A
lot of times, he'll just ask me to talk a case over with him. Sometimes
he'll even call me at home to run something by me. He'll get a case that's
really interesting. But with the phones all lit and dealing with clients and
running out to meetings, he doesn't have the time or even the
inclination to figure it out. I do. One time I was researching a motion for
summary judgment and light bulbs went off. I came up with a whole new
way of phrasing our argument and went running into his office to tell
him. He responded with "Wow!" That made my day—and the case.*

Small firms and solo practitioners also find that contract lawyers help them
provide better service by broadening their ability to provide technical expertise.
Richard Kaplan, a San Francisco solo practitioner, had just such an experience.

*A client of mine was an equipment supplier for a highly innovative
sewage refinement process project that turned into one of the largest
cost-overrun contracts in California history. When I got into the case, I*

was immediately befuddled by the architectural plans and engineering drawings. I was referred to a contract lawyer who had been a civil engineer for ten years, an associate in a downtown law firm for six, and now was working on his own.

Two or three days later, I laid out all those plans on the table for him. He was able to read those pages in five minutes and understood the concepts involved better than any of the other lawyers. The contract lawyer and I alternated five solid weeks of depositions in other parts of the state. The other lawyers, all from much larger firms, kidded me. "You've hired a ringer," they said. "That guy actually knows what he's talking about!"

Ultimately, the man really helped me make the case. He was able to provide insights into the project that made it clear in the course of one of the depositions where the real fault lay. In consequence of that, my client was able to work out a very favorable settlement. The whole case cost the client a tremendous amount of money but it worked out through a contract lawyer better than if I had hired the best political science or liberal arts law grad going. And I certainly couldn't have afforded to have an engineer/lawyer on staff full-time. Contract lawyering allowed me to have a specialist in my office "on loan," so to speak.

Samuel Frederick was able to provide a sophisticated product for a client in a cost effective way by hiring a contract lawyer:

One of my clients is a highly reputable, well-managed national subcontractor in large building construction. They got tired of having to deal with non-payment by general contractors and getting stiffed by the payment bonding companies. They asked me to design a payment bond enforcement procedure, taking a very business-like systems approach.

I have substantial litigation management experience, but not in the construction area. I've also done a lot of real estate work but without a big focus on construction. With my background, I had a good idea of how to handle the process but needed some specific questions answered. What are the forms that we use in the language of our contracts? What kind of notices do we send to the defaulting contractors and bonding companies? At what stage do we get counsel involved in certain states?

I hired a contract lawyer who had experience in construction litigation as well as knowledge of applicable statutes and cases. She did a lot of the research and provided a memorandum that was support for building the new policy. It was very cost effective. If my client had done this by hiring four law firms, one in each of the four states involved, they would have paid $100,000. They got it from us for a total of about $15,000.

LAWYERS WHO WANT TO INCREASE THEIR CAREER SATISFACTION

"Think about how pleasant your practice would be if you could take a break from boring and routine work and not sacrifice income," says Portland, Oregon, contract lawyer Katherine Foldes. Contract lawyers enable hiring lawyers like Trisha Mathers to focus on the aspects of practice they enjoy most without losing profit.

Legal research and writing is one area of practice that many hiring lawyers would prefer not to handle. For practitioners like Daniel Edwards, the choice is based on the economics. For those who relish oral presentations and attorney-client interaction, legal research and writing is drudgery at best. "A day in the library is a day in hell for me," says Mathers. Fortunately, for the past five years she has worked with a contract lawyer who is brilliant at legal analysis but who refuses to set foot in the courthouse or speak to a client. Assigning the work that doesn't interest her to a qualified contract lawyer has liberated Mathers to do what she does best.

In some cases, the benefit of increased job satisfaction extends to other employees as well. Counsel for the BOC Group were overwhelmed by work generated by the sale of one company division. To ease the pressure, Patricia E. Fleming hired a contract lawyer to handle day-to-day matters. When the sale was completed, the lawyer who had previously handled these routine matters was loath to accept them back. He wanted to move into more sophisticated and independent work, but the department still needed someone in a support role. Fleming hired the contract lawyer as a permanent part-time employee to fill this role.

Contract lawyers also provide an opportunity for solo and small-firm practitioners to juggle part-time or flexible schedules. Two Seattle bankruptcy lawyers wanted to maintain an alternative practice. They both worked four days per week; one left in mid-afternoon during the school year so she could be home with her children. They hired an experienced bankruptcy lawyer to come in two days per week on a contract basis to create the equivalent of two full-time practices.

BENEFITS OF CONTRACT LAWYERS

Hiring lawyers control costs and enhance profits by:
- avoiding the higher cost of adding a new permanent lawyer to the staff;
- charging more per hour to the client than the contract lawyer costs;
- reducing outside legal fees paid by in-house legal departments and government agencies;
- taking on cases they would have declined because of staffing shortages.

They manage growth by:
- hiring contract lawyers to handle extraordinary workloads;
- avoiding the need to lay off or downsize if their workload should later decrease;
- determining whether there is enough work on a long-term basis to warrant a permanent hire;
- avoiding the hasty hire of a new associate or partner when another suddenly leaves the firm.

Hiring lawyers increase flexibility by:
- Covering normal fluctuations in workload without increasing fixed overhead;
- Temporarily broadening the scope of their practices;
- Filling in a service gap with a contract lawyer rather than moving an associate without adequate experience into that slot;
- Using contract lawyers to cover scheduling conflicts.

They improve client service by:
- Passing cost savings for routine work on to the client;
- Making partner experience and oversight more cost-effective;
- Broadening their ability to provide technical expertise;
- Providing a sophisticated product for a client in a cost-effective way.

And they increase career satisfaction by:
- Focusing on aspects of practice they most enjoy without losing profit;
- Billing the necessary hours without exhausting their permanent staff;
- Making part-time or flexible schedules feasible.

II

WEIGHING THE RISKS

Contract lawyers can be lifesavers, but they're not the solution to every practice problem and sometimes their use can create new problems. We found, however, that myths about problems with contract lawyers seldom have much to do with reality.

Before you judge the value of this practice option, it's important to separate the myths from the realities of working with contract lawyers. Here, lawyers who have used contract lawyers tell you the real story.

MYTH: ONLY A BUNCH OF "LOSER LAWYERS" WOULD WORK ON A TEMPORARY BASIS.

"Many lawyers believe that only the dregs of the profession would do this kind of work," notes Linda Gill Taylor. Laura Black of Special Counsel in Baltimore repeatedly hears the comment, "If she's any good, why would she be working as a temp?" And Trisha Mathers says, "I constantly confront attitudes that contract lawyers couldn't possibly be good lawyers because they haven't signed up for life with an established law firm."

The skeptics do not have experience in today's contract lawyer market. "In my younger days, every time we'd hire clerical assistance on a temporary basis it would be a disaster," says Paul Mishkin. "What I didn't realize is that the world has changed. There are plenty of not just good, but really superb, lawyers out there who are pursuing other interests and don't want to be stuck on a permanent basis with a law firm." Robert M. Abrahams, a partner in New York firm Schulte, Roth & Zabel, concurs. "I invariably receive a stack of résumés of lawyers overqualified for every temporary position, who are available at mid-level associate-range rates."[1] Thomas Evans of New York's Mudge, Rose, Guthrie, Alexander & Ferdon says:

---

1. Samuel A. Frederick, "Teaming Up with Temporary Lawyers," *The American Lawyer,* May 1995.

> *I started with a predisposition against temporary attorneys—I was*
> *worried they would not be professionally qualified. Instead, I had very*
> *great success with them in an extremely complex litigation matter over*
> *a two-year period. During the course of their work, I offered three or*
> *four of them permanent jobs with the firm.[2]*

"Some firms think becoming a contract lawyer is an admission of inadequacy," notes Jed Rakoff, a partner with New York's Fried, Frank, Harris, Shriver & Jacobson. "The fear is that almost everyone who is a contract lawyer for some reason has not fit into the normal law firm progression, either by choice or because of various personality quirks. But it's baloney to think only someone who came up in the firm in the normal way can do the job right."

In fact, many, if not most, contract lawyers are first-rate lawyers. Richard Kaplan describes the contract lawyers he has worked with over the past ten years: "Almost everybody has been at a very competent level, some at an ultra-competent, superb level." Eric Walker, co-founder of San Francisco's Lawsmiths agency, observes:

> *The traits that define the quality lawyer—intelligence, initiative,*
> *adaptability, self-confidence, energy—are the very traits of the lawyer*
> *most likely to try this relatively new approach to practice. Perhaps*
> *nothing . . . is more important than emphasizing the inapplicability of*
> *the old stereotype of contractor lawyers as the hangers-on of the*
> *profession; they are today, by and large, the exact opposite—its cream.[3]*

MYTH: CONTRACT EMPLOYMENT IS NOT A PROFESSIONAL WAY TO WORK. IT DEGRADES THE PROFESSION.

See response in Chapter 4 at page 32.

MYTH: I CAN'T AFFORD THE GOING RATE.

A $50 per hour billing rate for an experienced associate can sound like a lot of money when you take a $45,000 annual associate salary and divide it by an 1,800 annual billable hour quota. Why pay a contract lawyer $50 per hour when you could replace his work with another associate earning only $25 hourly? Because you are not paying $25 per hour for the associate with a $45,000 salary; you are actually paying $35 to $55 per hour.

---

2. Samuel A. Frederick, "Temporary Attorneys: Here to Stay," unpublished manuscript, 1994.

3. Eric Walker, "The Contractor Lawyer: A Career Alternative," *Breaking Traditions* (ABA 1993).

An employee receives more than just a salary. Other cash outlays are made—state, local and federal employer taxes; health, disability and life insurance; family leave compensation; malpractice coverage; CLE subsidy; retirement plan participation; bonuses and severance payments. In addition, intangible employee costs can be substantial: recruiting, training, periodic evaluations, payroll processing and tax reporting and the potential for wrongful termination litigation. None of those obligations are incurred when the assistance is rendered by an independent contractor. "I have a fixed obligation," Richard Kaplan observes. "When that project's over, it's a warm handshake and good-bye."

The calculations at page 133 demonstrate how a $45,000 salary translates into an hourly rate of $36 to $38 when employer-paid taxes and benefits are taken into consideration. Overhead attribution, recruiting costs and family leave benefits can raise the rate to almost $60 per hour. Of course, associate salaries far exceed $45,000 in most parts of the country, so the savings are even greater. That's why a $50 per hour contract lawyer can make a lot of sense.

These hourly rate comparisons are especially significant when in-house budget trends are considered. From 1992 to 1993, outside counsel costs increased by more than 40 percent, primarily in the litigation area, while in-house legal department budgets were virtually unchanged.[4] General counsel have discovered that they can substantially decrease both outside counsel and litigation costs by hiring contract lawyers to handle such routine matters as reviewing documents for privilege and relevancy, handling uncomplicated securities filings and real estate transactions, monitoring labor and EEOC compliance, and implementing software licensing matters.

The savings are even greater, though, when *annual* salary is considered. Most contract lawyer relationships comprise a series of $250 to $2,500 projects, rather than a $60,000 to $100,000 per year guarantee. If the contract lawyer proves worthy of the initial investment, another similar commitment is made. If not—to paraphrase Richard Kaplan—it's a "cool" handshake and good-bye. Not so, of course, with the $45,000 associate. That lawyer generally gets many months to prove himself while the firm "papers the file" before asking him to leave, and, of course, another three to six months of job-hunting assistance or severance pay.

The overall affordability of contract lawyers versus permanent employees exceeds simple salary equivalents. Employers need not compensate the contract

---

4. According to Arthur Andersen & Co's 1994 General Counsel Survey for the *Corporate Legal Times* as reported in "Outside Costs Take Larger Part of Corporate Legal Budgets," *National Law Journal*, September 19, 1994.

HOURLY EQUIVALENT
CALCULATIONS

Salary of $45,000 salary ÷ 95% of 1,800 or		1,710 =	$ 26.32
Social security at 7.65% (1995)	= $ 3,442.50 ÷	1,710 =	$ 2.01
Medicare at 2.65% (1995)	= $ 1,192.50 ÷	1,710 =	$ .70
State employment taxes estimated at 3% of $45,000	= $ 1,350 ÷	1,710 =	$ .79
Medical/dental insurance at $1,800 yearly average	= $ 1,800 ÷	1,710 =	$ 1.05
Disability/life insurance package at $1,200 anually	= $ 1,200 ÷	1,710 =	$ .70
Retirement plan at 8% to 15% of $45,000 = $3,600 - $ 6,750	÷	1,710 = $ 2.11 to	$ 3.95
Annual malpractice insurance premium at $2,500	÷	1,710 =	$ 1.46
CLE expense = 15 credits at $20 per credit hour or $300	÷	1,710 =	.18
State, local and ABA or specialty bar dues at $850 annually	÷	1,710 =	.50

SUBTOTAL $35.82 TO 37.66

Overhead costs for secretarial assistance, equipment costs, additional telephone lines, office space, furniture, at 56% of $45,000	= $ 25,200 ÷	1,710 =	$ 14.74

SUBTOTAL $50.56 TO 52.40

Family leave, 427.5 hours at $35.12 = $15,013.80 ÷ 3,420 (amortized over 2 years) =		$ 4.39
Recruiting costs at 25% of $45,000 = $11,250 ÷ 5,130 (amortized over 3 years) =		$ 2.19

GRAND TOTAL $57.14 TO $58.98

lawyer for unproductive time. A contract lawyer is paid only for hours actually worked—most of which will be billed to the client—or only for the percentage of total hours that the contract lawyer feels comfortable billing. (Contract lawyers, like other lawyers, often trim hours, excising wasted time and research dead-ends, before submitting a bill.) Because they are usually overqualified for the assignment, they need little orientation and almost no training.

Contract lawyers can also be more productive because they don't have the social relationships at the office that permanent employees enjoy. "They are paid by the hour," says one hiring lawyer. "There's no chatting around the water cooler." One industry source, in fact, estimates that 21 percent of the savings from temporary help stems from eliminating payment for unproductive time. Indeed, employers tend to be so satisfied with productivity that an estimated 50 percent to 75 percent of temporary workers nationwide are offered full-time positions at some point during their "temp" careers.[5]

MYTH: USING CONTRACT LAWYERS WILL DISGRACE THE FIRM.

Some of the most successful large firms in the country (New York's Fried, Frank, Harris, Shriver & Jacobson and San Francisco's Morrison & Foerster, as examples) use contract lawyers regularly. So do Fortune 500 companies (Arco, The Irvine Company, General Electric Company). Savvy small firms and solo practitioners use them to stay small (or solo) yet avoid having to turn away work when they're busy.

MYTH: CLIENTS MAY WORRY THEY'RE GETTING SECOND-RATE WORK.

Sue Samuelson, a partner-level contract lawyer, heard through the grapevine at one firm where she worked that some of the lawyers strongly protested her presence. They were unhappy that someone not "on track" with the firm was working for their clients; they thought it would reflect badly on the quality of their organization. In fact, the client highly valued her work. When the case settled, the firm found additional projects for her and eventually hired her as a permanent part-time employee.

As Samuelson's experience demonstrates, fears that clients will not accept contract lawyers have proved unfounded. Although some lawyers choose not to tell their clients about the assistance they receive from contract lawyers, we heard no examples of clients' rebelling against the use of contract lawyers when they did find out. Not only have cost-conscious clients wholeheartedly endorsed the practice of hiring contract lawyers, but many now demand that the law firms they retain reduce costs by employing them.

It's no wonder that clients have accepted the idea. They have nothing to worry about, as long as hiring lawyers take a few simple precautions. First, hire the most qualified candidate and tell the client the contract lawyer was hired because of that level of expertise. Jed Rakoff suggests that this tactic will overcome any potential client objections. Or ask the client to approve the credentials of any contract lawyer, and assure the client that all work will be handled with your supervision. (Chapters 14 and 17 expand upon the issue of client notification.)

Where ethically permissible, you can avoid the issue altogether. Simply state in your retainer agreement that some work may be performed by outside contractors under your supervision. Samuel Frederick says:

---

5.   Only 20 percent accept. David Nye, *Alternative Staffing Strategies* (BNA 1988).

In most cases, firms work with established clients who have a high regard for their work. They apparently care little which individual performs the work as long as the firm chooses the lawyer and remains responsible for the work. Clients may even welcome the use of contract lawyers due to the improved firm response time and decrease in cost which they confer.

MYTH: THEY'LL EXPOSE YOU TO EXCESSIVE LIABILITY.

This is a complete myth. Our research uncovered no reported decisions anywhere in the country based on the work of a contract lawyer. We heard of only two claims. One was a disciplinary complaint filed by opposing counsel to disqualify a law firm that used a contract lawyer. The other was an insurance claim involving misrepresentation by a former contract lawyer who worked inside a law firm for a long period of time; the agent who told us about this claim could not tell us where or when it was filed. For more information about your risk—or lack of it—in this area, read the analysis of malpractice coverage and risk assessment in Chapter 19 starting at page 217.

MYTH: YOU'LL RUN INTO TOO MANY CONFLICTS PROBLEMS.

The possibility of a conflict of interest is always there, but the availability of a large number of contract lawyers in any particular area lessens its significance. Even in small markets, you can substantially reduce the risk. Robert Thomas hires contract lawyers to work only for his firm, guaranteeing them an acceptable minimum number of hours per week to assure their loyalty. If this isn't possible, an individual conflicts check should suffice. (See Chapter 17 for discussion of conflict of interest issues.)

MYTH: THEIR PRESENCE WILL DISRUPT OFFICE OPERATIONS AND
DECREASE PERMANENT STAFF MORALE.

"In my younger days," says Paul Mishkin, "every secretary we hired on a temporary basis would spend the first part of the morning figuring out which chair she wanted and where to get the coffee, and complaining about everything we weren't providing."

The opposite seems to be true of contract lawyers. "We worried about their acceptance by other associates," says Jed Rakoff. "But they had no problems, maybe because they were not seen as a threat to making partner." In fact, contract lawyers often insulate permanent associates from the tedium of document review and due-diligence projects. They can also be assigned to long-term, out-of-town projects to protect associates from being separated from their families. "Associates should be saying, 'Gee, you thought enough of me to get me some help. I appreciate the fact that I don't have to stay here until 10:00 p.m. every day'," says James Ounsworth, general counsel for Safeguard Scientifics.[6]

MYTH: THEY'LL WALK AWAY WITH YOUR CLIENTS.

"I'd love some clients to walk away with a contract lawyer," jokes Daniel Edwards. "So far, I've had no such luck!" His experience is the norm. Most contract lawyers choose this work arrangement for one of three reasons: to find another permanent job after leaving or being laid off from a prior position; to work fewer hours and have more control over their time; or to supplement their private practice income. The first two types of contract lawyers, who make up the majority of the market, have no impetus to steal a client. Even the third, those with their own practices, should realize that other lawyers will often be their primary source of client referrals; they'd be foolish to alienate a colleague.

At another level, however, the contract lawyer may not be the problem. If a contract lawyer walks away with your client, maybe that's where the client belonged. "It's a free world," notes Robert Thomas. "If contract lawyers are doing better jobs, the clients *should* be with them."

San Francisco contract lawyer Steven Weinstein tells a story that illustrates this point. He was involved in closing a deal on the sale of a radio station. The partner who ordinarily would have handled the matter had a vacation scheduled and "barked out" a few orders before he left. Weinstein managed to close the deal with "inordinate intense effort." After the deal closed, he was congratulated by one of the client's managers who thought he'd done a better job than the partner who went on vacation. "I was told afterwards that the firm might have some more work for me to do but I never heard from them," says Weinstein. "Much later, I ran into a summer law clerk who told me that word had gotten to the top people in the firm that the client thought I'd outshined the partner. It caused them such consternation that they didn't want to hire me to do anything else."

SOME MYTH; SOME REALITY: YOU CAN'T KNOW WHAT KIND OF WORK YOU'RE GOING TO GET.

Tom Watters of Los Angeles was in trial when an appellate brief with a short time for response arrived in the office. Having had one good experience with a contract

---

6. "Temp Time: Are You Ready?," *Corporate Legal Times*, September 1994.

lawyer hired through a reputable local agency, he decided to hire another to complete what he saw as a straightforward legal writing task. A contract lawyer convinced Watters he could complete the assignment. Watters explained that he needed the brief done by the next Friday. The contract lawyer said he had plenty of time available; a one-week deadline would be absolutely no problem. At the end of the week, when Watters asked for the draft, the contract lawyer had almost no work product. Watters and an associate spent the weekend churning out the brief themselves.

Contract lawyers are no different from the overall lawyer population: there will be more than a few brilliant practitioners as well as some real flakes. The fact that (as with most things in life) there are no guarantees troubles some lawyers. "We cannot afford to have a major client's case damaged by some unproven 'rent-a-lawyer,'" said a lawyer with a mid-sized Southern California law firm.[7]

Hiring a new contract lawyer involves as many unknowns as bringing in a new associate; there's no guarantee that an associate will live up to your expectations either—and associates are a much more expensive investment. You can minimize your risk by taking the same precautions in selecting a contract lawyer that you would when hiring an associate. Daniel Edwards discovered that "appropriate interviewing and giving appropriate guidance" are crucial. "The biggest mistake I made early on," he said, "was failing to provide clear objectives and time constraints." With a contract lawyer, you can assign one discrete project and wait for the results before investing any further. You can also hire a lawyer who is overqualified for the first assignment.

When you get a contract lawyer who can't do the job, your remedy is simple—don't use him again. If you hire an associate who lets you down, on the other hand, you may be stuck for a while.

SOME MYTH; SOME REALITY: THEY'RE SHORT-TERMERS AND AREN'T DEPENDABLE.

There's fear that contract lawyers' lack of long-term commitment to the firm will cause them to slack off and do only half a job. Dorothy Streutker confronted this attitude in one of her early assignments. The partner she worked with at a prominent San Francisco law firm had low expectations of anybody who would serve in a contract capacity. "He figured I was going to be a clock watcher," she recounts. "When I arrived at 7 a.m. the very first day and stayed late, he was impressed."

Daniel Edwards, on the other hand, actually experienced the short-termer's attitude.

---

7. James Law, "Marketing Attorneys for Temporary Assignments," *California Law & Business*, October 3, 1988.

I hired a former appellate court clerk to assist me in trial. I assumed
she'd be all caught up in the case; that she'd be charging forth and
burning the midnight oil like I was, that she would show up in court half
dead like I would. But I realized later that she looked at the assignment
as a job, not a commitment . . . which meant that one morning she woke
up not feeling very well and just didn't show up that day. I've had to
reconcile myself to the fact that contract lawyers are not going to have
the same commitment to the case that I have. They're going to look
upon the assignment strictly as a certain amount of time invested in a
project that's going to pay them money. You're really going to get
burned if you don't accept that.

Others would call Edwards' experience an exception to a well-established rule. Laura Black contends that contract lawyers "offer efficiency to new projects, tackling them with wide-eyed motivation because each is new and exciting and has an end." More importantly, their motivation is always to get more work: either a permanent position or additional temporary assignments. "Contract lawyers seem more willing to please because they know that if they don't do a good job, they're not going to continue to get work," says Robert Thomas. "Whereas associates are here long-term and chug along, contract attorneys have to prove themselves with each project." They have as much motivation to impress you with their ability as a permanent employee, and possibly more.

And, points out Jed Rakoff, "Some associates don't have a real psychological commitment to the work either." When associates burn out or become dissatisfied, their work quantity always decreases and sometimes the quality does as well. By hiring contract lawyers—or offering contract terms to permanent employees who have lost their passion for the work—you may circumvent that problem.

SOME MYTH; SOME REALITY: IT'S HARDER TO HANDLE RUSHES WITH TEMPS.

If you want something done in a rush, there's a fair chance you won't be able to get it done as fast as you'd like. But even this depends upon the attitude and style of the lawyer.[8] Richard Kaplan called one contract lawyer at home on a Sunday morning (Kaplan was out of town at a bar conference) to ask her to prepare a motion for a temporary restraining order. The work was ready for him when he got

---

8. And perhaps whether you have a contract lawyer placement agency at your disposal. "Agencies thrive on rushes," says Laura Black. "We often get a call at 5:00 p.m. to get someone who can write a brief by the next morning."

back to the office Monday evening. He remodeled it a bit, went into court Tuesday, and got his order.

Another time, though, Kaplan needed help with a commercial client who was trying to decide whether to get involved with "some heavy duty" litigation. He tried to reach a contract lawyer he'd used before who was, as he put it, "very casual about time." "She was on a mountain top for some event—I called it the harmonica vibrations—where the planets were in some weird relationship to the earth and the moon and for all I know Arcturus." By the time she returned, the client had decided not to pursue litigation and Kaplan lost what might have been a big case.

On the other hand, Portland, Oregon, contract lawyer Laurie Craghead finds that she's more diligent about deadlines and speed than many of her law firm clients:

> *I try to be conscientious and get the work done as fast as possible but everybody else's deadlines are not necessarily the same as mine. I've told one lawyer that I need this and that information or I can't get going on a document. I called last week. I called this week. I can't get the information so I can't do the work. Or I gave documents to another lawyer two weeks ago for approval. I've called three times and left messages but he hasn't responded.*

REALITY: YOU MIGHT GET OVERLY DEPENDENT ON THEM.

Some firms use contract lawyers as a substitute for establishing a clerkship or hiring a new associate. Contract lawyers then complain that the firms get upset because they're not available on demand even though the firms have been unwilling to make any fixed time commitments to them. For example, one small law firm asked two lawyers to come into the office two days per week. If the firm had work for them, they got paid. If not, the contract lawyers returned home, out the price of the commute. When one of the lawyers had been without assignments from the firm for several weeks, she began to accept projects from other lawyers. The firm was so upset with her unavailability for a rush a month later that it terminated the relationship with her. Obviously, if you want a consistent relationship, you'll have to pay for it with a permanent salary or guarantee of payment whether or not there's work.

REALITY: YOU MAY EXPERIENCE A LACK OF CONTINUITY.

You can't always get the same person back to pick up a project where it was left off. You can't always brainstorm or discuss the case with the contract lawyer on the spot when you get an idea. This problem can be remedied by maintaining long-term relationships with several contract lawyers and asking them to be available by telephone for consultations (to be billed at their regular hourly rates).

Ann Arbor practitioner Chris Green has been using Eric Ebel's research and writing services for nearly ten years; they have the kind of relationship where she freely telephones him to "kick around an issue" or get his impression of an analysis she'd like to use. Pat McGraw, an insurance defense lawyer in Saginaw, Michigan, also turns to Ebel on occasion. "I appreciate the chance to bounce ideas off someone else before trial," says McGraw. "I'll tell Eric about a particular strategy I want to try. Eric will tell me when I can't. He's so up on the research that he can tell me if my case is wrong or the old way of doing something."

REALITY: IT'S HARDER TO CRITIQUE AND FOLLOW-UP THEIR WORK.

Portland, Oregon, solo practitioner Dick Maizels has run into this problem:

> *Sometimes, I want to go back and say, "Wait a minute, I don't like this," but I don't have the opportunity. I haven't completed the project but the contract lawyer has already moved on to something else and doesn't want to interrupt the current project to come back and rehash what's happened in the past.*

Not all lawyers are as understanding as Maizels. Contract lawyer Edgar Risko completed a one-shot research project for a firm in Seattle; then accepted a long-term assignment working on a big case in San Francisco. Two weeks later, the Seattle firm tried to follow up on the project. Even though Risko had left a San Francisco contact number on his answering machine, the law firm chose to leave a message on his Seattle line and was angered that he didn't retrieve the message until several days later.

Obviously, immediate follow-up is important. When you ask that a deadline be met, you need to honor that deadline as well. If possible, ask for the project to be turned in before your deadline, with the understanding that the contract lawyer will be available for follow-up, if necessary, over the next few days or weeks.

YOU CAN BE SURE THAT:

- Contract lawyers are not losers.
- Working with contract lawyers does not degrade the profession.
- The going rate for most contract lawyers is a bargain.
- Using contract lawyers will not disgrace the firm.
- Clients will accept your use of contract lawyers.
- Contract lawyers will not increase your exposure to liability.
- Contract lawyers will not disrupt your office.
- Contract lawyers will not steal your clients.

BUT BE AWARE THAT:

- There are no guarantees about work quality.
- Some may have a "short-termer's" attitude.
- Sometimes it's hard to handle rush jobs with contract lawyers.
- You might get too dependent on them.
- You may experience a lack of continuity.
- It's harder to follow up their work with them.

12

CAN YOU USE CONTRACT HELP?

You've been practicing law for years without using contract lawyers. Why would you want to hire one now? Because hiring a lawyer to assist you on a part-time, intermittent or temporary basis makes you more efficient and profitable, and less harried, in the practice of law.

Practitioners convinced of the value of contract lawyer arrangements have found a variety of ways to integrate this type of help into their operations:

- *Baker, Brattain & Huguelet of Anchorage keeps itself small without sacrificing stimulating work by hiring lawyers to assist on an as-needed basis. The firm tells applicants point-blank that it will never add associates or partners to the firm. With experienced practitioners available to help on a variety of projects, the existing partners handle complex litigation matters while providing high-quality, competitively-priced service to their clients.*

- *When Charlotte Tuyman was general counsel for a large manufacturing company in Tennessee, she reduced outside counsel costs by hiring a battery of contract lawyers to review boxes of documents and work up a product development chronology. Paralegals might have done the work at a slightly lower cost, but she knew experienced lawyers would pick up things paralegals would miss while screening out matters that less experienced lawyers would have included.*

- *Chris Green has decided that the "up front" work she prefers—client contact, court appearances, negotiations—is incompatible with the "background" work—research, writing and legal analysis—so necessary to competent handling of a case. "The up-front work moves at such a fast pace that it's tough to slow down for the kind of methodical analysis that can really make or break a case," she observes. "The more active one gets*

CHECK AS MANY OF THESE AS HAVE
APPLIED TO YOU IN THE LAST YEAR:

❑ Your billable hours increased enough to make you feel overworked, but not enough to justify hiring another associate.

❑ You turned down income-generating work because you didn't have sufficient staff or expertise to handle the matter.

❑ A client complained about your delay in attending to his problem, or you had to make excuses for not doing what you'd promised.

❑ You took on a matter that made such extraordinary demands on your time for several months that you felt you were neglecting other matters.

❑ An issue outside your area of expertise arose in the middle of a case, and neither you nor anyone else at your firm had time to explore it adequately.

❑ The court set an accelerated trial date in one of your cases and it conflicted with a series of depositions you had scheduled in another case.

❑ You needed someone to assist you in a second chair role during a complicated trial.

❑ You procrastinated or lost your temper when facing projects or tasks you disliked or weren't interested in.

❑ The external demands of your practice—telephone calls, court appearances, client conferences, settlement negotiations, staff training, performance reviews—took so much of your time and attention that you didn't have adequate opportunity to concentrate on the legal issues and strategies of your cases.

❑ You (or a partner) wanted to take parental leave, vacation or even a sabbatical, but didn't because you wouldn't have had adequate coverage during the absence.

❑ You dreamed about scaling back your practice so you could devote more time to your family, a side business, or a hobby.

❑ Your firm took on a case in which opposing counsel appeared to have six or seven lawyers to your one working around the clock.

❑ The associate who was assisting you on a major deal broke her leg in a skiing accident (or got food poisoning or lost a close relative to cancer) a week before the closing.

❑ As corporate counsel, you assigned major litigation to outside counsel and were astounded when you received the first bills for discovery.

❑ Your corporate law department or government agency was not budgeted for another employee but did have additional funds available in a consulting, contingent or slush fund category to hire extra help to handle overload.

If you checked even one of these statements, you have good reason to develop a relationship with a contract lawyer. If you checked more than one, you should do it now!

in trial work, the less able one is to write a persuasive brief." When the pace gets too furious, she calls upon the contract legal services of Eric Ebel to write major portions of a trial brief or critique her trial strategy. "He's saved my neck more than once," she admits.

HIRING FOR A BROAD RANGE OF PROBLEMS

Every practicing lawyer knows the shame of procrastination. One file screams for attention, but the lawyer either has no clue what to do with it or has no interest in facing it. In 99 cases out of 100, a contract lawyer could take care of the problems the lawyer has been avoiding.

In fact, one of the greatest benefits of temporary professional help comes to those practitioners who admit that a contract lawyer can perform an essential task sooner—or better—than they. Richard Kaplan relies on the services of a "master writer" to produce winning summary judgment and appeal briefs. Werner Lewin of San Francisco's Attorney Assistance tells of a contract lawyer, hired to write the brief in a state court appeal, who later successfully argued the next appeal to the U.S. Supreme Court. Arthur Yost was nearing retirement when he started a successful long-term relationship with a contract lawyer who offered to organize a file for an impending trial. Dady Blake established a solo practice one year out of law school. She turns to more experienced contract lawyers for advice on litigation procedures and critiques of her drafting efforts.

Mark Reeve, who combines contract work with a solo practice, reviewed environmental reports and drafted language to cover environmental issues for the purchase of a manufacturing facility. Cincinnati contract lawyer Molly Tami researched the law of fraud in ten states and prepared a chart that compared the elements of fraud among them. A lawyer handling a number of class action lawsuits against insurance companies used the chart as an exhibit to a crucial memorandum of points and authorities.

HIRING FOR SPECIAL EXPERTISE

Corporate legal departments and law firms with cases outside their specialty need to consider whether hiring a contract lawyer in-house makes more sense than referring a matter to outside counsel. James A. Ounsworth has developed this policy: "If we have an issue which demands high quality, for example, a rights offering, the

THE RANGE OF CONTRACT ASSIGNMENTS

LEGAL RESEARCH
- Discrete issues
- Comprehensive analysis and overview
- Arcane areas of law

PERSUASIVE WRITING
- Memoranda in support of or in opposition to motions
- Trial briefs
- Appellate briefs
- Settlement conference, arbitration or mediation submissions

PREPARATION OF OTHER LITIGATION DOCUMENTS
- Complaint, amended complaint
- Answer, affirmative defenses, counterclaims
- Interrogatories, requests for admission, document requests
- Jury instructions
- Orders and judgments

DOCUMENT REVIEW AND ANALYSIS
- Your client's, to produce in response to adversary's request
- Your adversary's, produced in response to your request
- Your own, to prepare a chronology or overview of key events

APPEARANCES
- Take or defend depositions
- Judgment debtor exams
- Routine motions, status conferences
- Substantive motions
- Administrative hearings
- Arbitration, mediation, settlement conference
- Trial
- Appellate argument

PREPARATION OR REVIEW OF NON-LITIGATION DOCUMENTS
- Corporate articles, by-laws, minutes, resolutions
- Partnership agreements
- Deeds, mortgages, trust deeds
- Loan documents
- Wills and trusts
- Prenuptial agreements
- Securities filings
- Plan and disclosure statement for chapter 11 bankruptcy

GENERAL ASSISTANCE
- Organize a file in preparation for trial
- Interview witnesses
- Take a second seat at trial
- Help out on transactional work
- Prepare an initial draft of the article, book or CLE materials you agreed to produce

EXPERT ASSISTANCE
- Brainstorm or give strategy advice on complex or unusual problems
- Fill in for vacation, sabbatical, family leave, hiring gaps
- Handle the specialized aspects (e.g., tax, environmental) of a matter
- Make use of a non-law professional background (e.g., medicine, accounting, engineering, computers) to assist in technical areas
- Carry a business purchase and sale or real estate deal through to closing

cost of outside counsel is worth it. We [also] use outside counsel for cutting-edge work. Otherwise, we do the work in-house, filling in the gaps with contract attorneys."[1]

Firms often hire contract specialists to handle contested divorce and child custody cases, taxation and estate planning issues, appellate work, complex leasing transactions, software licensing review, securities offerings, business acquisitions with heavy due diligence requirements, and loan documentation. General business practitioner Dora Hobart regularly hires contract specialists to handle personal legal matters for her clientele. When a client with a substantial estate asks for a will, Hobart asks a contract lawyer placement agency to find a specialist in estate planning. The contract lawyer has no client contact; all communication is handled through Hobart, who is ultimately responsible for the work of the contract lawyer, even though she has no way of knowing whether the estate plan is accurate or appropriate.

There are obvious risks to this type of arrangement. Tom Watters says he would never hire a contract lawyer to handle a matter outside his area of expertise. "I can't know if the contract lawyer knows what he's doing. It's a very risky way to grow. My name is on the work and I'd be on the hook."

Watters' blanket rejection of the use of an expert in an area he knows nothing about seems misguided given that lawyers often hire other *firms* to serve just this function. It should be no harder to learn about the reputation and malpractice coverage of a contract lawyer than of a law firm. There are many situations when the most prudent course would be to hire a qualified contract lawyer rather than work in an area beyond your expertise. This option avoids the risk of losing the client altogether that you would take if you decided instead to refer the matter to an outside firm.

For example, it is common for domestic relations lawyers to hire someone else—sometimes a lawyer, sometimes an accountant—to draft qualified domestic relations orders. These documents require such specialized knowledge of pension law that most domestic relations lawyers do not feel competent to handle them. Similarly, the resolution of a property division issue in a divorce can have unforeseen consequences in a subsequent bankruptcy case. Chapter 13 bankruptcy may follow a divorce, and many matrimonial lawyers don't understand the Bankruptcy Code well enough to anticipate and plan for the consequences.

In transactional work, it is not unusual for the lawyer with primary responsibility to seek expert advice on tax, environmental, or other regulatory issues. The lawyer who is not expert in these areas may not even be able to determine whether such issues exist. Should she, out of concern that a contract lawyer is an "unknown quantity," attempt to handle these issues herself? In the litigation arena, would Richard

---

1. "Temp Time: Are You Ready?," *Corporate Legal Times,* September 1994.

Kaplan have been better off refusing to rely on the "unknown" expertise of the lawyer and former engineer he hired to help with a complex construction case?

We have spoken to and heard about many contract lawyers who achieved success precisely because they offer an expertise or skill the hiring lawyer lacks. Rather than reject the idea outright because of perceived risks, take the following precautions if you need to hire an expert:

- *First, investigate the qualifications of the expert more rigorously than you would the qualifications of someone you hire for a straightforward research or writing assignment.*
- *Second, make sure your contract specifies that the expert bears responsibility for his work.*
- *Third, obtain your client's consent to the referral.*
- *Finally, require any contract lawyer with expertise beyond your own to be independently insured.*

13

FINDING THE RIGHT CONTRACT LAWYER

It's a mistake to regard contract lawyers as fungible commodities. Their skills, personalities and work styles are as diverse as those of any other group of lawyers. Therefore, investing time in the selection process is one of the best ways to assure a match with your needs.

If you've never worked with contract lawyers, or if you've worked with them but had unhappy results, you'll need to think through your search process. To develop successful and productive relationships, follow the steps outlined in this chapter.

1. *Identify your needs.*
2. *Define the ideal contract lawyer to help you meet those needs.*
3. *Let others help you locate candidates.*
4. *Weigh each applicant's suitability.*
5. *Select the applicant who is closest to your ideal.*
6. *Test your selection with a small, non-emergency project.*

IDENTIFY YOUR NEEDS

Do you habitually rewrite anything drafted by another lawyer? Do you spend the day meeting with clients and wrangling with opposing counsel over the telephone when you should be preparing for the next day's depositions? Many potential hiring lawyers miss the benefits of contract help by holding on to the all-too-common reluctance to ask for or accept help—or even to admit that they *need* any. "Lawyers aren't used to asking for help," says Robert Thomas. "They just work harder." As co-owner of a contract lawyer placement agency in Seattle, Thomas found law firm administrators to be more receptive than lawyers to the idea of hiring contract help. The administrators "tended to be the ones who were around when the lawyers were saying, 'I'm dying.'" They recognized the inefficiencies and impracticality of handling everything independently.

To overcome this barrier, identify the parts of your practice you dread or avoid, whether a subject matter like bankruptcy or probate or such tasks as legal research and writing, deposition coverage, motion practice, document production or routine discovery pleadings. Some of you will spend hours in the law library or on the Internet but let those "While You Were Out" messages gather on your desk. Others will gladly let phone calls and emergency conferences with clients interrupt your days so that you never get around to filing a summary judgment motion. Think about the entries on your to-do list that get transferred from week to week and are completed only under duress. Could you be procrastinating?

The best cure for procrastination is to stop seeing it as a personal failing, and acknowledge it as a sign that you need to be off-loading parts of your practice. Recall one work project you currently are avoiding. (If you can't think of one that's pending, describe the last project you avoided.) What specifically do you have to do to complete this project? List each step in the approximate order it needs to be taken. Identify what, if any, parts of the project you have done before. Decide which parts of the project appeal to you and which do not. Think about hiring a contract lawyer to help with the less appealing projects or parts of projects.

Procrastination may be every lawyer's dirty little secret, but it's not the only reason you need contract lawyer help. Scheduling decisions beyond your control may require that you be in two places at one time. If you're going into a big trial, it may not be humanly possible for you to prepare all your witnesses *and* write the trial brief, motions *in limine* and jury instructions. Chapters 10 and 12 describe many common scenarios in which hiring lawyers need help—and get it from contract lawyers. Which of them sound familiar to you?

Look at your calendar for the next couple of weeks. Is there a scheduling conflict you hope will disappear, or a big project you can't block out enough time to complete? Think about your last vacation. What kept you at the office until 10:00 p.m. the night before you left on a 7:00 a.m. flight?

Use your answers to these questions, a review of the uses of contract lawyers in Chapter 12 at page 145, and the results of your procrastination exercise, to identify your needs.

DEFINE THE IDEAL CONTRACT LAWYER TO HELP YOU MEET YOUR NEEDS.

Keeping your needs in mind, think about the right contract lawyer to help you. John R. Gailey, III, general counsel and secretary of The West Company, knows his requirements:

> *One, the attorney must have specialized knowledge. Two, the attorney must be available long-term because the cost-effective lawyering comes with experience with our company. Three, they must subscribe to the available resources because in specialized areas, I need somebody who keeps up to speed with changing laws.*[1]

Are you looking for an introverted researcher, or a charismatic personality to charm a difficult client or tame a contentious opponent? Do you prefer a "take the ball and run with it" lawyer, or would you rather supervise the work as closely as you would that of a new associate? Are you seeking contract assistance so you can get the whole project off your mind, or do you want a helper for your work on the case? Stated another way, do you want a contract lawyer to whom you can state the problem and expect to be provided a solution? Or would you prefer to give precise instructions, requesting, for example, a memo on a narrow issue of law, or a trial notebook assembled according to your model?

There's also the detail-oriented versus big-picture style split: here you should find a lawyer who's *not* like you. If you let your work pile up whenever it deals with technical issues, look for someone who loves that kind of detail to come into your office regularly to help you catch up.

Then consider such qualifications as educational credentials, work experience, seniority, supervisory ability and technical or language capabilities.

GOOD CREDENTIALS

If you swear by such credentials as law review, Order of Coif, graduation from a top ten law school, or an apprenticeship at an AmLaw 100 law firm, by all means look for those achievements in your contract lawyer. Bear in mind, though, that lawyers with those credentials may charge more than their humbler colleagues and that many fine practitioners did not excel in law school or practice at one of the "best" firms. "You are making the presumption that people who have trucked

---

1.   "Temp Time: Are You Ready?," *Corporate Legal Times*, September 1994.

through a major firm have learned certain things," says James Ounsworth. "But I am always concerned about these badges of supposed quality: particular law schools, particular law firms. If I can make an analogy with sports, a lot of great professional athletes sometimes come out of 'so-so' undergraduate schools."[2]

Finally, match the credentials to the need. If you want someone to cover numerous but routine court appearances, a lawyer who participated in an indigent defense program, or prosecuted drunk driving offenses for the district attorney, will be better suited to the assignment than a former big-firm associate who has seen the inside of a courtroom, if at all, as a bag-carrier in a mega-case.

WORK EXPERIENCE

Consider whether you need an experienced or entry-level lawyer, paralegal, legal research service or litigation management assistance. It often makes sense to select a contract lawyer who is overqualified for the project, but don't ask a specialist to handle paralegal-level work. The experienced lawyer may be able to complete the work more efficiently and accurately than a beginner, but if the assignment is truly "entry-level," you may also get resentment, or an uninspired work product.

Similarly, new admittees may charge attractively low hourly rates, but be aware that you're paying for their training. Most experienced practitioners have forgotten what it's like to be green, and therefore have unrealistic expectations about a recent graduate's ability to handle discovery work or even "simple" legal research. Try to remember the first time *you* had to write a set of interrogatories[3] or draft a memorandum of points and authorities. You can hire recent graduates for research projects, document organization, trial assistance and other routine matters, but you must monitor their progress, supervise them as closely as you would a new associate and expect them to learn by making mistakes.

SUBSTANTIVE PRACTICE AREA

If you need someone to run your practice while you're on vacation or parental leave, look for a lawyer with comparable practice experience and a compatible

---

2. Id.

3. Deborah Arron vividly recalls her first assignment as an associate with Seattle firm, William, Kastner & Gibbs—drafting a set of interrogatories for the defense in a products liability case. She spent two weeks in the library comparing three sets of "standard" interrogatories, trying to figure out why each question was asked and which should be included in this set. Ultimately, she decided to copy most of one set and add a few more special questions. The firm chalked up the 50 wasted hours to education; most hiring lawyers would not be as charitable.

practice style. The more personal the nature of your practice, the more important this tip. (See discussion in the next sub-section.)

Appropriate experience is also a factor if you need help in an area such as tax or environmental regulation, where the inexperienced lawyer can spend days just getting oriented. Former placement agency owner and lawyer Ellen Alexander was once able to locate a contract lawyer with experience on several railroad bankruptcies, to work with lawyers who were experienced in bankruptcy but had never handled one involving a railroad.

Many contract lawyers refuse to do criminal or domestic relations work, while others do almost nothing but. In contrast, it doesn't take years of specialized experience to develop an argument on contract interpretation. Decide at the beginning whether your project is one that truly requires familiarity with the practice area, or whether it is one that any lawyer schooled in traditional research methods could successfully tackle.

STYLE

If you have a low-key personality and pride yourself on your reasonableness and courtesy, the last person you'll want standing in for you is a mad-dog litigator. The reverse is true as well, according to Ellen Alexander:

> We were always looking for good, strong domestic relations lawyers to take over cases for lawyers who were not interested in doing that kind of work. Our problem was finding a person whose philosophy fit that of the lawyer who was trying to delegate the work. Some lawyers had very firm ideas about the adversarial nature of domestic work. You could not send them someone who wanted to talk mediation.

Style may be less of an issue for behind-the-scenes projects, but even there it should not be ignored. (See discussions below on pressure and writing ability.)

PRESSURE AND SPEED

Two kinds of lawyers operate in the profession: those who perform well under pressure—and may even need it to get things done—and those who avoid it at all costs. If you habitually wait until the last minute yourself, you probably also wait until the last minute to find help. You'll need to stay in touch with contract lawyers who welcome "super-rush" projects.

If you're likely to need someone to handle rush projects, evaluate candidates for rapid response time from your first contact with them. Was the lawyer easy to reach? Did the lawyer respond promptly to your call, and any subsequent requests for information? Did he quickly provide you with a résumé or sample work product? Be certain, though, to tell the contract lawyer you need help with high-pressure assignments. Some, as New York contract lawyer Cecelie Berry points out, have chosen contract work precisely to avoid such situations:

> *If there is even a remote possibility of high-pressure assignments, court appearances, depositions or drafting of Supreme Court briefs, the temporary attorney should be so informed. A temporary attorney might not be interested in what might otherwise be considered a great career opportunity. Understanding that [some] temporary lawyers have purposely sought to limit their commitment to legal practice is essential to avoiding disappointment on the part of the firm.[4]*

WRITING ABILITY

Don't make the mistake of undervaluing "research and writing"—it can win the case for you. You may love to write and appreciate powerful prose, but as your practice has grown you've gotten too caught up in making deals, conducting trials, or developing client relations to spend the time you need to turn out a polished piece of work. If you hire contract lawyers to do the writing you'd like to do but don't have time for, you must review their writing samples with care. Would you be proud to sign your name to this one? The "masterful" writer Richard Kaplan relies on is "every bit as good a lawyer as I am; I'm flattered to think that I'm as good a writer as he is."

ORAL SKILLS

You need a contract lawyer with good oral skills if she will appear for you in court, attend meetings or depositions, or talk directly with your clients. You don't need to watch the lawyer argue an appeal to assess her skills, though. Simply observe how articulate and persuasive she is in interacting with you. You can expect the same kind of performance in carrying out work assignments.

INSURANCE STATUS

If you intend to rely upon the special expertise of a contract lawyer, pay attention to coverage for professional negligence. Ordinarily, your supervision of the lawyer will place liability on your shoulders; your reliance upon the advice of the contract

---

4. Cecelie S. Berry, "Temporary Lawyers: The Do's and Don'ts," *New York Law Journal*, April 17, 1989.

lawyer specialist could shift the burden. In either case, though, if the contract lawyer is uninsured, you face possible exposure. (See Chapter 19 for further information.)

LET OTHERS HELP YOU LOCATE CANDIDATES.

It's best to consider any prospective contract lawyer as someone with whom you'll maintain a long-term relationship, and to approach the process of finding good candidates as seriously as if you were looking for a new associate. Your chances of finding the right contract lawyer are related to how much time (or money) you invest in the process. In other words, you can either pay for the services of a qualified agency, or spend time making inquiries on your own.

In large cities, there are two groups of contract lawyers: those who work through agencies and those who don't. You'll find mostly experienced practitioners with impressive credentials through agencies; applicants with lesser experience or credentials will often find you. Don't let this generalization prejudice you against non-agency contract lawyers. Only a small fraction of contract lawyers work through agencies. (See Chapter 21.) Many of those with shining credentials find work on their own as well as through agencies, and many lawyers who find work only on

WHERE TO FIND CONTRACT LAWYERS

CONTRACT LAWYER PLACEMENT AGENCIES
- Local if any
- Regional
- National for specialized needs

PERSONAL CONTACTS
- At your firm
- In your building
- At other firms or companies
- Through law school career services/placement offices
- At bar association and other law-related events

READ RÉSUMÉS
- Check unsolicited résumés.
- Save the best.

CHECK THE CLASSIFIED ADS IN:
- Bar publications
- The Sunday paper
- Law school alumni bulletins

their own are equally competent. In legal markets without agencies, of course, contract lawyers find work through their own efforts.

If you need a specialized practitioner in an obscure area of law, asking a contract lawyer placement agency—even one with headquarters far from your geographic location—to conduct a national search is a logical choice. Agencies can also be helpful in locating candidates with specific backgrounds—for example, management of environmental litigation or courtroom experience in asbestos litigation defense. For routine litigation, and legal research assistance, you can usually find qualified applicants on your own, though an agency may save you time. Mike Evers, a placement specialist in Chicago, admits that "lawyers never need to use agencies to find entry-level candidates."

USING AN AGENCY

Working through an agency saves you time, because most agencies maintain pools of at least 35 prescreened lawyers. Not all agencies will be equally helpful, though. Chapter 21 suggests ways to choose an agency and best use its services. Appendix 5 lists contract lawyer agencies nationwide.

ON YOUR OWN

You might think that placing a classified ad is the easiest way to find a qualified contract lawyer. Think again. You'll be inundated with résumés from lawyers seeking permanent employment who hope this temporary opportunity will give them an advantage should you decide to hire another associate. Rather than rely on this inefficient and impersonal search method, tap into your network of colleagues.

- *Think about lawyers you know who have taken off time to raise children and might be eager to return to work part-time or intermittently.*
- *Consider practitioners who have recently left firms to start their own practices, or who recently opened solo practices in your building. If they're not available to do the work themselves, they may know of lawyers who are.*
- *Check with other lawyers in your firm or building; they may have worked with good contract lawyers in the past, or know of someone else who has.*
- *Call friends and colleagues at other firms or companies like yours and ask if they can recommend good contract lawyers.*
- *Finally, stay alert at bar association meetings, CLE programs and other gatherings of lawyers for word-of-mouth recommendations.*

If you're new to your legal community or your telephone calls haven't been effective, try these methods:

- *Review the classified ads in your state and local bar publications for lawyers seeking contract assignments. These lawyers make a business of contract work; some place ads as much to remind past customers of their availability as to solicit new ones. They tend to be reliable service providers if their ads have been running regularly for six months or more. You may also find ads placed by lawyers searching for full-time work—especially those who have recently moved to the area and have not yet developed contacts; they may also be willing to work on a contract basis.*
- *Watch your mail. If your office is like most in the country, you receive a steady stream of letters and résumés from lawyers looking for jobs. "I constantly get résumés from lawyers looking for either contract or full-time work," says Daniel Edwards. "They're clearly inundating all the lawyers in the Yellow Pages with their résumé. I've gotten to the point where I read the first line and if I see a résumé attached it usually just gets tossed. Sometimes they don't even get out of the envelope." Rather than tossing these letters in the recycling box, read them through and save those from lawyers who offer only contract services. Then when a need develops, you'll have a pool of candidates to interview.*
- *Law schools can often tell you which graduates have started solo practices or are available for contract assignments. People who work in career services (sometimes called placement) offices usually know which new admittees are available for legal research and writing assignments, and what experienced alumni might be open to contract assignments.*
- *As a last resort, check with legal headhunters in your area. Some make temporary placements upon request. If not, they may provide names of lawyers they haven't been able to place—although possibly for a fee.*

WEIGH EACH APPLICANT'S SUITABILITY.

Checking each applicant's credentials and conducting personal interviews may sound like a lot of work if all you have in mind is a 15-hour project, but it's worth it. Doing the spadework should only take an hour or two; balance this against the cost of a project that's poorly done, a client who's unhappy with the result, or your own loss of a weekend as you repair the damage. And remember that if you select well you can establish a relationship that will endure far beyond the first project.

But impermanence can also be a benefit of hiring a contract lawyer: you don't need to assure a perfect match because the relationship is easily terminated if the fit isn't right. Austin Reed, general counsel of Pittston Co., saved both money and time when he hired a contract lawyer because the interview "didn't focus so much on her long-term plans or how she would fit into the corporate culture, just her ability to handle the particular project." [5]

INTERVIEW THE LAWYER.

The best interview setting is a face-to-face meeting. Outline your needs first, then let the contract lawyer do most of the talking. And if you won't be working directly with the contract lawyer yourself, make certain that the lawyer who *will* be is involved in the interview process. Samuel Frederick remembers one case in which general counsel "metaphorically fell in love with" a contract lawyer and hired her. He then turned her over to work with one of his subordinates. That lawyer couldn't stand her, so the placement was a failure and the hiring process had to be repeated.

Observe the candidate's listening skills and note non-verbal clues. Guarded or inconsistent answers could signal problems with the candidate's representations about credentials and experience. Nonresponsive answers, or responses that indicate the candidate did not understand your concerns, may presage problems following instructions or understanding the nature of an assignment.

Since good communication is the foundation of an effective working relationship, look for contract lawyers who listen attentively and ask questions easily. "Contract lawyers have to be eager to please," says Ellen Alexander. "They have to be willing to sacrifice more than an associate does." Werner Lewin recommends "self-starters who take as much pride in the work they do for you as they would if the work were their own." Both experts are describing a humility that is the foundation of effective teamwork, an ability to set aside one's own ego for the good of the project. That humility translates into an attitude reflected by contract lawyer Dorothy Streutker's observation: "I'm not afraid to say, 'Gee, I don't know how to do this,' or 'I can't figure out how to make a phone call on your telephone system.'"

Tom Singman was hired for a contract position in Oakland, California, because the partner assumed his being a fellow alumnus of the University of Michigan meant they were compatible enough to develop a good working relationship. The assumption worked for that hiring lawyer, but it won't necessarily work for you. Describe

---

5. Amy Stevens, "Big Companies Hire More Lawyer-Temps," *Wall Street Journal*, September 22, 1994.

your own working style to the contract lawyer and, if he'll be working on-site, the essentials of firm culture. As the same time, observe his personality and think about whether you'll be comfortable working with him.

Make certain as well that you listen to what the contract lawyer says. Jim Finerman told one hiring lawyer that he was willing to do only office work: no depositions, court appearances or other "public duties." The law firm hired him to work on a large case. Later, the hiring lawyer was disturbed when Finerman refused to take a deposition or go to court, telling the placement agency that he "didn't specifically know" Finerman's limitations.

Lawyers in rural areas who need a good researcher with access to a better equipped law library probably won't be able to meet qualified applicants in person. The same applies to lawyers who need out-of-town deposition coverage or document review. In those situations, rely upon the services of either a respected contract lawyer placement agency or a combination of a thorough telephone interview, positive references and a credentials check.

CONFIRM COMPATIBILITY.

You should be able to tell in the course of the interview whether you are comfortable with the contract lawyer's personality. But if he'll be working on-site with lawyers other than you, fit with the firm style is also an issue. Edwin Heller of New York's Fried, Frank, Harris, Shriver & Jacobson says: "Be aware that an attorney who is highly qualified does not necessarily share your firm culture—the values, the intensity, the goals of the firm." He cited the unfortunate incident of a contract lawyer with outstanding credentials who invested too much time in producing "perfect" work—so perfect that the firm's client refused to pay the bill for the many hours it consumed.[6]

"In some law firms, you've got to be ready to work your ass off even if you're a contract lawyer," notes Samuel Frederick. "Someone who wants to be very strict about hours or who comes from a more laid back environment may not work." Likewise, an over-thorough contract lawyer working for a firm that prides itself on cost-efficiency, or a button-down type working in an office of jeans-clad practitioners, will cause problems.

CONFIRM CREDENTIALS.

Unless you know the lawyer personally, or the lawyer has been sent by an agency that does this for you, you'll want to confirm that the lawyer actually has the

---

6. Samuel A. Frederick, "Temporary Attorneys: Here to Stay," unpublished manuscript, 1994.

CHECKLIST FOR SCREENING CONTRACT LAWYERS

VERIFY:
- Law school graduation, any honors listed on résumé
- Admission to bar; good standing
- Two former employers
- Reason for leaving last position
- Whether complaints or malpractice claims are pending

REQUEST AND REVIEW:
- Writing samples
- Project list

REFERENCES:
- Ask for several names
- Call any you know and respect
- Ask respected colleagues whether they know the candidate's work
- Ask about the candidate's reputation for being responsible, reliable, punctual

INTERVIEW:
- Confirm a compatible personality
- Discuss contract lawyer's preferences regarding:
  - Working under pressure
  - Dealing with technical issues
  - Client contact, court appearances
- Evaluate such communications skills as:
  - Openness, readiness to ask questions
  - Eloquence and expressiveness
  - Persuasiveness
  - Ability to listen, responsiveness
- Determine contract lawyer's availability
  - Long-term
  - For rush projects
  - On short notice
- Discuss computer usage and compatibility

credentials and experience represented. Verify law school graduation and admission to the bar. Check at least two employer references. Ask for and review writing samples and other work product if writing will be an important part of the assignment.

Credentials and experience are the easiest qualities to investigate. "For lawyers with substantial experience, I am impressed with success as a lawyer prior to being a contract lawyer," says Robert Thomas. Recent graduates are judged on traditional law school markers such as class standing, the reputation of the law school, law review, moot court and trial practice participation, clerkships and other honors and awards. After a lawyer has practiced for a few years, the traditional markers become less important than experience, reputation and favorable references. All of these facts can be learned from a résumé.

"I look at the résumé to see if they're smarter than me," says Dick Maizels. "Most of the time they are, so I use them." "Basically, I want people who choose to be contract lawyers, not those who have been forced into it," admits Thomas. "If they're hungry due to no fault of their own that's good; it pushes them to achieve. If they're hungry because they haven't done well at what they were doing, I'm not interested."

These inquiries may assure high quality work, but intelligence is not the only qualification. Also important is experience that matches your needs and a personal style that instills confidence. If experience in a particular area of law is essential, you might ask for a list of projects the contract lawyer has completed in that area. Or you could, in the interview, engage the lawyer in discussion of a recent development in the law.

You should also take steps to minimize the chances your association with the contract lawyer will result in liability or exposure. Ascertain why the lawyer left his previous positions. Find out whether any complaints or proceedings are pending against him. Ask the contract lawyer whether he is aware of any ongoing investigations involving him or his current or former partners, or check with the contract lawyer's insurance carrier for the same information.

DISCUSS OFFICE TECHNOLOGY, ESPECIALLY COMPUTER EQUIPMENT.

"It is absolutely critical that the contract attorney have the ability to interface with us through PC WordPerfect and have an availability to our commercial loan officers," says Michelle Petrilli, chief marketing counsel at PNC Bank.[7] Tom Watters, in contrast, states that most lawyers in his firm don't use computers, so "computer literacy or familiarity with our system" is not a requirement. Make certain the contract lawyer understands your technology needs, and apply the standard that works for you.

CHECK FOR CONFLICTS.

Before you tell the lawyer about the case, you must make sure there are no conflicts problems. Inform the contract lawyer of the identity of all parties, counsel and potential parties *before* going into background information that could contain client confidences. If the contract lawyer will be working long-term on many matters for the firm—whether on site or out of a separate office—a more extensive conflicts check may be necessary. See Chapter 17 for a detailed discussion of conflicts of interest and other ethical issues.

SELECT THE APPLICANT WHO IS CLOSEST TO YOUR IDEAL.

When an arcane regulatory issue arises and you need a contract lawyer to deal

---

7.   "Temp Time: Are You Ready?,"*supra* n. 1.

WHICH CRITERIA ARE MOST IMPORTANT TO YOU?

CREDENTIALS
- Years of experience
- Prestigious institutions (law school, firm, corporation)
- Honors and awards
- Outstanding references

AREAS OF EXPERIENCE OR EXPERTISE
- Substantive law
- Particular court (e.g., bankruptcy, appellate)
- Drafting skills (negotiated or form agreements)
- Writing ability
- Oral skills
- Aptitude for dealing with technical issues
- Attention to detail

PERSONAL QUALITIES:
- Responsible, reliable, punctual
- Compatible with your personal style
- Truly stimulated by the law and how it works
- Able to communicate well
- Able to work under pressure
- Able to absorb information quickly
- Creative
- Able to think fast on his feet
- Able to work independently
- Able to follow instructions

with it, you're unlikely to find a candidate who spent several years in-house with a major corporation dealing with the same regulations. More likely, you'll find several résumés that differ as to years of practice experience and hourly rate charged, but which do not indicate familiarity with that area of law. If by some fluke, you do come across the perfect credentials, the person bearing them might make your eyeballs itch or might not be available when you need her. On the other hand, the shiny-faced recent graduate who charges only $15 per hour and has a can-do, eager-to-please attitude may make you want to say "yes" against your better judgment.

Perfection doesn't exist in the real world. That's why it's important for you to know yourself and your needs well enough to be able to choose among imperfect alternatives. In recommending that you use our checklists and heed our advice in hiring contract lawyers, we aren't suggesting that the perfect match exists, let alone that it will present itself in your office at the crucial moment. We do believe, however, that the more informed your decisionmaking process, the better the results are likely to be. So, now that you've defined the project and identified your expectations, reviewed résumés, checked references, and interviewed applicants, it's time to use common sense to match your needs to the contract lawyers you interview.

If, for example, you decide after much consideration that a glittering résumé is the one thing you must have, then you have an objective basis for making a choice. If (perhaps more realistically) you've identified the ability to write cogently under pressure as the most important quality in a contract lawyer, you can take steps to determine which of the available candidates does that best. If you need someone to step into your creditors' rights practice while you're on sabbatical, a seasoned bankruptcy practitioner will be a better choice than either a whiz-bang writer or a Harvard Law School graduate who practiced securities law in a prestigious Wall Street firm. If you'd like a contract lawyer whom you can ease into a full-time position when there's enough work, the lawyer who's combining contract work with a solo practice is not your best bet, no matter how perfect she is in other ways.

Only you can decide, given your situation, what the most important criteria are. We can help by identifying as many as we're aware of, and urging you to think through what they mean to you. As an exercise, pick at random a project you are currently working on. Imagine there's an emergency and you must hire a contract lawyer to complete it. Then consider the criteria on page 161 and decide which three would be most important to you in choosing a contract lawyer to do the work.

TEST YOUR SELECTION WITH A SMALL, NON-EMERGENCY PROJECT.

Once you've made a tentative selection, assign the lawyer a small project that is not critical to the success of the matter and has no immediate deadline. This way you can judge the quality of the lawyer's work product and compatibility with your practice style with a minimum of risk, and avoid the surprise of inadequate work when you don't have time for major revisions. If you're unhappy with the work product or other results, don't conclude that contract lawyers can't help you. Try working with another. Then later, when you need someone to handle a rush project or to assist with a high-level case, you'll spare yourself the stress of working with an unproven lawyer.

14

STRIKING A DEAL

To set an hourly rate or project fee, consider several factors: the nature of the assignment, the contract lawyer's background and established rates, the economics of your law practice, and your client's involvement in the decision.

Hiring lawyers and contract lawyers alike recognize that agreeing on the contract lawyer's rate is a key step in striking a deal. Likewise, both parties recognize that the contract lawyer's qualifications are a factor in this decision. Other factors play an important role as well: the nature of the assignment, the economics of your law practice and your relationship with your clients. Think through all of these issues before you agree on rates.

DEFINING THE ASSIGNMENT

There are several reasons to spend time defining the assignment. One (discussed in Chapter 13) is to decide who would be the ideal contract lawyer to complete it. Another (discussed in Chapter 15) is to ensure that the contract lawyer you've hired does exactly what you want him to do.

The reason applicable to this chapter is to help arrive at the right hourly rate (or flat fee) for the contract lawyer's work. Several aspects of the nature of the assignment affect the appropriate rate; note that they do not necessarily determine the rate.

LEVEL OF RESPONSIBILITY

How does the work the contract lawyer will do fit into the case or matter as a whole? For example, litigator Gretchen Sandvig has a big trial coming up in a breach of contract case. One of the issues is whether a person had apparent authority to bind a partnership. Sandvig decides to get help from a contract lawyer. Depending on how much responsibility she is willing (or needs) to delegate, she can ask the contract lawyer to:

- *Find and copy all the reported decisions in her state since 1985, and any leading decisions from earlier years, on apparent authority.*
- *Research apparent authority in her state and write an informal memo summarizing the law, which Sandvig can incorporate into the trial brief.*
- *Research the law and write the trial brief, covering all issues including apparent authority.*

Sandvig should be willing to pay higher rates as the level of responsibility she delegates to the contract lawyer increases.

LEVEL OF EXPERTISE

Related to the level of responsibility but distinct from it is the expertise required by the assignment. In litigation, for example, discovery work is usually seen as "low-level" and appellate work as high-level. But this rule does not apply to all situations, so analyze yours individually. What will you be asking the contract lawyer to do:

- *Work you'd delegate to a junior associate if one were available?*
- *Work you'd do yourself if only you had time?*
- *Work beyond your area of proficiency (for example, appellate work if you're a trial lawyer)?*

Again, you may be able to pay a lower rate for work you would feel comfortable delegating to an inexperienced lawyer than for work you would prefer to do yourself if you had the time. A higher rate is warranted when the contract lawyer has expertise you lack.

TIME FRAME

The time for completion of the project or assignment is not always a factor, but it can be. For example, if you are offering an assignment that will require full-time work (or close to it) over a period of several months, you can probably negotiate a lower hourly rate than if you are hiring someone to do a discrete ten- to 15-hour project. Being assured of steady work allows contract lawyers to charge somewhat less, because such a guarantee reduces the time they would otherwise lose to marketing or transition between projects.

At the other end of the scale, a high-pressure rush project with a fast turn-around time may command a somewhat higher hourly rate. If the contract lawyer has to drop everything to complete your project on time, the lawyer may want to be compensated for the disruption of his schedule. (The contract lawyer also might enjoy a strong bargaining position resulting from your desperation!) Not all contract lawyers request higher rates for rush projects, however.

WORK SITE

If the contract lawyer will work in your office, using your equipment and being assisted by your support staff, the rate paid the contract lawyer should be lower than for assignments the contract lawyer completes without using your facilities. The lower rate is to account for the portion of your overhead attributable to the contract lawyer's work.

COMPENSATING THE CONTRACT LAWYER

Nationally, contract lawyers charge from as little as $12.50 to more than $150 per hour, with most rates in the $30 to $65 range. Rates vary depending upon geography; specialty area, reputation, quality and experience of the contract lawyer; whether the hiring lawyer and contract lawyer have an existing relationship; the negotiating skills of the parties; whether or not a contract lawyer placement agency is involved; independent contractor versus employee status; and luck.

Rates at the high end of the scale are commanded by lawyers with recognized expertise, usually in a sophisticated specialty area. Their involvement is similar to that of a consulting expert or associated counsel. In the middle of the range are lawyers with substantial experience who are perhaps overqualified for their assignments.

Most lawyers willing to work at the bottom of the pay range are recent law school graduates with little or no experience who are trying to get a foot in the door or to learn about the practice of law from you. Lawyers who hire new admittees may be disappointed with their contract lawyer experience because of unrealistic expectations. "Some lawyers are looking for magic: a contract lawyer who will work for next to nothing, make no demands and produce excellent work," notes Los Angeles contract lawyer placement specialist Liz Elliott. "That's not a real-world scenario." Any lawyer hiring a recent graduate must be prepared to provide substantial supervision, instruction and one-on-one guidance—for example, discussion of sources that should be checked and the length of time the project should take. For $25 an hour you are not hiring someone who can work independently on a case.

A contract lawyer generally charges other lawyers less than what he could charge directly to a client. Why would a competent lawyer allow his or her time to be compensated at such a low rate? There are many good reasons.

- *The hourly rate received by the contract lawyer can equal or better the take-home pay of a full-time practitioner, when you consider the number of hours including non-chargeable time that a typical associate or partner works annually, and divide those hours into salary. "If I work 80 hours a week, I get paid for all of them," says San Francisco contract lawyer Deborah Trotter. "If an associate in a law firm works 80 hours, he or she just gets straight salary."* [1]

- *Many contract lawyers have home-based businesses, with little overhead to subtract from the hourly rate. Lee Archer, a New Orleans appellate specialist, uses the most up-to-date technology, but charges only $65 per hour for her expertise. "The reason I can keep my hourly rate so low is that my overhead is low."*

- *Lawyers tend to pay more promptly and reliably than other clients. Contract lawyers expect payment within a couple of weeks of the time the work is billed. If they don't get paid, they can refuse to provide further services.*

- *Contract lawyers who want to work part-time find that the hourly rates, combined with flexible work hours and location, yield a well-paid part-time job.*

- *Some contract lawyers are between jobs and need extra funds to keep them and their families afloat.*

SETTING AN HOURLY RATE

You may be willing to pay higher hourly rates to a contract lawyer who has had a longstanding good relationship with you or your firm, whether as a former associate or partner, as adversary or co-counsel or by way of other connections. You may be required to pay higher rates for a contract lawyer who works through an agency than for one you contract with directly, since the agency must be compensated for its search and screening work. At the other end of the scale, you may be able to negotiate a lower hourly rate if you're hiring several contract lawyers through one agency for a large-scale long-term project.

Although there is no universally accepted method for setting fair compensation of contract lawyers, the following formulas have been recommended.

---

1.   William Lewis & Nancy Schuman, *The Temp-Workers Handbook* (Amacom 1988).

- *Ask the contract lawyer to state a rate. If it seems reasonable, pay it without further negotiation. Experienced contract lawyers have researched the market and know how much they can command for their services.*
- *Pay the contract lawyer from one-third to one-half the hourly rate you would bill the client for the work of an associate or partner in your firm qualified to do the job. If the lawyer will be working in your office and using your clerical staff, pay the lower end of the scale. Contract lawyers who maintain their own offices should receive the higher hourly rate.*
- *Pay an hourly rate comparable to the salary plus benefits divided by average billable hours of an associate or partner with the necessary level of expertise to handle the job.*
- *Pay $5 to $15 per hour less than the rate a local contract lawyer placement agency would charge for a lawyer with the necessary background and experience to handle the assignment.*
- *Pay an hourly rate that allows you to retain as profit from ten to 33 percent of the fee charged to the client.*

See Chapter 7 on rate setting by contract lawyers for more detailed discussion of these rate-setting formulas.

Hourly rates are almost always negotiable. Some lawyers will accept less than their stated rate for the first project—to convince you they're really worth what they're asking. Many contract lawyers raise their rates as they gain confidence. To maintain a productive relationship with a contract lawyer you value, you may want to offer a higher rate. "One lawyer started me out a little lower than my normal rate, but when she realized she wasn't getting my attention, she raised the rate," says Susan Shulenberger, a contract lawyer for the past six years.

The hourly rate is not the only compensation issue to discuss. Let the contract lawyer know the intervals at which you expect to be billed (i.e., weekly, monthly, or at completion of the project) and ask how soon she expects to be paid. When the lawyer will be working on the premises, you also need to discuss whether meals and breaks will be compensated (usually no) or whether the lawyer will be paid for attending administrative functions such as department meetings or client luncheons (usually yes).

NEGOTIATING A FLAT FEE

If you want to negotiate a project fee, take care in defining the scope of the assignment. Most experienced contract lawyers have been burned on this enough times to be able to present a contract that specifically outlines their obligations and payment. If you are dealing with someone less experienced, draft your own letter of agreement spelling out precisely what you expect to be included in the project.

You might be tempted to define the project only by maximum hours to be spent, but it's better to define it by tasks and scope. For example, define a research project by stating the issue to be researched (e.g., duties of a small business to a pregnant employee), the breadth of the research (a thorough review of current state statutes and administrative regulations and applicable federal law, Shepardized to this month) and the final product (a memorandum that summarizes all responsibilities and cites supporting statutes, regulations and case interpretations). See sample engagement letter at page 243.

KEEP IN MIND THAT THE CHEAPEST CONTRACT LAWYER IS RARELY THE BEST

Some hiring lawyers forget that in contract lawyering, as in other facets of life, you get what you pay for. "There is a whole group of people out there who want a contract lawyer with fifth- or sixth-year associate level experience but offer to pay them first-year wages," says Robert Thomas, a former contract lawyer and past owner of a contract lawyer placement agency. "They end up with inexperienced people who don't meet their expectations and then blame that contract lawyer—or contract lawyers in general—for their bad experience."

Ellen Alexander reports that when she was running the agency with Thomas, "at least half the time" her customers opted for the lawyer with the cheapest hourly rate. This is almost always a mistake. A more experienced lawyer usually completes the project faster and more competently, especially if the job is in an area of specialty. Further, the tendency to choose the cheapest lawyer, which several agency owners have observed, is at odds with hiring lawyers' concerns about quality. A firm or lawyer that truly wants the best-qualified lawyer should hire on that basis even if the lawyer is more expensive. Richard Kaplan willingly pays $90 to $100 per hour for the services of a master writer. "This man recognizes his competence and very high skills, and for his services I pay more than I have for others," admits Kaplan. "To me, it's worth it."

Thomas suggests that you always hire a contract lawyer slightly overqualified for the assignment. "You'll pay more per hour but it's usually money well spent." An overqualified practitioner not only will work more efficiently, but will have the judgment to handle unexpected situations that could prejudice the client. Bay Area contract lawyer Dorothy Streutker was defending a routine deposition when her client admitted he had been convicted of a felony. Although Streutker's previous experience had been in commercial transactions, she had the presence of mind to ask for an immediate recess to confer with the client. In fact, the "felony" conviction was a juvenile offense and she was able to strike his answer from the record.

Anne Bowman, a lawyer with a forestry and environmental law practice, learned the folly of hiring the cheapest contract lawyer the hard way. She needed research in an esoteric area of environmental law and asked a local agency to provide her with several résumés. One was from an environmental law specialist, another from a lawyer with antitrust experience and Harvard Law Review credentials. The specialist charged $65 per hour and estimated he could complete the project in 15 to 20 hours. The Harvard graduate seemed a bargain at only $45 per hour so she hired him. It was a disaster: "He wandered around the library for 40 hours before he even found the right book!"

By suggesting that cheapest is usually not best, we do not mean to discourage the hiring of recent graduates. But be realistic when you do so. The lower rates inexperienced lawyers charge mean you'll have to spend more time describing the assignment and supervising the work; in effect, these lawyers are charging low rates in exchange for your training. (See "Tips for Working with Recent Graduates" in Chapter 15 at page 179.) If you are not prepared to spend the necessary time on guidance and oversight, you should not hire them. It is not fair—to the contract lawyer, the client or yourself—to hire a new graduate at a low rate and expect the same results in the same amount of time as would be produced by a seasoned practitioner.

There are, of course, times when the least expensive lawyer will serve your client best: when you need to represent your client in a distant court or at a deposition in a nonadversarial role; when you need basic research in a general area and plan to read all the cases yourself; or during trial, when you simply need another pair of eyes and ears to observe the jury and keep track of details. The important point is to be sure that the requirements of the assignment—rather than desire for a bargain— govern your decision.

CHARGING THE CLIENT

One advantage of using contract lawyers is that their modest rates give you great flexibility: you can realize profit from their work, or pass savings along to the client. In many instances you can do both. The following are ways hiring lawyers can approach the question of how much to charge the client.

MARK UP THE CONTRACT LAWYER'S HOURLY RATE BEFORE BILLING THE CLIENT.

Most hiring lawyers we talked to charge the hours worked by contract lawyers to their clients at rates higher than those they pay the contract lawyers.[2] This markup allows the hiring lawyer to be compensated for the delay between the time he pays the contract lawyer and the time the client pays him, as well as for the risk of nonpayment by the client. It also lets the hiring lawyer recover any overhead costs—and realize a profit. The theory is the same as that for associates: the firm bills them out at a rate that will enable the firm (1) to pay them what they deserve (or what the market demands), (2) to cover costs of employee benefits and over-head, and (3) to realize a profit.

Some hiring lawyers charge the contract lawyer's time at the hourly rate of the least experienced lawyer at the firm able to handle the job—which may be two or three times the rate the contract lawyer charges them. Others charge the contract lawyer's time at their own hourly rates, since the contract lawyer is doing work the hiring lawyer would otherwise have done himself. Still others mark up the contract lawyer's bill by some percentage (perhaps 20 to 50 percent) and charge that amount to the client. This system may still result in a rate to the client lower than the rate of a firm lawyer with comparable experience.

When contract lawyer Candice Kawata left her West Coast firm to pursue other interests, she agreed to continue handling one big case on a contract basis. The firm paid her $55 per hour, while billing her work to the client at her regular rate of $135 per hour. Because she was a known quantity, was familiar with the case, and was accustomed to dealing with the client, the firm had no need to oversee her work. Kawata worked out of her home office, dealt directly with the client, and made court appearances when necessary. The only thing she did not do was sign pleadings. "The firm made $80 of profit for every hour I billed," she notes.

Richard Kaplan always marks up the contract lawyer's rate, because this is "exactly what they do in the large law firms. It's called profit. We are in a capitalist system, supposedly," he observes. Kaplan has billed one contract lawyer out at his own rate, while paying the lawyer about half that. Rochelle Kosnitsky, who has a debt collection practice and a low hourly rate herself, works with Phoebe Conover, a contract lawyer whose rate is not much lower than her own. She marks up Conover's rate only 20 or 30 percent, so that the client pays a rate midway between Kosnitsky's and Conover's.

---

2. Some jurisdictions prohibit the mark-up of costs like fax charges, court reporting, and expert witness fees. Those same prohibitions might apply to contract lawyer services, especially if the contract lawyer is acting as a consulting expert. Check your state's requirements.

CHARGE THE CLIENT EXACTLY WHAT THE CONTRACT LAWYER CHARGED YOU.

Daniel Edwards would rather bill his client $25 per hour for research by a less experienced lawyer than do the work himself at a much higher rate. He figures that the client will save money even if the contract lawyer takes more time than Edwards would.

A few lawyers send the contract lawyer's bill directly to the client for payment. Many incorporate the bill into their regular statement instead, sometimes identifying the charge as contract assistance, in other cases identifying only the tasks performed without indicating who did the work. For example, one lawyer charges his clients the number of hours at his billing rate that equate with the contract lawyer's bill. That is, if the contract lawyer bills him ten hours at $50 per, the hiring lawyer will bill the client for five hours at his normal billing rate of $100 per hour.

Rochelle Kosnitsky once took on what looked like a simple breach of contract case and agreed to a contingent fee. When the case proved to be more complicated than anyone had anticipated, she turned to Phoebe Conover for research and analysis, but arranged for the client to reimburse her for her payments to Conover.

ABSORB SOME OR ALL OF THE COST OF THE CONTRACT LAWYER.

Dwight Benjamin, a very successful plaintiff's lawyer who works exclusively on contingent fee cases, hires contract lawyers only rarely. When he does, though, he simply pays their bills as his own business expenses, like his secretary's salary or the lease and service payments for his copy machine.

Pat McGraw of Saginaw, Michigan, might not charge the client for contract research assistance during trial if he hasn't told his client he might use outside help. He looks at the fairness of the overall bill at the end of the case before making this decision. If he asked a contract lawyer to look at an issue that turned out to be a dead end, he would not bill the client for the time. (Many lawyers would argue that the occasional dead end is essential to a thorough look at an issue, however, and should not be written off.) Dick Maizels sometimes assigns short research projects to contract lawyers on pro bono cases he has accepted; he pays them out of his own pocket. "Just because I was a dunderhead," he jokes, "I don't expect the contract lawyer to be the same!"

DISCUSSING THE ARRANGEMENT WITH THE CLIENT

Many lawyers fear their clients' reactions to their decision to use contract lawyers. If you are one of these lawyers, you should be aware most contract lawyer placement agencies report that their best customers are not law firms but in-house legal departments. In other words, your clients may be more prepared than you are to recognize the benefits of working with contract lawyers.

DISCLOSURE AS AN ETHICAL REQUIREMENT

The first client issue is what applicable ethics rules require in the way of disclosure. We discuss disclosure requirements in general and the position of the ABA in Chapter 17, but you'll need to review your jurisdiction's rules and decide for yourself how to proceed. In brief, the ABA states in Op. 88-356 that the Model Rules of Professional Conduct ("Model Rules") require disclosure and consent of the client *only* when the contract lawyer is working without your close supervision. Several state and local ethics opinions require disclosure of *any* use of a contract lawyer. (See Appendix 3.)

Rules on division of fees with lawyers not in the same firm also come into play. The ABA's position here (again expressed in Op. 88-356) seems to be that disclosure is required only when the *actual fee* paid by the client is divided with the contract attorney—as, for example, in a contingent fee situation. Of course, every fee charged to your client is subject to the requirement that it be reasonable according to Model Rule 1.5(a). Again, you must review the rules of your jurisdiction before making any decision on whether your contract lawyer arrangement requires disclosure to and consent of the client.

Do you need to tell the client how much you pay the contract lawyer? Probably not[3]—unless you either pass the bill on directly to the client for payment or bill the client for your payment to the contract lawyer as a cost. Even in the case of a "direct division of the actual fee paid by the client, such as percentage division of a contingent fee" (in which case Model Rule 1.5(e) requires disclosure and consent), ABA Op. 88-356 and the Model Rules do not require disclosure of *how* the fee is divided, so long as the total fee is reasonable.

Different states, of course, have different approaches to the issue, and it's essential for you to be familiar with your state's restrictions. In general, though, you'll satisfy ethical rules on division of fees if you (1) advise the client, preferably in a written retainer agreement, that some work may be performed by contract lawyers under your supervision, or (2) obtain your client's permission to assign work to a contract lawyer at a specific billing rate, even if that rate is higher than the rate you pay the contract lawyer. (See discussion of disclosure issues in Chapter 17.)

---

3. Again, such disclosure may be required under a state or local ethics opinion, although we believe this is rare.

DISCLOSURE AS A CLIENT RELATIONS ISSUE

Client relations are another matter. We believe "open communication regarding the [contract lawyer] arrangement is the best policy," as do the editors of the ABA's *Law Practice Management* magazine.[4] A client who learns about the hiring of a contract lawyer after the fact may feel duped, and might engage you in fee disputes or file ethical complaints. Without exception, the benefit of being straightforward is much greater than the risk of displeasing the client.[5]

Richard Kaplan agrees:

> *I always tell the client. They have a right to know. And they've never had a problem with it. They realize I'm not all things to all people. Of course, I tell them I supervise the contract lawyers and review their work carefully. But I figure if the client trusts me, the client should trust the people I trust as well.*

Jed Rakoff advises hiring top quality contract lawyers and telling clients they were hired for their expertise. He also remarks that it may be better to introduce the client to the contract lawyer first, so the client is not dealing with a phantom. This method worked for Rochelle Kosnitsky, when she hired Phoebe Conover to help with an unexpectedly complex collection case. Kosnitsky's client discussed the facts and obscure statutory issues directly with Conover on several occasions. At the end of the case, he complimented Kosnitsky on finding such able assistance.

Another tip is to remind your client that all lawyers are bound by the Rules of Professional Conduct and therefore must protect the client's confidences. If you are working on more than one case for the client, and the client has concerns about the contract lawyer's knowledge of or involvement in matters other than the one specifically assigned, explain your office's screening procedures. (See page 195 of Chapter 17.)

Also, explain in detail what supervision you will provide the contract lawyer; obviously, the more experienced the lawyer, the less oversight is necessary. Having inexperienced lawyers work on site, assuring the client that no pleadings or correspondence will leave the office without your review, and paying them as temporary hourly employees rather than independent contractors may also alleviate client concerns.

---

4. Sidebar to "Flexible Attorney Staffing," *Law Practice Management*, November/December 1991.

5. We believe that it's *always* best to disclose your use of contract lawyers, but that it's usually not necessary to disclose how much you pay them.

You can also explain to the client that associating a contract lawyer will reduce the client's cost (if true) while maintaining, or even improving, quality. Offer to pass on some cost saving to the client by billing the contract lawyer at less than the going rate for a lawyer with comparable experience. If you follow the rule of always hiring a contract lawyer who is overqualified for the project, you will impress the client with your efforts to provide the highest possible quality of legal work.

A potential client relations problem noted by the editors of *Law Practice Management* is the possibility that a competing law firm may "capitalize on your use of project attorneys as a basis for arguing you do not have adequate professional staff to provide for the client's needs." An insurance defense lawyer we interviewed echoed this fear. He worried that if a major client knew he was using the services of a contract lawyer, it would pull its business and place it with a firm that had the staff to handle the overload. You should be able to prevent client defection on this theory by pointing out that your having less staff and using contract lawyers only for peak times is good for the client. It enables you to keep your overhead low, and to charge contract lawyers at rates lower than you would for associates.

In some cases it may make sense to consult with your client on the best working arrangement for the contract lawyer. For example, in a document-intensive litigation matter, or when intellectual property or other proprietary information must be kept secure, it may be better for the contract lawyer to work on-site with the client. If immediate availability is a concern, either equip the contract lawyer with a fax machine, beeper or cellular telephone, or hire a contract lawyer with comparable accessibility.

DISCLOSURE IN THE ENGAGEMENT LETTER

The written retainer agreement could contain language like this:

> *During the course of our representation, it may be necessary [or advisable, or cost-effective] to delegate portions of this matter to outside lawyers retained for that purpose. [If this is the case, we will inform you in advance of the identity of the lawyers.] These lawyers, whom we refer to as contract lawyers, will have expertise commensurate with the tasks involved. [Tasks assigned to contract lawyers will be limited to factual and legal research, and the review and preparation of documents or pleadings.] [All work performed by contract lawyers will be supervised and reviewed by the partner-in-charge of your case. The firm assumes full responsibility for the quality and accuracy of any contract lawyer's work.] [No documents prepared by*

*contract lawyers will be filed with the court or sent to opposing counsel
without the review and signature of the partner-in-charge.]*

*Services performed by contract lawyers will be billed at $___ per
hour [or $___ per hour for partner-level work, $___ per hour for senior-
associate level work and $___ per hour for junior-associate level work].
This rate may be increased from time to time, but not more frequently
than annually. Notice of any rate increase will be given to you no later
than three (3) days before it takes effect.*

ASSURING INDEPENDENT CONTRACTOR STATUS

See Chapter 19.

CONFIRMING THE AGREEMENT IN WRITING

See Chapter 20.

15

OVERSEEING THE CONTRACT LAWYER ARRANGEMENT

After expending so much effort in finding the right contract lawyer and striking a deal, don't weaken the relationship with neglect. Open, courteous and continuous communication—with both the contract lawyer and your staff—will keep your investment paying off.

Miranda Bouton has been on assignment with a Fortune 100 company for over a year, working about 20 hours per week. In all that time, she has received no orientation to the office. No one has formally introduced her; as a result, the clerical staff refuse to help her. For many months, she lacked an identification card that would give her access to her office or enable her to walk around the building and speak to employees about projects she's handling. There were days when she had to sit in the lobby for hours because no one in her department was available to escort her in.

The hiring company lost many dollars to inefficiency because of its failure to incorporate Bouton into its operations. One vivid example occurred when Bouton was negotiating a sublease with Federal Express. The hiring company does not use Federal Express services; Federal Express does not recognize packages delivered by any other courier. She couldn't charge the delivery to her credit card because she was a non-person at the company—her time was billed to a contract lawyer placement agency—so her expenses would not be reimbursed. She remembers waiting outside the building for the Federal Express truck to arrive and using all her powers of persuasion to convince the truck driver to accept the package and bill delivery to Federal Express at the other end. "God forbid if the deadline had occurred over the weekend," she says.

The first four months, she worked at empty desks of other employees, if any were available. Company personnel and opposing counsel had to telephone her at home to keep in touch; she had to call home repeatedly during the day to retrieve messages. Finally, she convinced the company to provide her with her own computer and voice mail number. Now she doesn't have to come in every day to stay connected. By collecting her voice mail messages and telephoning others in and out of the company, she can stay on top of her assignments in less time and save the company money. If only she could get some secretarial assistance, her time would be even better used!

Oversight of the contract lawyer relationship is, as you can see, a bottom-line issue for hiring lawyers. Inadequate or inappropriate supervision creates counter-productive and costly inefficiencies. This chapter synthesizes the suggestions of those who have been on either end of enough mistakes to know how to avoid them.

DESCRIBE ASSIGNMENTS CLEARLY

Philadelphia practitioner Samuel Frederick believes there are two kinds of managers: those who want to own and control the project, and those who share the process by communicating and cooperating with their teams. Most lawyers are in the first category. These "black-box lawyers" accept an assignment from a client without asking many questions. They then mull over, study, research and process the assignment on their own and return with the answer—and a big bill. This work style leads to poor relationships with clients, with colleagues and with contract lawyers. If you want your relationships with contract lawyers to succeed, you must climb out of your black box before you hire.

Peter Ludwig, who accepted contract assignments in Denver when he returned to school for a teaching certificate, learned how damaging a "black box" lawyer can be. One time, he thought a conversation with a hiring lawyer was only preliminary; he did not understand the issues and had no idea that the hiring lawyer had given him an assignment. A couple of weeks later, the lawyer telephoned him, demanding to know where the brief was. The hiring lawyer thought he had been perfectly clear about his expectations.

Contract lawyer Elizabeth Bottman has found that most hiring lawyers do a poor job of explaining the assignment. "They often don't tell me enough about what they need, and what form they need it in." Luckily she's experienced enough to take charge of the discussion. "I listen to what they say and then I have to ask questions, and even interrupt them. What kind of motion do you need? By when do you need it? What's the maximum number of hours you're expecting?"

Rather than assuming contract lawyers can read your mind, as the lawyers working with Ludwig and Bottman did, take responsibility for communicating the scope and details of the assignment. If you have pondered the assignment and the level of assistance you expect, you should be able to convey both clearly to the contract lawyer. Often, you'll be hiring a contract lawyer to handle a last-minute assignment. Even so, don't let your lack of time cause you to stint on explaining the assignment. Be generous in orienting the contract lawyer to the project and you're more likely to be pleased with the result.

Recognize that different lawyers have different practice styles: don't expect the lawyer you hire to share yours. If you want the contract lawyer's product to conform to your style, provide him with samples of pleadings, briefs, settlement proposals, trial notebooks or whatever else you've assigned.

Clear communication between you and your contract lawyer is simply an extension of clear comunication between you and your client. Richard Kaplan describes a recent case in which his client was sued for "an indeterminate amount, but possibly as much as $30 million." Kaplan wanted to move for summary judgment, using a contract lawyer to write the brief. General counsel to the client agreed, but said he wanted the brief to be of "law review quality." Based on this description, the contract lawyer produced a brief that was "very academic and dry—not punchy," says Kaplan. The client demanded a substantially revised version. After much additional effort, Kaplan and the contract lawyer produced a brief that was scholarly but lively. Then the client complained about the cost—even though it had resulted from the client's own misleading instruction. But, Kaplan notes, "There were no complaints when we won the motion."

"Working with a contract lawyer takes a lot more guidance than taking someone in and turning them loose," says Robert Thomas. "First you need to clearly state your expectations, in terms of both time and quality. Then you should ask the contract lawyer to repeat what he understands about your expectations. Ask for his ideas on your objectives as well. When you have that kind of conversation, you have fewer problems as you go along."

Daniel Edwards learned the hard way how critical reciprocal communication is. He wanted to move against a default judgment taken in another county and asked a contract lawyer located there to review the file and answer some specific questions about the case. "I thought I was giving crystal clear guidance because the contract lawyer's head was bobbing up and down at all the appropriate times. But it became clear after the fact that he just didn't have a clue. He didn't understand the nature of judgments or the nature of defaults."

You can test the clarity of your instructions by following Samuel Frederick's advice. "Explain the factual context to the temporary attorney and, where research or other lengthy written work will be the end product, have the temporary attorney

TIPS FOR WORKING WITH RECENT GRADUATES

- Remember what it was like for you when you were a new lawyer. Treat the new admittee as you would have liked to be (or were) treated. Encourage him to ask questions and don't make him feel stupid for not knowing the answers.

- Ask whether the new lawyer is looking for a permanent job; clarify from the outset whether you (or your firm) can provide that opportunity. Remember that hiring an applicant initially on a contract basis is a good way to test his abilities and compatibility.

- Understand that in return for the low rate you pay a recent graduate, you must provide much more guidance and supervision, and more specific instructions, than you would for an experienced lawyer. Suggest sources and their locations when assigning research projects. Provide samples of all documents—even the most basic (e.g., interrogatories and requests for production, simple motions and complaints)—for the contract lawyer to use as models.

- Don't expect the entry-level lawyer to work as quickly, or produce as finished a product, as a lawyer with two or three years of experience.

- Help orient the lawyer to the real world of law practice. Many new admittees are simply not aware of the intensity with which most practitioners approach their work. If you're seeking a second chair at trial, tell applicants up front if you expect a 24-hour a day, "drag-yourself-to-the-courthouse-no-matter-how-sick-you-are" commitment and ask if they're up for that level of participation.

- Clarify your expectations about time to be spent on each project. Don't use vague terms like "as soon as you can" or "quick turnaround." Be specific instead, using deadlines like "tomorrow" or "by noon Friday."

- Spend time reviewing and critiquing any written product, and talk to the contract lawyer about ways to improve it, rather than simply rewriting it yourself. Discuss in the initial interview whether "training time"—like conferences spent going over completed assignments or explaining how to write a motion—will be compensated.

- Think of yourself as a role model for a future leader of the bar.

submit a statement of facts and list of issues presented, or an outline or list of issues for the document to be prepared, before beginning in-depth work."

Allocate plenty of time for questions, and confirm your expectations about the scope of and time to be invested in the project. If you are hiring the contract lawyer for a discrete project, but may have more work for him in the future, make that clear. If you're hiring for a series of projects, let him know how long you think the work will last. For example, "I think we can keep you busy for about 20 hours a week for at least the next three months."

If you work regularly with one or more contract lawyers, you will know what to expect from their work, and will develop a sense of how much time you'll need to spend on the project after the contract lawyer has completed it. Until then, assume you'll have to revise (or rewrite) whatever the contract lawyer gives you, and set the deadline to allow yourself time to do so.

With luck, the right contract lawyer, and good communication, you will get to the point where review and signature is all that's required. Anchorage practitioner Bob Baker does only "minor tweaking" of Shawn Mathis Isbell's work product before it goes out of his office. Contract lawyer Lee Archer of New Orleans prides herself on providing "appellate briefs and writ applications in final form to attorneys who do not want to do any revisions at all or to double check my research or judgment."

ORIENT THE CONTRACT LAWYER TO THE OFFICE

In your initial meeting, discuss administrative details like office hours and access, billing protocol and clerical assistance requirements. Discuss any of the following issues that apply to your situation:

- *Will the contract lawyer work on-site or from her own office? If the latter, what office facilities of yours will the contract lawyer be able to use— library, on-line research services, copier?*
- *Will the file remain in the office or will the contract lawyer be permitted to remove it? What parts of the file will be copied for the contract lawyer if the file remains with the firm?*
- *In what form do you need the work product to be submitted (e.g., draft hard copy only, draft hard copy plus computer disk, or final version ready for signing and filing)?*
- *Will the contract lawyer have direct client contact or communicate only through you?*
- *If the contract lawyer is to work on-site, what are your office hours and what hours do you expect the contract lawyer to be there? Will the contract lawyer have access to the office evenings and weekends?*
- *What level of secretarial, paralegal and other support will be available to the contract lawyer?*
- *Will any perquisites be provided—for example a car, car service or meals for late work hours? What about reimbursement for expenses? What supporting documentation does your accounting department require?*
- *What billing records do you expect the contract lawyer to provide?[1]*

---

1.   If you use a contract lawyer placement agency, it will handle these matters.

*Discuss what is billable to the client and what is billable to the firm and
when work reports or diaries are due. What are your deadlines for
submitting time sheets? When do you expect bills, and what is the office
procedure for paying them?*

■ *If this is an on-site, open-ended assignment, specify the minimum and
maximum number of billable hours you expect each week.*

Another topic of discussion might be how you introduce the contract lawyer to
colleagues and opposing counsel. Robert Thomas suggests keeping the relationship
vague, introducing the lawyer as being "with the firm." Others use the terms "legal
consultant," "special counsel," or "project attorney." You can say, "This is Lucy
Timberlake, a lawyer who's working with me on this case." Or you can be perfectly
open: "This is Lucy Timberlake, the best contract lawyer in Iowa City."

Do not, however, represent the lawyer as an associate. Many contract lawyers
have partnership-level experience and will be offended at this denigration of their
position. They may also be put off by what they see as your attempt to misrepresent
the size of your office. Most important, however, the designation can create ethical
problems for both the firm and the contract lawyer. For example, one law firm
included a contract lawyer who was also providing services to other lawyers as an
associate in its Martindale-Hubbell listing. Even though the contract lawyer worked
on only a few matters for the firm and did not have access to client files, the listing
itself created serious conflicts problems for her.

ADDRESS ASSOCIATE CONCERNS.

When you hire one or more contract lawyers for long-term assignments at your
office, your associates may resent them, or may worry about what the firm's use of
contract lawyers portends for their future. Or, like Jed Rakoff when he hired contract
lawyers at New York's Mudge Rose, you may expect resentment but receive none,
because your associates realize the contract lawyers are not competing for partnership slots.

Rather than leaving it to chance, you can alleviate associates' concerns by
addressing them openly. Explain that the contract lawyers have been hired to
reduce pressure on the permanent staff and to avoid the need for downsizing should
the workload decrease. Assure the associates that they will continue to get first
crack at the best projects. Explain that even though contract lawyers may receive
seemingly higher hourly rates of compensation, they are responsible for paying their
own taxes and expenses of doing business (bar dues, for example); they are not
compensated for vacations, holidays or sick leave; and they will not be considered

for partnership. Emphasize that the contract lawyers have been hired to improve the lives and working conditions of the firm's associates, as well as its partners.

SHOW RESPECT FOR CONTRACT LAWYERS.

No matter how impressive their credentials, lawyers who choose to work on a contract basis often confront the attitude that they're second-rate. "I've been to places where even the most minimal resources—office space, desk space, word processing—are not provided," says Steven Weinstein, who worked eight years in-house with Safeway and is operating as a contract lawyer to support a career transition into financial planning. "I almost quit one job because the secretary flat out refused to do anything for me when her boss was on the road for two weeks." The hiring lawyer will prevent disruption in the office both by modeling respectful behavior from the first contact and by specifically instructing the staff to cooperate.

Cecelie Berry, who worked as a contract lawyer in New York City, notes:

> *Employers must avoid two opposite but equally harmful pitfalls: the tendency not to accord the attorney the courtesies routinely extended to full-time professionals, and the temptation to regard temporary professionals as having the responsibilities and commitments of a partnership-track lawyer.*[2]

It's important to communicate directly with the clerical and professional staff about the contract lawyer's assignment, making clear their role in supporting the contract lawyer's work. As Cecelie Berry observed:

> *Staff are sometimes reluctant to type, copy or otherwise assist an unfamiliar attorney. When the temporary lawyer is introduced to the staff, the short-term nature of the assignment should be minimized and the matter the attorney is working on should be explained. Similarly the staff member should be introduced as an important resource in the firm's functioning.*[3]

It is also the hiring lawyer's responsibility to model accepting behavior in other ways. Janis Goldman, founder of the Washington, D.C., contract lawyer agency Lawyer's Lawyer, placed Irene Desjardins (pseudonym) in a long-term assignment

---

2.   Cecelie S. Berry, "Temporary Lawyers: The Do's and Don'ts," *New York Law Journal,* April 17, 1989.

3.   Id.

with the understanding that Desjardins would leave daily at 3:00 p.m. to attend soccer practice. A few weeks into the assignment, Desjardins called Goldman, concerned because the firm "looks at me funny when I leave every day." Goldman telephoned the firm, asking if they'd rather have a lawyer willing to work full-time or even overtime. She didn't want Desjardins to be treated with disrespect when she was living up to her agreement. The hiring lawyer apologized profusely. "I have a passion for soccer too," he explained. "I feel envious when she leaves, not annoyed."

From partners to clerical help, other staff members will observe the contract lawyer's comings and goings, and may resent the contract lawyer's perceived freedom and generous hourly wage. If you sense such resentment, remind the person that the contract lawyer's flexibility comes hand in hand with economic uncertainty. When the contract lawyer's hourly wage translates into enough money to justify hiring another associate, the lawyer will be out of work. If the associates were willing to accept the same risk, they could "enjoy" the same freedoms.

Don't worry that extending common courtesy to a contract lawyer will convert the relationship into one of employer and employee. In the event of an audit, your detailed oversight and control could result in such a ruling; providing contract lawyers access to the services they need should not. (Review Chapter 18 for a discussion of this issue.)

SCREEN THE CONTRACT LAWYER FROM ACCESS TO CLIENT INFORMATION.

To avoid potential conflict of interest problems, including firm disqualification stemming from a contract lawyer's imputed knowledge of the firm's entire client base, you must avoid exposing contract lawyers to matters other than the ones you have assigned to them. This is more of an issue with lawyers working on-site than with ones who come to the office only to pick up or drop off assignments. But even an off-site contract lawyer can be exposed to client files unnecessarily—for example, if you let him work in the firm library where files or drafts of documents are lying around, or if you leave him alone in your office, which has piles of loose documents on every surface. Read Chapter 17 on conflict of interest and other ethical issues and take appropriate steps.

MONITOR PERFORMANCE AND WORK PRODUCT

Former in-house counsel Shawn Mathis Isbell says:

> *Success with contract lawyers depends upon supervision. You need to be sure that they're pointed in the right direction, that they have clear directions and clearly-stated expectations. I tried to give clear job*

parameters and check in frequently to avoid having them head down the wrong track. Then, I tried to make myself available to answer questions when they arose.

Although we heard story after story of the superb work done by contract lawyers, there were also cautionary notes. Therefore, as we have stressed, unless you've worked directly with the lawyer already, you'll need to be vigilant at first. Assign finite parts of any project and carefully review the lawyer's work before use or delivery to the client. Once you are satisfied with the quality of the contract lawyer's work product, you can relax your vigilance.

Be sensitive about your oversight, though, if you're dealing with lawyers who are well established in the legal community, have partner-level experience and come with glowing recommendations from lawyers you know and respect. Senior level lawyers will be insulted if you treat them like first-year associates. Any efforts to oversee or manage the work of a lawyer who has expertise you don't have will probably be resented, and certainly be counterproductive. All you can or should do in these cases is to ensure that the lawyer meets your deadlines.

COMMUNICATE GOALS AND REQUIREMENTS ON AN ONGOING BASIS.
The first, best and most important rule for managing contract lawyers is to communicate with them freely. Tell them what you expect and when you expect it. Let them know if you're satisfied with their work and if you're not. Tell them when you think the project needs more work, and what you think it needs. Let contract lawyers know immediately if scheduling requirements change, if you learn new facts, if you discover a useful precedent, or if you decide to expand the scope of the project. Keep contract lawyers informed by placing them on relevant distribution lists.

Equally important, give contract lawyers your attention: offer plenty of opportunity for them to talk to you, and listen carefully to what they say—or don't say. You encourage communication when you make yourself available for their calls and return their calls promptly.

Solicit reports and other input as their work progresses and keep them informed about developments in the case. That way, the contract lawyers will feel part of your team and express more enthusiasm and commitment toward you, the case and the client. You'll also encourage "off-the-clock" thought about the case and may be the recipient of solid insight. More than one contract lawyer speaks with pride of coming up with the legal analysis or strategy that won a motion or triggered a favorable settlement. Be receptive to contract lawyers' ideas and open to their concerns about problems with positions you want to take.

OFF-SITE CONTRACT LAWYERS

For the contract lawyer working off-site in his own office, monitoring is largely a matter of staying in touch. Monitoring of performance is more important for the initial assignment, when the contract lawyer is proving himself. Once you have enough experience to develop trust and confidence in your contract lawyer, you needn't worry as much. One reason busy practitioners prefer working with trusted contract lawyers is this ability to give an assignment and get a satisfactory product by the time requested without having to prod or check up on the lawyer, or to worry about the end product.

When you start a relationship, however, a little worrying may prevent a bad outcome. Tom Watters soured on non-agency contract lawyers when he learned, on the day a draft of a responding appellate brief was promised, that the contract lawyer had completed nothing more than preliminary research. Watters might have avoided a weekend of frantic work had he called once or twice before the deadline to see how the lawyer was progressing. Then again, this particular lawyer might have failed to deliver despite close monitoring. This kind of experience is why we suggest you try to make the first assignment a low-pressure one.

Your goal should be to achieve as soon as possible a relationship that does not require close and constant supervision—since lack of supervision may be the essence of the appeal of such arrangements to both the independent-minded contract lawyer and the busy hiring lawyer. If you communicate fully at the beginning of the assignment, respond quickly to your contract lawyer's calls—which probably concern either substantive issues or the timing of the project—and touch base after receiving the work product, the rest should take care of itself.

ON-SITE CONTRACT LAWYERS

When contract lawyers work on the premises, monitoring is more important and must be more extensive. You'll need to address issues such as how they will be integrated into the workplace, who at the firm will be responsible for assigning work and ensuring its completion, how to avoid potential conflicts problems by limiting access to client files, and whether at some point a contract lawyer begins to look more like an employee than an independent contractor.

Oversight should begin at the first contact. Samuel Frederick suggests that each contract lawyer be "assigned to a specific partner or experienced associate for management and reporting purposes" to avoid conflicting or confusing directions about work product and time. James Ounsworth, general counsel of Safeguard Scientifics, Inc. says:

We've only used contract attorneys when someone would be in a supervisory role. We haven't just said, "Go do it," because they might not know what we're striving for. Plus, even though you may have a good feeling about them going into a project, you don't know how well a person will work out until you've actually worked with them.[4]

If contract lawyers will be working on a relatively long-term basis in-house, it's essential to incorporate them into the operation. Jess Womack, head of the environmental law department at Arco, emphasizes this:

You have to do a pretty darn good job of integrating the contract person into your operation if you want to get the full benefit of what the person can do for you. The name of the game at a corporation is knowing where the information is and then having the moxie to get it out of the people who have it. If you don't feel confident and comfortable going after folks, you won't get everything you need. The contract lawyer is not truly in-house. If you want them to function at the level you're paying them, they have to feel a sense of entitlement to speak with authority.

Whether or not the lawyer will be working in your offices, provide a tour of the premises including copying, word processing, mailroom and library facilities. If the project will require contact with one or more of these areas, emphasize those, and introduce the lawyer to all employees potentially involved in completing the project. Of course, make certain the contract lawyer has necessary access to your office including an identification card or badge, elevator card key and building or office key.

After they've been oriented to your office procedures and assigned a project, check in regularly until you feel confident about their work. Robert Thomas says:

We always start with a lot of supervision, no matter how much experience contract lawyers have, because we're starting with unknown quantities. As they prove themselves, they get to the point where they are working on their own. Eventually, if I ask for a summary judgment brief on a particular issue, the contract lawyer does all the research, I look it over and if it looks fine, I sign it.

---

4. "Temp Time: Are You Ready?," *Corporate Legal Times*, September 1994.

SET REGULAR MEETING TIMES.

Peter Zeughauser, senior vice-president and general counsel of The Irvine Company, takes this approach with a long-term contract lawyer. "In one piece of major litigation, we have a monthly all-lawyers meeting. The contract lawyer on the case puts together the agenda and attends every meeting. A lot of supervision comes out of that meeting. I also meet with her weekly."

Regular meetings, in person or by telephone, are especially important if the contract lawyer will be working off-site on a project with imminent deadlines or strict limits on hours to be billed. Encourage daily or weekly progress reports. Communicate regularly with the contract lawyer about her whereabouts and make certain she can be reached easily by telephone. On particularly urgent matters, consider lending the contract lawyer a cellular telephone or beeper.

Talk to the contract lawyer within a day or two after she has submitted any work product. If you're pleased with it, you should let her know. If you're not, it is important to discuss what you think is wrong, so the contract lawyer has time to fix it. If you delay discussion until your workload lessens (which may never happen!), the contract lawyer may have moved on to another assignment, and you will have lost the chance to get gaps filled or errors corrected.

REGULARLY REVIEW INDEPENDENT CONTRACTOR STATUS.

When a short-term assignment turns into a long-term relationship and the firm comes to rely on the contract lawyer's services, it's time to redefine the relationship. You may want to designate the contract lawyer a permanent hourly employee, a part-time employee, or perhaps "of counsel" to the firm. The onus is on the hiring lawyer to raise the issue and change the relationship, since the penalties of mischaracterizing the relationship are all yours. Don't assume that the word "contract" in "contract lawyer" will protect you against the IRS. The distinction between independent contractor and employee is a complex area of law, and there is currently no bright line test. (Read Chapter 18 for a thorough discussion of this issue.)

PAY PROMPTLY AND IN ACCORDANCE WITH YOUR AGREEMENT.

According to Samuel Frederick, the most common source of demotivation reported by contract lawyers is not being paid on time. You should have discussed at the beginning of the engagement, and memorialized in an engagement letter or retention agreement (see Chapter 20), how soon after receiving a bill you will pay the contract lawyer. If you anticipate difficulty in paying within the time requested,

SUGGESTIONS FOR WORKING WELL
WITH CONTRACT LAWYERS

DO:

- Be willing to ask for help.
- Define the assignment in your own mind.
- Decide what qualifications are important.
- Interview the candidates in person or by telephone.
- Check references if not using an agency.
- Be specific in communicating your expectations.
- Be clear about deadlines.
- Formalize the agreement in writing.
- Introduce the contract lawyer to your office staff.
- Explain office procedures.
- Treat the contract lawyer with respect.
- Address associate concerns.
- Screen them from client information.
- Monitor their performance carefully.
- Communicate regularly and listen well.
- Set regular meeting times.
- Review independent contractor status.
- Pay promptly according to agreement.
- Touch base after completion of the assignment.

DON'T:

- Wait till the very last minute to ask for help.
- Make hiring decisions based on rate alone.
- Make hiring decisions based on résumé alone.
- Expect contract lawyers to intuit your unspoken needs.
- Delay in returning contract lawyers' calls.
- Be stingy in answering contract lawyers' questions.

negotiate a different payment schedule *at the outset.* Portland contract lawyer Katherine Foldes, for example, suggested a longer payment term to a hiring lawyer who often paid late; in return, she charged a higher hourly rate. If a problem develops later, call the contract lawyer immediately and negotiate a schedule of partial payments or a short delay.

RELATED ISSUES

See Part IV for detailed treatment of issues of special concern to both hiring and contract lawyers, including conflicts of interest, malpractice insurance coverage, independent contractor status, retention agreements and contract lawyer placement agencies.

16

ENDING THE RELATIONSHIP

This chapter is short, but its message is important: when your relationship with a contract lawyer is over, say good-bye.

Even the best relationships come to an end, and saying good-bye is not a skill at which most lawyers excel. Bridget Fahey tells the following cautionary "bad ending" story:

A respected New England law firm found itself understaffed when a series of unforeseen events occurred: a junior associate left at the same time several major transactions came into the office and a partner decided to combine family leave with a long-overdue sabbatical. Fahey was offering her services as a contract lawyer but so far had received disappointingly meager assignments. In this case, the firm needed someone with just her background to step in immediately and help. Working on-site at the firm full-time for six months, Fahey was treated like an associate—her own office, voice-mail box and secretary, and her name on her office door—but was paid by the billable hour as an independent contractor.

No one at the firm told her when they expected her stay to end. After five months had passed, though, she noticed that the partners she worked with were avoiding her. She had day-to-day responsibility for a large deal on the verge of closing but couldn't get the supervising partner to answer her questions. The mysterious silence and inaccessibility continued until the deal closed. The very next day the managing partner took her to lunch and informed her that her time at the firm was at an end. They needed her office for another purpose.

Strictly speaking, the firm lived up to its side of the bargain, but Fahey was left feeling ill-used. She realized that the firm had decided to let her go long before anyone informed her of the decision, but had been concerned that she would abandon her responsibilities if she knew of their plans before the deal was closed. The firm's failure to communicate struck Fahey as insulting and unprofessional, and tainted the whole experience for her. The firm could have been open with her about its plans as soon as the decision was made. It could have requested that she remain through the crucial closing, and could even have offered her an increased rate if she was hesitant to do so. Such a course would have been better for both parties. Fahey would have left with a positive feeling about the experience, and the firm would have avoided the awkwardness its own partners clearly felt about how Fahey's termination was handled.

If you've hired a contract lawyer to complete one discrete project, the arrangement may be over when the project is finished. Presumably, though, you'll want to hire her again if you're happy with the work. Don't assume the contract lawyer will know how you feel; if you're pleased, tell her. "You did a terrific job on the partnership agreement. I may have a similar project for you next month. I hope you'll be able to take it on." Such comments let the lawyer know you consider the relationship to be continuing even though the specific project is finished. Then, if she is offered a big assignment "next month," she can check with you about your assignment before she accepts the other.

If the work was fine but your partner who was on family leave is about to return and you don't anticipate needing the contract lawyer to help in the future, extend the courtesy of letting the contract lawyer know. It's a small but meaningful gesture.

What if you aren't particularly thrilled with a contract lawyer's work? Don't act like the Cleveland firm that hired a former government lawyer without private practice experience to handle sophisticated discovery work in a complex commercial case. She was given an office, the file and cursory instructions. A week later, after spending 40 hours on a ten-hour project, she was given the boot. No explanation. No feedback. No chance to redeem herself. You don't have to give a contract lawyer a second chance, but at least treat her with courtesy.

Part IV

ISSUES
OF
JOINT
CONCERN

17

ETHICAL CONSIDERATIONS

The rules of ethics were not drafted with contract lawyers in mind, but they still apply to contract lawyers and their relationships with clients and other lawyers. Here we interpret the Rules of Professional Conduct in contract lawyer situations.

Contract lawyers, as licensed attorneys, are subject to the same ethical rules as other lawyers. This much is clear. The fact that the ABA's Model Rules of Professional Conduct (hereinafter Rules)—and corresponding state rules and codes[1]—were not drafted with contract lawyers in mind, however, has given rise to some controversy about how they apply. The involvement of agencies that place lawyers in temporary assignments—some owned and operated by licensed attorneys, others not—is another complicating factor.[2]

The most comprehensive treatment of ethical issues faced by contract lawyers is found in ABA Formal Opinion 88-356 ("Op. 88-356"). Although Op. 88-356 is not binding, several states have adopted some or all of its conclusions,[3] and it provides a useful structure for looking at the issues.

Op. 88-356 uses the term "temporary lawyer," defined as "a lawyer engaged by a firm for a limited period, either directly or through a lawyer placement agency." The ABA term excludes lawyers who work part-time or full-time for an extended period for one firm exclusively (although without contemplation of permanent employment), as well as those who have "of counsel" relationships or are associated as independent

---

1. Because of variations in state codes, we base our discussion on the ABA's Model Rules of Professional Conduct. As of 1995, two-thirds of jurisdictions had adopted standards based on the Rules. ABA Center for Professional Responsibility, Model Rules of Professional Conduct at viii (1995 ed.). Familiarize yourself with the ways your state's code of professional responsibility differs from the Model Rules.

2. We deal with these ethical questions in Chapter 21 on agencies.

3. State-by-state ethics opinions relating to contract lawyering are outlined in Appendix 3.

counsel on a particular case. Our definition of contract lawyer, in contrast, includes lawyers on temporary long-term assignment, and sometimes those identified as "of counsel" or "associated" counsel. (See Chapter 1 and Appendix 1.) Whether the temporary arrangement is long- or short-term, though, makes little difference in applying ethical precepts.

Issues of client confidentiality, conflicts of interest, disclosure and fee-splitting apply to all contract lawyers. With respect to agency involvement, the most hotly disputed issue is whether payment to an agency constitutes a division of fees with non-lawyers

CONFIDENTIALITY

The client of a contract lawyer is the client of the hiring lawyer. Both lawyers share the obligation of preserving that client's confidences. Op. 88-356 discusses the difference between the requirements of new Rule 1.6 (the obligation not to reveal information relating to representation of a client even if that information was not acquired in the course of the professional relationship) and former DR 4-101[4] (protecting information subject to attorney-client privilege and information gained in the course of the representation that would be embarrassing or that the client has asked be kept confidential).

The ABA notes that temporary lawyers' responsibilities with respect to client confidences depend upon the extent to which the lawyers can be deemed to be "associated with" a firm under Rule 1.10. "Association" depends on the nature of the relationship and may turn on whether contract lawyers have been screened from information relating to the firm's clients other than the ones on whose matters they have worked. For example, temporary lawyers who work in law firm offices on a number of different matters for several clients, under circumstances that would give them access to information about the firm's other clients and matters, will probably be deemed to be "associated with" the firm, unless the firm can demonstrate that the lawyers' access to client files was strictly limited.

If temporary lawyers are exposed to general client information and thus deemed to be "associated with" the firm, they cannot reveal information about *any* clients of the firm, whether or not the information was acquired through contact

---

4. References to "DR ___" are to the ABA's Model Code of Professional Responsibility, predecessor to the Model Rules of Professional Conduct. We have not studied the Model Code independently; references are to discussions of it in Op. 88-356.

with the firm. Temporary lawyers who work only on discrete matters and do not
have access to information about other clients of the firm are obligated to keep
confidential *all* information about the clients they have served, and any information
about other firm clients they learned from the firm.

State bar ethics opinions do not generally treat the subject with this level of
detail. *Kentucky* adopted the "confidentiality" portion of Op. 88-356 verbatim in
Oliver v. Board of Governors, Kentucky Bar Association, 779 S.W.2d 212, 219-20
(1989). *South Carolina* adopted Op. 88-256 in its entirety in its Advisory Opinion
91-09. *California*, in Formal Opinion 1992-126, notes that firms should screen
temporary lawyers from matters on which they are not working and reminds
attorneys of their duty to keep client confidences.

Although we have heard of at least one firm that decided not to hire contract
lawyers because of concerns about client confidences, this issue should not be
fraught with difficulty. Contract lawyers should be—and should be presumed to be—
as aware of their ethical duties as are other lawyers. "There is no reason to think
that temporary lawyers are more likely to breach their obligation of confidentiality
than regularly employed attorneys," assert Vincent Johnson and Virginia Coyle in
their comprehensive 1990 law review article.[5]

Both contract lawyers *and* hiring lawyers need to be extremely sensitive to their
duty to protect client confidences. If you are a hiring lawyer, ensure that contract
lawyers have access only to information necessary to complete the assigned
projects. Do not allow contract lawyers access to areas where files are kept. Do not
engage in conversations about unrelated cases within earshot of a contract lawyer.
When orienting staff to the presence of a contract lawyer—whether working on site
or outside the office—remind them of the need to preserve confidences of other
clients. Computer screens and wastebaskets can reveal confidential information;
remind the staff to turn off the screens when they're not around and to shred rather
than recycle paperwork containing confidential information. If the case involves
sensitive information, don't let the contract lawyer remove the file from the
premises but designate an isolated area on site where the contract lawyer can
review it. Such precautions will ensure that the contract lawyer does not have
access to information about firm clients other than those for whom he is working.

If you are a contract lawyer, remember that any clients for whom you work are
your clients even if you never have direct contact with them. When working on law
firm premises, make certain that your office contains files only for the cases you are

---

5. Vincent Johnson and Virginia Coyle, "On the Transformation of the Legal Profession: The Advent of
    Temporary Lawyering," 66 *Notre Dame Law Review* 359 (1990).

handling. If the hiring lawyer asks you to work in a room that contains other client files, don't open or look at them; ask that they be removed the moment you become aware of them. To provide comfort to hiring lawyers, include in your engagement letter an assurance that you understand your obligation to keep client confidences; you can also advise hiring lawyers to take the precautions outlined in the preceding paragraph.

CONFLICTS OF INTEREST

The typical contract lawyer will work for a variety of lawyers and law firms over the course of a career. As a result, more questions about real and possible conflicts of interest may present themselves than would be the case with lawyers who work for one firm during an entire career—and even for lawyers who change jobs four or five times in the course of a career. (Although *questions* about conflicts may arise more frequently, the actual *number* of conflicts may well be less for the contract lawyer than for the lawyer who frequently changes associations, because the contract lawyer may not be deemed to be associated with any of the law firms for which he works.) Categories of concern include not only the accuracy of conflicts-checking records, but also imputed disqualification and the question of when a contract lawyer should decline work even if there is no real or possible conflict.

Rules 1.7 and 1.9 cover conflicts of interest involving present and former clients. There are many similarities between Rule 1.7 (present clients) and Rule 1.9 (former clients).[6] The key difference is that representation adverse to a former client is prohibited only for the same or substantially related matters, while representation adverse to a present client may be prohibited even for unrelated matters.

According to Op. 88-356, "[i]t is clear that a temporary lawyer who works on a matter for a client of a firm with whom the temporary lawyer is temporarily associated 'represents' that client for purposes of Rules 1.7 and 1.9." Thus a lawyer who works on a matter for a client of one firm cannot thereafter work for a client of another firm on the same or a substantially related matter. For example, if Anita Ames did a project for Smith & Jones representing the wife in a divorce case in 1992, she should not undertake a project for Black & White representing the ex-husband in a post-divorce proceeding to adjust child support payments in 1993.

Op. 88-356 does not address the knottier problem of how long a client for whom a contract lawyer has handled only one discrete project remains a client. Does the

---

6. Hazard & Hodes, *The Law of Lawyering* 61.9:201 (2d ed. 1990 & Supps. through 1994).

client become "former" immediately upon completion of the project, enabling that contract lawyer to take on another project, on an unrelated matter, adverse to the client? Although that position is tenable, we advocate the more conservative approach of considering the client a "present" client until the conclusion of the matter on which the contract lawyer originally worked.[7]

This approach makes sense as a matter of customer relations as well. Suppose Smith & Jones hires Ames to investigate the facts and law and draft a complaint in the adverse possession case of *Fish v. Fowl.* Several months later, shortly before the trial, Black & White, representing a credit union with a security interest in Fish's minivan, asks Ames to help its client repossess the van. If Fish is considered a " former" client, Ames can accept the new assignment. But what happens if Smith & Jones later asks her to draft a trial memorandum in *Fish v. Fowl?* If she accepted that assignment, Fish would be a present client again, and representation of the credit union would become problematic under Rule 1.7. It would have been cleaner and simpler for Ames to have declined the Black & White project at the outset.

The area of imputed disqualification—treated in Rule 1.10—presents the most serious potential difficulties for both contract and hiring lawyers. Imputed disqualification develops as follows. If contract lawyer Ames does several projects on the premises of law firm Smith & Jones without being shielded from information about the firm's other clients and cases, knowledge of the firm's entire client base may be imputed to her. Should she then accept a project from Black & White, a firm representing one party in a case in which Smith & Jones represented the opposing party while Ames was working there, it would be possible for Black & White to be disqualified from representation on the basis of Ames' imputed knowledge, even if she had never worked on the case for either law firm.

Of course, neither contract lawyers nor the firms they assist want this sort of thing to happen. The ABA analyzes the situation by looking at the question of when a lawyer can be said to be "associated in" or "associated with a firm" under Rule 1.10—although it cautions that the "association" test is only a guideline, not a set rule. Thus if Ames had worked mostly out of her own office on one or more projects for Smith & Jones and each project had been discrete and separately assigned, she would most likely not be "associated with" that firm for conflicts purposes. If she had worked in the Smith & Jones office, however, her work on projects for numerous clients could result in her being deemed "associated with" the firm—unless, according to Op. 88-

---

7. Id. at 306 & n. 4 (1994 Supp.), discussing cases in which courts have held that longstanding clients of firms were still "present" clients even though they had no matters actually pending with the firms at the time.

356, Smith & Jones, through accurate records or otherwise, could demonstrate that she had no access to information relating to the representation of other firm clients and matters. If she had worked with Smith & Jones on only a single matter, and had no access to information relating to the representation of other firm clients and matters, Op. 88-356 again indicates that she "should not be deemed 'associated with' the firm generally for purposes of application of Rule 1.10."

Assume Ames worked on a divorce case in which Smith & Jones represented the wife and Black & White represented the husband. While the divorce was still pending, but after Ames had completed her assignment for Smith & Jones, Black & White called and asked if she could work on a project unrelated to the divorce and involving neither the husband nor the wife. According to the ABA, Ames should *not* take the assignment: "[I]t would be inadvisable for a second firm representing other parties in the same matter whose interests are directly adverse to those of the client of the first firm to engage the temporary lawyer during the pendency of the matter, even for working on other matters."

The ABA makes this recommendation because the "associated with" test is "only a guideline." Thus it is conceivable that Ames' work for Smith & Jones on the divorce would lead to disqualification of Black & White even though her work for Black & White was on an unrelated matter. Proper screening should be sufficient to avoid disqualification of either firm on the divorce matter, though, if Smith & Jones had hired Ames to assist in a matter involving a different client.

The ABA's recommendation could seriously limit contract lawyers' work options, especially in smaller legal markets. In jurisdictions that allow screening procedures to avoid problems of imputed disqualification,[8] the ABA's approach would actually make it harder for a contract lawyer to work for different firms than it is for an associate or partner to change firms. In these states, if an associate left Smith & Jones and went to work for Black & White, the potential for imputed disqualification would be handled by screening the associate from all matters involving Smith &

---

8. Several states have rejected the concept of screening the lawyer to prevent imputed disqualification of the new firm. Appendix 4 summarizes some recent rulings on all sides of the issue, but the list is not complete. You'll need to learn what the rule is where you practice before deciding how to proceed in situations like the hypothetical examples.

   In 1997, the ALI members working on the *Restatement of the Law Governing Lawyers* voted to include a section that permits screening to avoid imputed disqualification, but only when the confidential information known by the personally-disqualified lawyer is unlikely to be significant in the subsequent matter. The *Restatement* had been approved for publication but was not yet on the shelves as of October 1998.

Jones. There is no reason to forbid the same course of action to a contract lawyer—especially one who may not even be "associated with" the old firm. Where screening to avoid imputed disqualification is an approved practice, ethical concerns could be met by disclosing the circumstances to all parties; with their consent and with suitable screening measures, the contract lawyer should be able to accept the project from Black & White.

Office share arrangements can also present imputed disqualification issues.[9] In fact the ABA in Op. 88-356 reasoned that the discussion of office sharing in the Comment to Rule 1.10 could provide guidance for the temporary lawyer situation. Two lawyers who share office space and occasionally consult with or assist one another are not ordinarily considered a "firm," but if they present themselves to the public in a way that suggests they are a firm, or conduct themselves as a firm, they should be regarded as one for purposes of applying ethical rules. Also relevant to the determination are the terms of any formal agreement between them and whether they have access to one another's files and thus to confidential information about the other's clients.

The rule in California (Formal Opinion 1997-150) is that lawyers who share office space or staff must ensure that the public is not misled about their relationship, and must employ safeguards and structure their practices in a way that will protect the confidentiality of their clients' information. An office share arrangement can cause concern even where boundaries are strictly observed. Bob Webster of San Francisco's The Lawsmiths agency tells of a contract lawyer who was turned down for a project because he shared space with a solo practitioner peripherally involved in a case with the hiring firm—even though it was not the case for which the firm wanted to hire the contract lawyer.

Only a few states have directly addressed the problem of conflicts. The *Oregon* Code of Professional Responsibility contains a definition of "firm member" that excludes office sharers or lawyers working with the firm on a limited basis, unless there are "indicia sufficient to establish a defacto law firm among the lawyers involved." Oregon DR 10-101(A). Both *Kentucky* (in the *Oliver* case) and *South Carolina* (in Opinion 91-09) have adopted Op. 88-356 with respect to conflicts issues. *New Hampshire*, in Opinion 1993-94/8, cautions that a lawyer who offers "pro tempore" coverage of court hearings on a regular basis may be considered part of the firm for conflicts purposes.

The *California* State Bar Standing Committee on Professional Responsibility and

---

9. In Appendix 2 we suggest that some contract lawyers may want to enter into office share arrangements in which they perform contract work in exchange for all or a portion of the rent.

Conduct, in Formal Opinion 1992-126, notes that the firm must make a concerted effort to screen the contract lawyer from confidential information that is not essential to the project, and that the contract lawyer must be mindful of the rule that confidential information of a former client may not be used against that client. Both hiring firm and contract lawyer bear responsibility for checking conflicts, and a review of prior clients and cases should be part of the hiring process. The contract lawyer should keep a record of clients and matters worked on, but, suggests the California Committee, the hiring firm has the most direct obligation to monitor conflicts.

Both hiring and contract lawyers need systems for avoiding conflicts problems. Lawyers and law firms using contract lawyers should maintain complete records showing clients and matters for which each contract lawyer has worked. Be sure to tell the contract lawyer the names of clients, opposing party or parties, opposing counsel and any potential parties *before* discussing the substance of the assignment. Once the assignment has begun, take positive steps to screen the contract lawyer from all information relating to clients for which that lawyer does not work, and keep a record of the precautions taken.

The contract lawyer should also maintain a conflicts checking system. First, keep a complete record of all cases handled and law firms served throughout your legal career. When a potential hiring lawyer calls, ask *immediately* for the names of the client and all opposing parties, as well as any potential parties. If you get a call from a firm that's on the other side of a case you worked on in the past, and the case is still pending, either decline the assignment (per the recommendation of Op. 88-356) or (if you can resolve imputed disqualification issues) disclose your involvement and obtain the consent of all parties.

As a contract lawyer, make every effort to avoid exposure to information relating to other firm clients. You may need to remind the firm of the need to screen you; you can also refuse to work in a room or office containing other client files. Address conflicts checking and screening to avoid imputed disqualification in the engagement letter.

In many situations there won't be a clear-cut right answer. Familiarize yourself with applicable sections of your state code of professional responsibility and any pertinent ethics opinions, and discuss your concerns with bar association lawyers available for advice on ethics questions.

DISCLOSURE TO CLIENTS

When must a lawyer or firm disclose to a client that a contract lawyer is doing some of the work, and when must the firm obtain the client's consent before assigning the work? Must any disclosure include details of the compensation arrangement between hiring and contract lawyer?

The ABA's Op. 88-356, relying on Rules 7.5(d), 1.2(a) and 1.4, concludes that client consent must be obtained whenever "the temporary lawyer is performing independent work for a client *without the close supervision* of a lawyer associated with the law firm" because the client "cannot reasonably be deemed to have consented to the involvement of the independent lawyer." In contrast, no disclosure is necessary "where the temporary lawyer is working *under the direct supervision* of a lawyer associated with the firm." Furthermore, the hiring lawyer need not tell the client anything about its compensation of contract lawyers working either independently or under supervision, if the compensation paid is reasonable for the services rendered and there is no direct division of the fees paid by the client. (See discussion of fee splitting that follows for a more detailed analysis of this issue.)

Some state and local bars, in contrast, take the position that use of a contract or temporary lawyer must *always* be disclosed to clients. *Illinois* State Bar Opinion No. 92-7 (1992), dealing with hiring contract lawyers for court calls and other routine appearances, notes that [Illinois] Rule 1.1(c) requires the client's consent before delegating work to a lawyer not of the firm. *Ohio* Opinion 90-23, concerning temporary placement agencies, states that the temporary relationship must be disclosed to the client. *New Hampshire* Opinion 1989-90/9, also concerning agencies, requires that the temporary arrangement be disclosed to the firm's clients, the agency's insurer and creditors of both the firm and the agency. *New York City (Bar)* Opinion 1989-2 emphasizes the law firm's obligation to make full disclosure and obtain consent from clients for use of contract lawyers. In *Kentucky*, under the *Oliver* case, the use of a temporary lawyer must always be disclosed to the client. Finally, a conservative reading of the requirements on division of fees (below) suggests disclosure is necessary whenever the contract lawyer's work is paid for (even indirectly) by the client.

The *Los Angeles* County Bar Association, in Formal Opinion 473 (1993), lists five questions about delegation of work. A positive answer to any one of the questions requires disclosure:

- *Does the arrangement alter responsibility for the client's matter?*
- *Is the new lawyer performing a significant portion or aspect of the work?*
- *Has staffing of the matter been changed from what the client was originally told or what the client requested of the lawyer or firm?*
- *Is staffing of the matter different from the client's reasonable expectation?*
- *Does the change in staffing increase the cost to the client for the work performed?*

The opinion also says that use of a lawyer with less expertise or experience may require disclosure. See also *California* Opinion 1994-138, stating disclosure is required if the arrangement represents a "significant development" in the matter.

If you're not practicing in a state with an ethics opinion or decision on the subject, review your state's rules and act in accordance with them. Even if the rules do not require disclosure of the hiring of a supervised contract lawyer, client relations usually make disclosure a good idea. Certainly, if the firm's bill will reflect the contract lawyer's time, it's best to tell the client about the arrangement before the bill is sent. (See sample disclosure language for a standard retainer agreement on page 174.) By presenting the choice in a positive light—as a cost-effective way to obtain experienced and well-qualified assistance—you can improve client relations rather than risk harming them.

DIVISION OF FEES

Ethical restrictions on fee-splitting arise in two situations: those in which an agency places the contract lawyer and receives compensation from the hiring lawyer or firm (Rule 5.4(a) governing division of fees with non-lawyers), and those in which the firm pays the contract lawyer a portion of the fee it receives from the client (Rule 1.5(e) on division of fees with other lawyers). Most state bar opinions relating to contract lawyers were issued in response to questions about contract lawyer placement agencies; an inordinately large proportion of their agonizing concerns how the agencies will be compensated. The second situation has, in contrast, scarcely been addressed at all.

The ABA opined in Op. 88-356 that "an arrangement whereby a law firm pays to a temporary lawyer compensation in a fixed dollar amount or at an hourly rate and pays a placement agency a fee based upon a percentage of the lawyer's compensation" does not constitute proscribed sharing of legal fees with non-lawyers. The rationale is that the fee to the agency is not a legal fee but compensation for locating, recruiting, screening and placing the lawyer.

Several states that have considered the issue are more troubled by the arrangement and either suggest or require that the agency be paid separately. *California* Formal Opinion 1992-126, for example, recommends that the hiring firm pay the contract lawyer directly and make a separate payment to the agency. Similarly, *Connecticut* Informal Opinion 88-15 assumes the agency is paid separately from the lawyers. *Kentucky,* in the *Oliver* case, requires that the agency and the contract lawyer be paid separately. *New Hampshire* requires, per Opinion 1989-90/9, that the firm not divide legal fees with an agency (or employee leasing company) "directly or indirectly." The *District of Columbia* prohibits basing agency fees on what the client pays to the firm for the legal services rendered, and implies that the agency fee should be distinguished from and paid separately from that to the temporary lawyer. Similarly, *North Carolina*'s Opinion 104 states that the fees paid to a leasing company— similar in many ways to an agency—must not be tied to the fees paid to the firm.

On the other hand, *Ohio* (Opinion 90-23) simply requires that any fee structure developed not involve fee-splitting. *South Carolina* (Opinion 91-09) follows ABA Op. 88-356. The *New York City* Bar (Opinion 1989-2) allows the agency to be compensated as a percentage of the contract lawyer's pay, noting that this is still not a payment for legal services.

What about the contract lawyer who works directly with another lawyer and, as is a common practice, charges the lawyer a percentage of the rate at which the lawyer then bills the services to the client? Is this arrangement considered "fee splitting"? Opinion 88-356 does not provide a clear answer: "If . . . the arrangement between the firm and the temporary lawyer involves a *direct division of the actual fee paid by the client,* such as percentage division of a contingent fee, then Rule 1.5(e)(1) requires the consent of the client and satisfaction of the other requirements of the Rule regardless of the extent of the supervision." On the other hand, says Op. 88-356, if a lawyer or firm "simply pays the temporary lawyer reasonable compensation . . . *and does not charge the payments thereafter to the client as a disbursement,*" there is no need to inform the client. Rule 1.5(e) does not apply "because the gross fee the client pays the firm is not shared with the temporary lawyer."

Op. 88-356 thus defines the two extremes of the continuum: the out-of-pocket payment not passed on to the client in any form but paid out of the lawyer's or firm's profits, which does not require disclosure, and the percentage splitting of a contingent fee actually received by the firm, which does require disclosure. Most contract lawyer arrangements do not fit either extreme. Contract lawyers generally provide their services directly to the hiring lawyer and expect payment whether or not the hiring lawyer is paid by the client. Most hiring lawyers bill their clients for the contract lawyer's time, but increase the hourly rate rather than pass the cost directly on as a disbursement. Neither Op. 88-356 nor any state or local bar opinion addresses this situation.

The careful hiring lawyer should also study ABA Opinion 93-379, which addresses numerous billing queries. This opinion stresses the lawyer's obligation to disclose to the client "the basis for the fee and other charges." It also discusses the lawyer's duty not to make false statements about her services and the need to render statements that "adequately inform" the client. Applying its conclusions to the contract lawyer context suggests simply that client billings should show who did the work, how long each lawyer spent and each lawyer's billing rate. It would thus be unethical for a hiring lawyer to transform 20 hours of a contract lawyer's time at $60 per hour into 20 hours of his own time at $180 per hour. The bill could, however, show 20 hours of the contract lawyer's time at $120 per hour and two hours of the hiring lawyer's time (at $180 per hour) reviewing the contract lawyer's work.

ABA Opinion 94-388 is also worth consulting. It states that when a lawyer or firm "associates" or "affiliates" with another firm, the lawyer must disclose "the exact nature of the relationship" between the firms "and the extent to which resources of another firm will be available." Further, says the opinion, "[a] client whose fee is shared must receive a complete explanation of the sharing arrangement and the arrangement cannot be implemented if the client objects."

Reading this opinion with Opinion 88-356 suggests that the less a contract lawyer looks like an employee and the more she looks like another law firm, the higher the duty of disclosure.

The Comment to Rule 1.5 may resolve the dilemma in favor of disclosure. It defines a division of fees as "a single billing to a client covering the fee of two or more lawyers who are not in the same firm." Although the Comment goes on to discuss contingent fee arrangements, this definition arguably fits the arrangement in which a firm pays a contract lawyer, then bills the client for the contract lawyer's time at the same or a higher rate. Rule 1.5(e) would then require that a contract lawyer's time be billed to the client only after disclosure and agreement. If the fee paid to the contract lawyer and passed onto the client is not "in proportion to the services performed" by that lawyer, the client must consent in writing.[10]

Some might disagree with this analysis, claiming that the contract lawyer is not "billing" the client (that is, expecting to be paid by the client); rather the contract lawyer submits his or her bill to, and expects to be paid by, the hiring lawyer. Arthur Garwin, professionalism counsel for the ABA's Center for Professional Responsibility, asserts that, "If outside counsel is paid on a non-contingent hourly basis, this is not considered a division of fees."[11]

Erring on the side of conservatism, lawyers using contract lawyers should make a habit of obtaining the informed consent of their clients in all cases. Even if not

---

10. According to the Comment to Rule 1.5, disclosure to the client of the share each lawyer is to receive is not required. Note, however, that the ALI's *Restatement of the Law Governing Lawyers* (approved in 1998) requires that clients be informed not only of the fact of a fee division but also of "the terms of the division."

11. Arthur Garwin, "The Right to (Extra) Counsel," *ABA Journal*, June 1994.

required by the Rules of Professional Conduct, this policy will enhance client relations and avoid later misunderstandings.

DUTIES TO PROVIDE COMPETENT REPRESENTATION AND TO SUPERVISE

Judging by ethics programs and commentary, lawyers are not especially concerned about Rule 1.1, the duty to provide competent representation. Yet lawyers have been disciplined for violating this rule (sometimes with a finding that their fees were unreasonable). Even less appreciated is Rule 5.1, which places responsibility on a supervising lawyer for the unethical actions of the lawyers she supervises. In the contract lawyer context, these rules need to be taken seriously. Read together, they suggest that a hiring lawyer has a duty to hire qualified contract lawyers and to provide meaningful supervision if she hires inexperienced ones.

Hiring lawyer Irene often works with contract lawyer Gregory, who is fresh out of school. If Irene asks Gregory to draft a partnership agreement (something he has never done before), she needs to spend more than just a few minutes explaining the assignment. She should give him examples of good agreements, go over the points that need to be covered, suggest decisions relating to partnership issues for him to read and carefully review his work after he completes it. If she discovers that he left out a key provision, or treated an important issue in a way that invites future disputes, she should tell Gregory what he did wrong and suggest ways to correct the mistakes.

This sounds like no more than common sense and good management practice. In the 1990s, though, market pressures tempt many experienced lawyers to skimp on training and supervising beginners. "My client can't pay for Gregory's learning time," Irene might protest. Or, "I just don't have any extra hours to spend on Gregory. Besides, didn't I hire him so he could save *me* time?"

If Irene truly feels this way, she should hire a more experienced lawyer to help her. Even in that case, though, she must assure herself that the lawyer is competent. Not to do so risks malpractice liability as well as violation of the rules of ethics. She can't escape responsibility for the acts of lawyers she hires to help her.

This should not stop Irene from using contract lawyers, however. If she explains the assignment well to Gregory, and points him in the right direction, he will spend less time on the project and deliver a better product. If Irene has to write off a few hours of his learning time, the cost to her will be minor in comparison to the cost of a job poorly done, the weekend she spends repairing the damage or a client who defects. And if Irene takes time to train Gregory well, her effort should be hand-somely repaid—by Gregory's gratitude, her own satisfaction and the good work Gregory accomplishes under her tutelage.

Consider another scenario. Irene is facing an unusual bankruptcy issue, and the bankruptcy lawyer she usually calls with questions is on sabbatical. She asks Gregory to research the issue and suggest a course of action. Gregory is a bank-ruptcy bonehead—he never even took a course on bankruptcy in law school—and Irene's knowledge of the area is limited to what she has gleaned from her conversa-tions with her expert adviser. Irene and Gregory both risk malpractice liability if harm to the client results. Since Irene is incapable of adequately supervising Gregory's work, neither would be deemed to be providing competent counsel; thus both would also violate the rules of ethics.[12]

If Irene, instead of relying on Gregory, turns to Hugo, an experienced bankruptcy lawyer, competency and supervision are no longer issues, but Irene's disclosure to the client about Hugo's participation should meet the standard for associating another law firm set forth in ABA Opinion 94-388, and satisfy Rule 1.5 as well.

The problem of the under-supervised, inexperienced lawyer is not limited to sole practitioners who hire contract lawyers. Lawyers in mid-sized and large firms may neglect associate training in favor of billing more hours themselves.

But the days when these rules were ignored may be ending. In May, 1996, the New York courts changed the state's rules of ethics to impose responsibility on *law firms* for the unethical conduct of lawyers practicing under their auspices. They also added a rule requiring adequate supervision of the work of firm lawyers. A 1994 law review article[13] suggests that rules on competency and the duty to supervise could be used to pressure law firms to correct the problem of inadequate training (and mentoring) of their new lawyers. Hiring lawyers and contract lawyers would be wise to take heed of these trends.

CONSIDERATION OF OTHER ISSUES

The resolution of many ethics issues turns on the nature of the relationship

---

12. See *In re Odman*, 687 P.2d 153 (Or. 1984), in which a lawyer was disciplined for undertaking estate work and performing it incompetently. The opinion notes that he took no steps to educate himself, and his associates were recent law school graduates who could not provide the expertise he lacked.

13. Irwin Miller, "Preventing Misconduct by Promoting the Ethics of Attorneys' Supervisory Duties," 70 *Notre Dame Law Review* 259 (1994).

between contract lawyer and hiring lawyer or firm. The degree of closeness, and the extent of supervision, as well as the particular jurisdiction you're working in, will dictate how to handle questions of conflicts, confidences and disclosure to clients. These factors have implications for the other topics treated in this section as well.

18

INDEPENDENT CONTRACTOR
OR EMPLOYEE?

*Be warned. The distinction between independent contractor and
employee is one of the great gray areas of the law. We shed what light we
can on a controversial but important part of the contract lawyer scene.*

In 1994, the Internal Revenue Service targeted attorneys for increased audit
scrutiny. The IRS has also stepped up its enforcement efforts with respect to the
"misclassification" of employees as independent contractors. These two trends,
taken together, make the distinction between independent contractor and
employee a crucial one for contract and hiring lawyers. The distinction can have
serious tax consequences, as well as liability implications[1]

Many contract lawyers we talked to consider themselves independent
contractors, and are treated as such by the agencies and hiring lawyers with whom
they work. But there are almost as many contract lawyer arrangements as there are
contract lawyers. Angela works exclusively out of her own office, using her own
equipment, on short-term projects for a variety of different lawyers and law firms.
Derek takes on full-time long-term assignments—from three months to a year or
more—and works on the premises of the hiring lawyers, using their equipment, relying on their support staff and subject to their direction and control. Martin shares
office space with several other lawyers and receives contract assignments as a
result of that arrangement. He is expected to be available to work for these lawyers
at specified times; he has invested in his own equipment, has his own telephone and
fax lines, and accepts work from other lawyers and clients as well.

The more independently contract lawyers work, the less likely they are to be
classified as employees. Thus Angela is probably an independent contractor, and
Derek is almost certainly an employee. Martin is a tougher case. It's possible the IRS

---

1. This chapter addresses the federal tax issues. See Chapter 19 for discussion of malpractice liability.

would consider him an employee of the lawyers he shares space with but an independent contractor with respect to other hiring lawyers.[2]

As of this writing, we know of no situation in which the IRS has publicly announced, or a court has held, that a contract lawyer who holds himself out as an independent contractor is actually an employee. Although some observers are sanguine about the issue and believe that the IRS is unlikely aggressively to recharacterize contract lawyers as employees,[3] we recommend caution. Contract lawyers and hiring lawyers should recognize the factors the IRS uses in its determinations, federal common law distinctions between employee and independent contractor status, and applicable state statutes or common law. There is no bright-line test; our aim here is to alert you to the issues. If you think you have cause for concern, do additional research yourself or consult your tax advisor.

WHAT THE DISTINCTION MEANS FOR HIRING LAWYERS

If the IRS audits you and determines that your "contract lawyer" is an employee rather than an independent contractor, you could face the following assessments:

- *The employer portion of the employee's social security taxes (7.65%);*
- *The employee portion of social security taxes (7.65%);*
- *The employee's required withholding (up to 28%);*
- *Federal Unemployment Tax Assessment (FUTA) up to about $65;*
- *A fine for failure to withhold the employer's share of social security taxes, up to 20 percent of the 7.65% the employer owes;*
- *A fine of 1.5 percent for not withholding federal income taxes;*
- *Interest on deficiencies;*
- *Additional fines up to three percent of the amount owed, and double the social security penalty on the employee's share, for failure to file 1099 reporting forms as required.*

If the hiring lawyer's mistake is deemed to be willful, the fines are even tougher.

---

2. It is possible to be an employee of one firm and an independent contractor with others.

3. "To date, the Internal Revenue Service has not pursued firms hiring temporary attorneys (unlike most other categories of temporary workers) so initial concerns [over the tax implications] have faded." Samuel A. Frederick, "Controlling Compensation Costs by Using Temporary Attorneys," *Law Practice Management*, July/August 1995.

The fact that the "employee" actually paid some of these taxes does not reduce the penalty. If you believe the IRS is wrong, you can take it to court, seeking rulings on whether the workers are employees and whether you are entitled to "safe harbor" under section 530 of the Revenue Act of 1978. To get into U.S. District Court or the Court of Federal Claims, you must have paid the taxes the IRS claims were owed and seek a refund. To get into U.S. Tax Court, you need not have paid. Although the courts may have a more liberal reading than the IRS of what constitutes an independent contractor, there are no guarantees. The battle may well be more expensive than acquiescence.

WHAT THE DISTINCTION MEANS FOR CONTRACT LAWYERS

Unless you are a determined maverick, being classified as an employee isn't the worst thing that could happen to you. If you believe your relationship with one or more hiring lawyers borders on employer-employee, bring up the subject. It may be in both your interests to recognize the employee relationship formally, in which case the firm will deposit Social Security taxes and withhold income taxes, and may provide malpractice coverage as well. You may also receive employee benefits like sick leave, vacation pay and participation in the firm retirement plan.

Your characterization as an employee can, however, limit your ability to deduct certain expenses (for example, travel and parking, or those of your home office). Be aware also that if you work for more than one firm in the course of a year, you'll need to take steps to adjust the amount of taxes withheld from your paycheck, since each firm will withhold taxes on the basis of a figure much less than your total annual income.

If you are truly self-employed, you can take advantage of the tax benefits of that status by deducting all your business expenses and writing off half the Social Security tax you pay. (An employee, in contrast, can deduct business expenses only to the extent they exceed two percent of adjusted gross income.) But recognize your responsibilities. You must file quarterly tax returns, pay for all your own professional expenses (bar dues, for example) and pay both employer's and employee's share of Social Security tax. (See budget discussion in Chapter 9.)

HOW TO TELL AN EMPLOYEE FROM AN INDEPENDENT CONTRACTOR

No federal statute explains the distinction between independent contractors and employees.[4] Rather, the categories are said to derive from the common law. Unfortunately, few reported decisions deal with professionals of any sort; none we've found deal with lawyers at all, let alone contract lawyers. Thus we are in the dubious position of having to rely on IRS pronouncement, regulation and uncodified statute rather than the decisions that should make up the common law.

THE IRS'S 20 FACTORS

The 20 factors used by the IRS to decide independent contractor status are not part of any statute or regulation; rather they are the IRS's interpretation of the federal common law. They are to be "used as guidelines to determine whether sufficient control is present to establish an employer-employee relationship. . . . Not every factor is applicable in every situation, and the degree of importance of each factor varies depending on the type of work and individual circumstances." The 20 factors are reprinted on page 213.

Many sources cite the 20 factors as if they were "the law." They are not. Revenue rulings do not have the force of law, or even as much weight as a regulation, although courts do give them some deference. And while the IRS, author of the 20 factors, is the decisionmaker at the audit level, if you challenge the audit result you will go to federal court. The court will apply what *it* sees as the common law (or perhaps the "safe-harbor" provision of the Internal Revenue Code, discussed below).

There are additional problems with relying on the 20 factors. Many of the factors simply don't work for contract lawyers. For example, their services are arguably "integral" to the hiring lawyer's business because both contract and hiring lawyers provide legal services. Further, a particular contract lawyer often will be hired because of his or her expertise or abilities, so the hiring lawyer expects the contract lawyer's services to be rendered personally. Contract lawyers—if they do good work—develop continuing relationships with the firms that use them. Most lawyers—and most contract lawyers—bill their work by the hour. And law firms typically pass on to their clients such expenses as travel, copying charges, the costs of on-line legal research, and charges for long distance telephone calls and faxes;

---

4. Federal statutes typically define "employee" as "an individual employed by an employer." See 29 U.S.C. §1002(6). There is no applicable federal definition of independent contractor. From time to time a legislative definition of independent contractor for tax purposes is proposed. For example, the Independent Contractor Tax Fairness Act of 1995 would have classified as an independent contractor a worker who (1) could suffer a loss or make a profit, or (2) had a separate place of business with significant investment in facilities or tools, or (3) made her services available to the general public, or (4) was paid on commission.

many contract lawyers as well bill hiring lawyers for some or all of these expenses. Thus there are several factors that few contract lawyers will be able to satisfy.

This does not mean, however, that all contract lawyers must be classified and treated as employees. The 20 factors don't all have the same weight, and all don't have to be satisfied. Indeed, virtually no taxpayer will be able to meet all twenty.[5] Even IRS examiners concede that some factors weigh more heavily than others.

The 20 factors have also been criticized as illogical. One commentator has observed that the factors consolidate three alternative common law tests: the control test, the organization test and the economic realities test.[6] Under common law it should be necessary to satisfy only one of the three tests, but the IRS seems to require that all three be satisfied. Several of the factors are subject to criticism as meaningless, in that they are present to some degree in all contractual relationships. For example, all contracts contain requirements, which, according to the IRS, can be seen as "instructions" indicative of control. The "integration" factor is likewise an empty one, as no business retains workers, whether as independent contractors or employees, to do something that is not necessary to the business operations. And most contracts require formal or informal oral or written reports.[7]

It is also recognized, however, that one factor alone—making one's services available to the public—can be dispositive of independent contractor status. This factor, together with accepting work from several clients during the same period of time and not being "required" to work full-time for any one of them, add up to the "independent trade" factor, a label used by the *Restatement (Second) of Agency* §220. Advertisements, business cards and a business telephone line are examples of the ways a contract lawyer offers services to the public. Payment of one's own professional dues and malpractice insurance premiums are also evidence of having an independent trade.

As noted in BNA *Employment Status*, principles contained in *Restatement* §220 explain better than the IRS how to identify the control indicative of a common-law master-servant relationship. As the *Restatement* explains in a comment to §220, a master-servant (or employer-employee) relationship is one in which the actor's physical activities and time are surrendered to the control of the master, rather than

---

5. Nancye Faulkner Belding, "Independent Contractors Cost Less Than Employees — But What Are They?" *Corporate Legal Times*, September 1992.

6. Rick A. Pacynski, "Legal Challenges in Using Independent Contractors," *Michigan Bar Journal* 671, 673, July 1993.

7. *See* Marmoll, 391-2nd T.M., *Employment Status — Independent Contractor v. Employee* (BNA 1993 & Supp. 1997) (cited as BNA *Employment Status*).

THE IRS'S 20 FACTORS

Revenue Ruling 87-41, 1987-1 CB 296, reprinted in IRS Publication 937—Employment Taxes and Information Returns—lists the following factors to distinguish an employee from an independent contractor:

1. **Instructions.** An employee must comply with instructions about when, where, and how to work. Even if no instructions are given, the control factor is present if the employer has the right to control how the work results are achieved.

2. **Training.** An employee may be trained to perform services in a particular manner. Independent contractors ordinarily use their own methods and receive no training from the purchasers of their services.

3. **Integration.** An employee's services are usually integrated into the business operations because the services are important to the success or continuation of the business. This shows that the employee is subject to direction and control.

4. **Services rendered personally.** An employee renders services personally. This shows that the employer is interested in the methods as well as the results.

5. **Hiring assistants.** An employee works for an employer who hires, supervises and pays workers. An independent contractor can hire, supervise, and pay assistants under a contract that requires him or her to provide materials and labor and to be responsible only for the result.

6. **Continuing relationship.** An employee generally has a continuing relationship with an employer. A continuing relationship may exist even if work is performed at recurring although irregular intervals.

7. **Set hours of work.** An employee usually has set hours of work established by an employer. An independent contractor generally can set his or her own work hours.

8. **Full-time required.** An employee may be required to work or be available full-time. This indicates control by the employer. An independent contractor can work when and for whom he chooses.

9. **Work done on premises.** An employee usually works on the premises of an employer, or works on a route or at a location designated by an employer.

10. **Order or sequence set.** An employee may be required to perform services in the order or sequence set by an employer. This shows that the employee is subject to direction and control.

11. **Reports.** An employee may be required to submit reports to an employer. This shows that the employer maintains a degree of control.

12. **Payments.** An employee is paid by the hour, week or month. An independent contractor is usually paid by the job or on a straight commission.

13. **Expenses.** An employee's business and travel expenses are generally paid by an employer. This shows that the employee is subject to regulation and control.

14. **Tools and materials.** An employee is normally furnished significant tools, materials and other equipment by an employer.

15. **Investment.** An independent contractor has a significant investment in the facilities he or she uses in performing services for someone else.

16. **Profit or loss.** An independent contractor can make a profit or suffer a loss.

17. **Works for more than one person or firm.** An independent contractor is generally free to provide his or her services to two or more unrelated persons or firms at the same time.

18. **Offers services to general public.** An independent contractor makes his or her services available to the general public.

19. **Right to fire.** An employee can be fired by an employer. An independent contractor cannot be fired so long as he or she produces a result that meets the specifications of the contract.

20. **Right to quit.** An employee can quit his or her job at any time without incurring liability. An independent contractor usually agrees to complete a specific job and is responsible for its satisfactory completion, or is legally obligated to make good for failure to complete it.

one in which services are provided pursuant to an agreement to accomplish results, or to use care and skill in accomplishing results.

An independent contractor is like a plumber, says Linda Marks, work options consultant and co-author of *Negotiating Time: New Scheduling Options in the Legal Profession.*

> *You call the plumber and say, "Here's my problem. Please fix it." How the problem gets fixed is up to the plumber. The independent contractor calls the shots, deciding what he or she does or does not want to do. An employee, on the other hand, would be told what steps to take to fix the pipe.*

This approach would permit almost every contract lawyer to claim independent contractor status, except those who are hired to sit in an office and do whatever needs doing for certain hours of the day and days of the week.

Finally, courts and even the IRS will apply factors other than those listed in Revenue Ruling 87-41. The one most relevant to the contract lawyer is skill. According to the *Restatement,* less skilled workers are more likely to be employees, whereas more skilled workers, especially licensed professionals, are likely to qualify as independent contractors. Additional relevant factors are what the parties intend (as set forth in an engagement letter, perhaps), who is responsible for the worker's insurance coverage, and who pays the worker's license fees and taxes.

If you're concerned about whether a relationship is that of employer-employee, you can use Form SS-8 to describe the arrangement and solicit an opinion from the IRS. But first acquaint yourself with the 20 factors so you'll have some sense of how the IRS will apply them. No matter how carefully you complete the form to comply with the 20 factors, experienced tax lawyers observe that nine times out of ten the IRS will come down in favor of "employee" status.[8] Filing a Form SS-8 may also invite an audit.

FEDERAL STATUTES, REGULATIONS AND DECISIONAL LAW

Regulations. Although little in the statutes, regulations or reported decisions gives assurance about the status of contract lawyer arrangements, 26 CFR 631.3121(d)-1, titled "Who are employees?," does offer some guidance. Subsection (c) of this regulation discusses "common law employees," emphasizing "the right to control and direct the individual who performs the services, not only as to the result

---

8. "Independent Contractors Cost Less Than Employees — But What Are They?," *supra* (quoting Illinois lawyer Nancy Joerg).

to be accomplished by the work but also as to the details and means by which that result is accomplished."

Factors mentioned in the regulation as indicative of an employer-employee relationship include the right to fire, and the furnishing of tools and a place to work. The regulation also states:

> *Individuals such as physicians, lawyers, dentists, veterinarians, construction contractors, public stenographers and auctioneers,* engaged in the pursuit of an independent trade, business or profession in which they offer their services to the public, *are independent contractors and not employees.*

Decisions Based on Common Law. Most reported decisions concern situations so different from the contract lawyer arrangement that they offer little guidance in this area. Typical cases involve, for example, truckers who hire drivers and people to load and unload trucks, cab drivers, construction workers and installers of doors and windows. Further (as in other areas of the law), different courts considering similar fact patterns have been known to reach different conclusions. The few reported decisions on attorneys (which are very old) generally support the idea of the attorney's independence.[9]

A 1997 decision concerning an emergency room physician is also instructive. In *Cilecek v. Inova Health System Services,* 115 F.3d 256 (4th Cir. 1997), the court applied general principles of agency law to decide that the physician, who had sued under Title VII of the Civil Rights Act of 1964, was an independent contractor without the right to seek relief under that statute. The court said: "Cilecek exercised an independence . . . that enabled him to determine his hours, his income, and who he worked for. These are core incidents of a work relationship that are inconsistent with employee status." 115 F.3d at 261.

Revenue Rulings. Three Revenue Rulings on the independent contractor status of lawyers are probably the most helpful precedent. In Rev. Rul. 68-323, 1968-1 CB 432, the IRS ruled that an attorney engaged by a corporation and paid an annual retainer to defend it in any suit that might be brought against it during the year was *not an employee* of the corporation. He was not subject to direction and control by the corporation, and his work for the corporation was performed in the course of his independent profession in which he offered his services to the public.

In Rev. Rul. 70-546, 1970-2 CB 205, the IRS ruled that a lawyer hired by the state

---

9. See discussion in BNA *Employment Status* at p. A-39.

to collect delinquent taxes was *not a state employee*. Again, the attorney was not subject to the direction or control of the state in performing the tax-collection services, and he was not an officer of the state or any political subdivision of it. Instead, he was seen as carrying on a trade or business.

In contrast, the IRS in Rev. Rul. 68-324, 1968-1 CB 433, found an associate at a law firm who was paid a fixed annual salary, was furnished with an office and a secretary, was required to work stated hours, and worked mostly on assignments from other lawyers in the firm *was an employee*, even though the firm sometimes assigned cases that he handled independently and from which he retained the fees.

Revenue Ruling 66-274, 1966-2 CB, concerning a physician who performed services as director of a hospital's department of pathology, is also interesting. The IRS noted that normally professionals in practice who offer their services to the public are independent contractors, but the degree of control and supervision exercised over such a professional is relevant. This physician was an independent contractor and not an employee of the hospital, because he was permitted to perform services for others, hired and paid his own associates, was paid on a percentage basis (that is, not salaried and no guaranteed minimum), was not required to comply with the hospital's rules for its employees and was not entitled to such employment benefits as vacation pay, sick leave and retirement pay. The pathology director's situation is similar in many ways to contract lawyer arrangements.

Safe Harbor Provision. Many recent court decisions apply the so-called Safe Harbor provision, section 530 of the Revenue Act of 1978, which was never codified but can be found in a note to 28 USCA 63401. This provision is intended to save employers from being penalized for failing to treat workers as employees if certain conditions are satisfied. If (1) all tax returns filed by the employer for the period at issue were consistent with non-employee status (specifically, Forms 1099 were filed for payments in excess of $600), (2) the employer had a "reasonable basis"[10] for not treating the worker as an employee, and (3) the employer did not treat any similarly situated workers as employees, the employer will not be liable for taxes for that period.

---

10. A "reasonable basis" can be reasonable reliance on (1) judicial precedent or published rulings, (2) a previous IRS audit (not necessarily for employment tax purposes) if the audit resulted in no assessment attributable to employment tax treatment of workers in similar positions, or (3) longstanding recognized practice of a significant segment of the industry. Absent such reasonable reliance, the taxpayer may be entitled to section 530 relief if it can demonstrate in some other manner that there was a reasonable basis for not treating the worker as an employee. Rev. Proc. 85-18, 1985-1 CB 518.

Up until 1996, the IRS contended that §530 applied *only if the worker was in fact an employee.* Some courts, however, applied the Safe Harbor provision as if it were an alternative to the common-law analysis—that is, an alternative basis for finding that workers are independent contractors, rather than a basis for escaping penalties for misclassification.

In *Critical Care Register Nursing, Inc. v. U.S.*, 776 F. Supp. 1025 (E.D. Pa. 1991), for example, the court, applying the Safe Harbor provision, held that the plaintiff, an agency that supplied temporary nursing staff to hospitals, had a reasonable basis for treating the nurses as independent contractors. The court mentioned the following factors: The agency did not have any right to direct or control the work the nurses actually did, the nurses performed no services on Critical Care's premises, and the nurses were free to choose when and for whom they would work.

In other words, even though this was a §530 Safe Harbor case, the court treated the question as whether the nurses met the common law definition of independent contractor. Although the IRS filed notice of nonacquiescence in this decision—signifying its intent to litigate the issue again—at least one contract lawyer placement agency owner relies on *Critical Care* for the proposition that contract lawyers who find work through agencies are unlikely to be tagged as "employees."

The IRS stance on limiting the scope of section 530 was widely criticized, and as a result, the IRS announced that beginning January 1, 1997, it would no longer require a taxpayer to concede that its workers are employees to obtain section 530 relief. (See BNA *Employment Status* at A-4 & n.4.)

STATE STATUTES AND DECISIONS

Consideration of how the states define independent contractor (and penalize misclassification) is beyond the scope of this book. More material exists to interpret state requirements, and penalties for running afoul of the law are less terrifying than those in the federal system. In some cases, there is actually a statutory definition. The bad news is that state standards are not necessarily the same as federal, so it is possible for someone to be an independent contractor under state law but not under federal law. If you are (or work with) a contract lawyer who appears to be an independent contractor under federal law, you'll need to check relevant state law to make sure the arrangement meets those criteria as well.

PRECAUTIONS FOR HIRING LAWYERS

If you work with contract lawyers and you believe them to be independent contractors, treat them that way. Don't micromanage their work, says Richard J. Block, corporate counsel for Nissin Foods in Fort Lee, New Jersey, and chair of the Sole Practitioners Subcommittee of the American Corporate Counsel Association's (ACCA) Small Law Department Committee. "Overall direction, of course, should be given; but it is best to let temps manage themselves to the extent they can."[11]

On a more tangible level, confirm that the contract lawyer is operating as a business with all applicable business licenses, and that he intends to be responsible for all taxes. Don't provide the contract lawyer with business cards or list him on your stationery, pay his health insurance, let him participate in the firm 401(k) plan, or pay his bar dues or individual liability insurance. Most important, don't withhold taxes or provide W-2 forms. Rather, obtain the lawyer's Social Security number (on Form W-9) at the outset[12] and file a Form 1099 at the end of the year, even if the total amount you paid the contract lawyer was under the $600 mandatory filing figure. Send a copy of Form 1099 to the contract lawyer.

If you hire outside lawyers to be in the office for certain hours and days for a prolonged period, to handle whatever work is needed at the direction of associates or partners of the firm, and as a result these lawyers cannot accept work from other hiring lawyers, the lawyers are probably employees. You may want to enter into temporary employment agreements with lawyers who work on terms such as these.

If you use an agency to hire contract lawyers who fit the definition of employee, don't assume that the agency insulates you from tax liability. Find out whether the agency treats the lawyers as employees and withholds taxes. If it does, you will not have to. But ethics rules could make it problematic for agencies to treat contract lawyers as employees. Several states have ethics rules or opinions that require the agency to be paid separately from the contract lawyer. (We go into more detail on this subject in Chapters 17 and 21, and Appendix 3.) If you work in such a state, or if the agency you use treats the contract lawyers as independent contractors, you'll need to make your own determination about whether to treat the contract lawyer as an employee.

---

11. Richard J. Block, "Temporary Help Provides Both Talent and Savings," *National Law Journal*, October 17, 1994.

12. We interviewed one contract lawyer, placed with a law firm by a contract lawyer placement agency for three months, who refused to provide his social security number to the agency and objected to its attempt to file a Form 1099. He did not want to have to declare the income and felt the agency should have paid him as an employee.

PRECAUTIONS FOR CONTRACT LAWYERS

If you want to be characterized as an independent contractor, try to meet most if not all of the following conditions:

- *Work primarily out of your own office;*
- *Use your own equipment and support staff or services;*
- *Maintain a business license and pay all applicable state and local business taxes;*
- *Keep yourself insured for professional negligence;*
- *Print business cards and stationery;*
- *Maintain a separate business telephone line;*
- *Hire yourself out on a project-by-project basis;*
- *Offer your services to the public by maintaining a continuing classified advertisement in your state or local bar publication, posting notices at law libraries, or sending brochures or fliers to potential customers;*
- *Give your Social Security number to all hiring lawyers so they can complete Forms 1099. Make sure that they understand your status and the legal basis for it, and that they treat you consistently with that status.*

CONSIDERATION OF OTHER ISSUES

No one claims the employee/independent contractor distinction is an easy one. If you're involved in a situation that straddles the line, it may help to think about the other issues discussed in this section. Contract lawyers who are not deemed to be "associated with" a firm for purposes of client confidences and conflicts of interest, and who are so minimally supervised by the hiring lawyer that disclosure to the client is required, are probably independent contractors. So are contract lawyers who work sufficiently independently of hiring lawyers to require their own malpractice insurance.

19

MALPRACTICE LIABILITY AND COVERAGE

The lack of consistency in the areas of malpractice liability and coverage demands that both hiring and contract lawyers be aware of the risks of the relationship, monitor insurance coverage issues and practice malpractice avoidance.

When we researched the first edition of this book in 1995, we asked malpractice carriers about their policies toward contract lawyer coverage and whether they had experienced any claims stemming from the contract lawyer relationship. No company reported a claim. As a result, we had difficulty getting clear answers about coverage. There seemed to be no reason to develop coverage policies because there had been no claims to stimulate the analysis.

In 1998, our discussions with the companies were more fruitful. Although there was still no evidence of any claims based on the work of a contract lawyer, most carriers had defined coverage for the acts of temporary attorneys and independent contractor lawyers, mostly at the behest of the law firms they insure. Without any underwriting analysis of the risk, however, coverage tended to be limited and still in flux.

Since most malpractice policies were drafted with the traditional relationships of law firm, partner and associate in mind, the nontraditional relationships of contract lawyer to hiring lawyer to client have created continuing interpretation challenges for hiring lawyers, contract lawyers and insurance carriers. Due to the evolving state of malpractice coverage, and the ever-present need to prevent any claims at all, we suggest approaching liability concerns as follows:

1. *Consider the risk. What is the nature of the relationship between hiring and contract lawyer and how is liability likely to be allocated in the event*

*of a claim? Does the relationship warrant separate insurance coverage
for the contract lawyer? What other risk factors are implicated?*

2. *Find out how the carriers involved treat the relationship, and
what steps they require you to take to extend coverage.*

3. *Finally, remember the truism that an ounce of prevention is worth a
pound of cure, and invest in some common sense precautions against
malpractice claims.*

WHO BEARS THE RISK?

Keith, the plaintiff's lawyer in a common law fraud case, hired Caleb to prepare
papers opposing a motion for summary judgment after the plaintiff made statements
in a deposition that presented a statute of limitations problem. Caleb prepared an
affidavit in which the plaintiff contradicted the damaging deposition testimony.
In his research, however, he failed to find a line of cases about the circumstances in
which an affidavit contradicting earlier sworn testimony can be used to raise an
issue of fact precluding summary judgment. If this mistake were to result in
malpractice liability, who would be responsible?

Rosemary, who represented the wife, asked Heather to help draft an agreement
for division of marital property in a divorce case. Rosemary negotiated the terms,
but Heather was supposed to make sure that the agreement covered everything.
Later, when the husband filed for bankruptcy, Rosemary learned that Heather had
missed—and the agreement therefore did not mention—a substantial joint debt;
because of the husband's bankruptcy, the wife was now on the hook. If the wife
sues, who is at fault—Rosemary or Heather? Assume the same facts except that
Heather *had* informed Rosemary of the joint debt and mentioned it in a memo
listing unresolved issues. Rosemary nevertheless left it out of the agreement. Is
Heather at risk?

In most cases the hiring lawyer will be liable to the client for any professional
negligence on the part of a contract lawyer. The hiring lawyer's liability is based
on theories of failure to supervise adequately and respondeat superior (vicarious
liability):

> *In contrast to . . . process servers, a temporary lawyer would arguably
> be considered an agent of the client attorney for liability purposes.
> Liability should attach to the client attorney just as it would in the case
> of errors committed by employed attorneys or office staff. See* Stinson v.

Brand, *738 S.W.2d 186 (Tenn. 1987). Of course, liability might [also] inure for failing to supervise those employees adequately. See* Gautam v. DeLuca, *521 A.2d 1343 (N.J. 1987).*[1]

In some jurisdictions, the hiring lawyer could also become liable for the negligent hiring of a contract lawyer. See *Duggins v. Guardianship of Washington,* 632 So.2d 420 (Miss. 1993), in which an attorney was found liable for the acts of counsel he had associated and relied upon as an expert.

The allocation of malpractice liability depends on the hiring lawyer-contract lawyer relationship. Many hiring lawyers assume that they will be at risk for the mistakes of their contract lawyers, and indeed, the more closely they work with or supervise the contract lawyers the safer this assumption is. Thus, if in the first example, Keith had given Caleb an outline of the issues, had spot-checked Caleb's research, and rewritten the work product to present the arguments more forcefully, Keith would likely bear the risk of malpractice liability.

Many contract lawyers also assume that for purposes of malpractice liability their acts will be attributed to the hiring lawyers—and in many cases this assumption will also be correct. If in the second example Heather worked only from facts that Rosemary provided, any liability would probably be Rosemary's. If, however, Heather was a bankruptcy expert whom Rosemary had retained, with the client's consent, to "bankruptcy-proof" the settlement, Heather would be the one in trouble. If Rosemary failed to obtain the client's approval and consent prior to retaining Heather, Rosemary could be liable to her client under the theory of negligent hiring. Heather could also be at risk to the client, even if not an "expert," if she worked independently of Rosemary, Rosemary relied on her to develop the factual side of the case and the client had approved the arrangement. In the variation on this example—in which Heather advised Rosemary of the missing debt but Rosemary denied it—Rosemary would blame Heather, in which case Heather would need legal representation even if she weren't ultimately responsible to the client.

Even a low-risk profile presents potential for exposure to a lawsuit. And as every practicing lawyer knows, being sued can be almost as damaging—both financially and psychologically—as being held responsible. As a result, both contract and hiring lawyers ought to be vigilant in determining the need for and availability of

---

1. From an edited excerpt of a presentation delivered by Thomas W. Wilson, a partner in the law firm of Wilson, Elser, Moskowitz, Edelman & Dicker in New York City, at the Spring 1992 National Legal Malpractice Conference sponsored by the American Bar Association's Standing Committee on Lawyers' Professional Liability.

individual coverage. The first step is to define the relationship and think about how it affects the level of risk for both lawyers.

IS THE CONTRACT LAWYER "ASSOCIATED WITH" THE HIRING LAWYER?

For conflicts purposes, both hiring and contract lawyers will need to decide whether the contract lawyer will be deemed "associated with" the hiring lawyer or firm. The ABA in Op. 88-356 (see Chapter 17) says that this is determined by "a functional analysis of the facts and circumstances involved in the relationship," a statement that by itself is not especially helpful. Op. 88-356 does suggest that if the parties present themselves to the public as belonging to the same firm, or "conduct themselves as a firm," they should be regarded as one, at least for purposes of ethics rules on conflicts of interest.

Similarly, a contract lawyer who looks like an associate of a hiring lawyer or firm—that is, one who works in an office on the firm's premises or is assigned work to help with general overflow rather than discrete projects—is less likely to be subject to individual malpractice liability than is a contract lawyer who works independently outside the firm structure.

EMPLOYEE OR INDEPENDENT CONTRACTOR?

The negligent acts of a contract lawyer paid as an employee by the hiring lawyer for IRS purposes will be attributed to the hiring lawyer. The work of one characterized as an independent contractor for IRS purposes will often be attributed to the hiring lawyer as well, unless the independent contractor acts as a consulting specialist, handles the work without any oversight by the hiring lawyer and the hiring lawyer obtains the client's consent to the relationship. Liability for the acts of a contract lawyer paid as an employee by a temporary placement agency would probably be analyzed like that of an independent contractor.

LEVEL OF RESPONSIBILITY—DEGREE OF SUPERVISION

If the contract lawyer does not work so closely with the hiring lawyer as to pass the "associated with" test, and looks more like an independent contractor than an employee, consider the amount of responsibility delegated to the contract lawyer. How crucial to the outcome of the case are the matters the contract lawyer has been asked to cover? Are briefs written by a contract lawyer signed and filed after only cursory review; are they superficially revised to conform to the firm's style; or are they restructured and rewritten to present the arguments differently? Does the hiring lawyer check the work product for missed arguments or misstated law? The more closely the hiring lawyer supervises and reviews the contract lawyer's work and the less responsibility the hiring lawyer delegates to the contract lawyer, the less concerned the hiring lawyer needs to be about whether the contract lawyer is independently insured. The acts of a contract lawyer who works under the supervision and control of a hiring lawyer are likely to be attributed to the hiring lawyer through the doctrine of vicarious liability. (The high level of supervision that can make a contract lawyer less likely to need separate coverage may also result in IRS classification of the lawyer as an employee. See Chapter 18.)

You might also analyze the liability exposure of contract lawyers by studying the Oregon system. The Oregon State Bar requires all active, licensed lawyers to carry insurance through the state's Professional Liability Fund (PLF), but it makes the "law clerk exemption" available to lawyers who do not engage in the private practice of law. That is, lawyers who do not (1) hold themselves out to clients as attorneys, (2) sign court papers or appear in court, (3) sign correspondence as attorneys or appear as attorneys on firm letterhead, and (4) whose work is supervised and reviewed by a PLF-covered attorney, can remain licensed members of the bar without purchasing insurance.

In fashioning the requirements for the law clerk exemption, the PLF intended to define a situation with minimum malpractice liability risk. Many successful Oregon contract lawyers have elected the law clerk exemption. They cannot represent any clients on their own, and must advise every hiring lawyer of their uninsured "law clerk" status. Contract lawyers who accept assignments with the same parameters are not likely to be held responsible to the client for their professional negligence.

HAS THE HIRING LAWYER OBTAINED THE CLIENT'S CONSENT TO USE CONTRACT LAWYERS?

A lawyer who hires an independent contractor with special expertise may also be exposed to liability for the independent contractor's work if the lawyer fails to obtain the client's consent.

> *The general rule seems to be that "except for delegation within the law firm, a lawyer does not have the inherent authority to associate outside counsel or to refer the client's representation. If the client's consent is not obtained for an association or referral, then vicarious liability is the rule." This rule is important because it suggests that if a firm retains a temporary attorney over whom it exerts no control in performing legal work on the matter in question, it faces vicarious liability for the temporary attorney's negligence when the client fails to consent to the use of the temporary attorney. In other words, unless there is client*

consent, the firm cannot avoid liability by arguing the temporary
attorney was an independent contractor.[2]

ASSESSING OTHER RISK FACTORS

If the nature of the relationship is such that the contract lawyer's acts may not
be attributed to the hiring lawyer for liability purposes, consider other factors
affecting malpractice risk and the need for coverage.

PRACTICE AREA
Certain practice areas are currently considered riskier than others.
Underwriters rate domestic relations, estate planning, probate and trust, personal
injury, real estate, commercial and environmental law as raising more concerns
about claims than other subject matters. The ABA's study of malpractice claims in
the mid-1980s showed that 25 percent of claims arose out of plaintiff's personal
injury representation. Real estate work accounted for another 23 percent of claims;
bankruptcy and collections for 11 percent; family law eight percent and estates and
probate seven percent. All other areas combined accounted for 26 percent of
claims.[3] The ABA cautions that these statistics may be misleading for a number of
reasons, in particular the lack of comparable statistics showing what proportion
of all legal activity was devoted to each practice area during the relevant period.
At a minimum, though, this information can help you assess the relative risk of your
practice area.

The carriers also want to assure that their insureds practice within their areas
of expertise. Handling too many subject matter areas at once—as one insurance
representative put it, attempting to be "all things to all people"—will place a law firm
or lawyer in a high risk category.

OFFICE PROCEDURES
According to ABA statistics, over 21 percent of malpractice claims arise from

---

2. "Two Alternative Ways Lawyers Can Practice Law: 'Temping' and 'Joint Venturing,'" George C. Rochas
    & Daniel B. Trinkle, *New Problems...Creative Solutions: Emerging Trends in Lawyers' Professional
    Liability,* ABA National Legal Malpractice Conference, September 17-19, 1997, quoting 1 R. Mallen & J.
    Smith, *Legal Malpractice* sec. 5.9 at 386 (4th ed. 1996).

3. ABA Standing Committee on Lawyers' Professional Liability, *Characteristics of Legal Malpractice:
    Report of the National Legal Malpractice Data Center* Table 1 (1989) (cited as *ABA Report*).

missed deadlines.[4] Meeting court deadlines, making proper service, and ensuring that all parties receive appropriate notice are some of the routine office tasks (often delegated to paralegals and secretaries) that, if neglected, give rise to these claims. Most contract lawyers do not take care of these "details"—and therefore should be at a low risk for liability resulting from those types of mistakes. If contract lawyers will be responsible for such tasks, the hiring lawyer should make certain the contract lawyer has his own coverage, or take steps to extend coverage under the firm's policy.

PROBLEM CLIENTS

Another common source of malpractice claims is choosing the wrong clients—or letting the wrong clients choose you.[5] The *ABA Desk Guide* notes failure to "qualify" clients as the number one malpractice trap. Contract lawyers have no control over the clients hiring lawyers accept, but they can control the role they assume in those cases. Working for lawyers who handle high-risk clients or cases is another reason for contract lawyers to obtain individual coverage and to confirm that the hiring lawyers are insured.

LEGAL RESEARCH

Contrary to the perception of many lawyers that legal research and writing is a "low-risk" function, the *ABA Report* cited failure to know or properly apply the law as a major source of malpractice claims, accounting for just under ten percent. The *ABA Desk Guide* lists "Inadequate Research and Investigation" as malpractice trap number five. A 1991 law review article[6] compiles reported decisions on whether lawyers' research efforts were "adequate" to avoid malpractice liability. In several cases, malpractice liability has been premised on inadequate legal research. It is not hard to imagine a situation—like the example involving Keith and Caleb—in which a contract lawyer misses an argument and the hiring lawyer does not catch the omission.

PERSONAL PROBLEMS

Alcoholism and drug abuse are major malpractice risk factors. According to the *ABA Desk Guide*, studies in California and Oregon have shown substance abuse is

---

4. ABA Standing Committee on Lawyers' Professional Liability, *The Lawyer's Desk Guide to Legal Malpractice* 21 (1992) (cited as *ABA Desk Guide*).

5. Ronald E. Mallen and Jeffrey M. Smith, *Legal Malpractice* (West 3d ed. 1989 & Supp. 1993).

6. Mark J. Newman, "Attorney Research Malpractice," 32 *Law Office Economics and Management* 85 (1991).

a factor in 60 percent of disciplinary proceedings (which are a fairly reliable malpractice indicator).

COMFORT LEVEL

Legal arguments aside, every lawyer should follow his or her own gut instincts. Do what feels right for you. If, as the hiring lawyer, you are certain that you are ultimately responsible and your insurance will cover any exposure, don't worry about whether your contract lawyer has separate coverage.

If you are a contract lawyer with no assets and no immediate prospect of accumulating a nest egg, you may be comfortable "going bare" because you have nothing to lose. You may also choose not to purchase coverage if it is common for lawyers practicing in your geographic area[7] or substantive area to be uninsured. On the other hand, if you enjoy using your judgment on cases, advising clients and arguing substantive motions, if you're practicing in a geographic area where most active lawyers have coverage, or if your tolerance for risk is low, you'll want to accept only assignments for which you know you have coverage.

MALPRACTICE COVERAGE

You're a contract lawyer who's concerned enough about your liability risk to want coverage. Or you're a hiring lawyer who uses contract lawyers and are worried about coverage for their acts. What do you do?

THE STATUS OF CONTRACT LAWYER COVERAGE AT THE END OF 1998

In 1995, we heard horror stories from both contract and hiring lawyers about their experiences getting coverage from insurance carriers. One hiring lawyer with an unblemished claims history had her limits reduced from $1,000,000 to $100,000 solely because she used "too many" contract lawyers—even though four out of five of the contract lawyers were separately insured. A solo practitioner who did contract work when her practice was young was offered affordable coverage that excluded claims stemming from her prior contract work, or a $6,300 premium for full coverage! Carriers told hiring lawyers that errors and omissions of contract lawyers would be covered only if they were categorized as "of counsel" to the firm.

---

7. Mid-1980s estimates of the number of lawyers without insurance in any locality ranged from 20 percent to 45 percent. Debra Cassens Moss, "Going Bare," *ABA Journal*, December 1987.

Things have changed in 1998. The state of coverage essentially boils down to this:

- *Hiring lawyers can easily obtain coverage for the work of the contract lawyers they hire.*
- *Contract lawyers can obtain individual coverage (including costs of defense) only if they work as employees of, or of counsel to, a hiring firm (or perhaps a placement agency) or, in some cases, are developing a solo practice.*

HIRING LAWYER COVERAGE

Hiring lawyers can usually obtain full coverage for claims arising out of the work of the contract lawyers they use. Coverage is specifically extended under some policies if the contract lawyer works as a temporary employee or "of counsel" to the firm, that is, working on a more or less permanent association with the firm on particular cases. Contract employees and "of counsel" lawyers are also individually covered for work performed for the insured law firm within the policy period.

Most insurance companies also cover errors and omissions of the "independent contractor" lawyers their insureds use "if the law firm becomes legally obligated to pay as a result of wrongful acts of the independent contractor."[8] This coverage is standard in some policies; in others, the law firm must request a special endorsement. Some carriers do not require the insured lawyer to notify them of the presence of a contract lawyer after the policy period has begun. If the association continues into the next policy year, a full premium will often be charged for continued coverage. The independent contractor is not individually insured unless mentioned by name in the policy, sometimes for an additional premium.

Other carriers will insure the work of a lawyer working on a project basis only if the firm informs the carrier of the contract lawyer's assistance on the project. If the lawyer's involvement is minimal, the carrier will extend coverage without additional charge. If the work is extensive (defined perhaps as more than 20 hours a month for a year), the carrier will assess an additional premium. In most cases, this coverage protects only the hiring entity, not the contract lawyer. In other words, the contract lawyer is still individually responsible for costs of defense and for liability.

A complication occurs when a contract lawyer working for a law firm is paid as an employee by a contract lawyer placement agency. The law firm cannot claim the contract lawyer as its employee, thereby extending coverage under that provision of

---

8. A quotation from the CNA interpretations of their standard policy.

its professional negligence policy. The contract lawyer is also not working as an independent contractor, as that term is defined by the IRS (see Chapter 18). In this situation, you must make certain that your policy covers, or request an endorsement from your insurance carrier for, liability stemming from the work of "temporary attorneys" or "contract staff," without regard to their status as employee or independent contractor.

At least one contract lawyer placement agency that pays its contract lawyers as employees has purchased supplemental errors and omissions coverage for the negligent acts of its employees. Jodi L. Nadler, co-founder of Law Pros Legal Placement Services, Inc. in New Jersey, says their E & O insurance covers liability for both their internal and external employees, based on the theory of respondeat superior. She requires her law firm customers to advise their malpractice carrier of their hiring of contract or temporary staff and to sign a contract that guarantees that the work of the contract lawyer will be supervised by the law firm.

"Regardless of the relationship, if the outside attorneys at issue are to be covered by a primary firm's carrier, the safest method is to name them on the primary policy," says Anne W. Hill of the Reciprocal Group.[9] Coverage for the acts of contract lawyers—whether temporary employees of the law firm, employees of the agency, or independent contractors—will then be spelled out in the policy.

CONTRACT LAWYER COVERAGE

Contract lawyers who work as employees of hiring lawyers are covered for their malpractice exposure as long as the hiring firm has satisfied the insurer's requirements. Some contract lawyers receive coverage from the placement agencies that pay them as employees. A contract lawyer can obtain individual coverage outside of the employee (or "of counsel" relationship) only if his or her contract work merely supplements the development of a solo practice. As examples, Corregis covers its insured sole practitioners for all claims; Reliance National specifically excludes from coverage any independent contractor assignments.

None of the insurance companies currently write policies for lawyers who work only for other lawyers on an independent contractor basis. Their reasoning is this: Since contract lawyers generally do not control the progress of the matters on which they work, there is no way to assess the risk. By extending coverage to the contract lawyer, the insurance company would expose itself to the bad practice

---

9. "Understanding Risk in the Brave New World of Lawyers for Hire: Vicarious Liability and Malpractice Insurance," *New Problems...Creative Solutions: Emerging Trends in Lawyers' Professional Liability,* Fall 1997, ABA National Legal Malpractice Conference, September 17-19, 1997.

habits of uninsured practitioners who use the contract lawyers' services. (One representative suspected, however, that if there had been any claims involving the work of independent contractors, most policies would specifically exclude the arrangement from coverage.)

Another representative stated that his company "underwrites the culture of a law firm," specifically one that operates as a "cohesive unit over time." The carriers assume that lawyers who resort to contract assistance are either of poor quality or so overextended they cannot provide the oversight necessary to assure adequate work product. The hiring of a contract lawyer supposedly detracts from cohesiveness and is thus undesirable.

Other concerns include:

- *the difficulty with conflicts checks in multi-party cases when the contract lawyer has previously worked for a large law firm or a firm with a large number of individual clients (even though associates and partners of large law firms seem to be able to move freely among law firms without being subject to the same concern);*
- *the potential for misrepresentation when one lawyer uses contract lawyers to appear to the public to be a full-service law firm;.*
- *the possibility of unintended exposure under claims-made policies for the work of a contract lawyer completed prior to his relationship with the current firm.*

The reluctance expressed by most of the carriers, however, reflected a bias against lawyers practicing without fully-staffed offices, and a negative stereotype of lawyers who choose to hire contract lawyers. One account executive expressed the belief that most contract lawyers are either new admittees seeking work from established practitioners at paralegal rates or experienced practitioners who believe "other things are more important than practicing law." Another stated that contract lawyers who work on short-term assignments with a variety of different law firms aren't likely to be conscientious because, unlike associates in law firms, they don't risk the wrath of a senior partner if they do a bad job. Similarly, insurance company representatives expressed the belief that contract lawyers don't have the level of interest and fear that drives lawyers who are ultimately responsible to clients.

Others expressed concerns that contract lawyers are less dedicated and focused; they won't maintain adequate conflicts checking or tickler systems; and because they work without clerical assistance, they don't have systems to assure deadlines are met. The fact that many work part-time is also seen as a negative:

Carriers are afraid part-time lawyers will be too distracted by another venture to pay adequate attention to their legal work and won't keep up with recent developments.

PROBLEMS WITH RATIONALES FOR DECLINING COVERAGE

These excuses for refusing coverage are not well reasoned. Carriers can ask contract lawyers the same questions they pose to other lawyers—for example, what conflicts-checking and tickler systems they have in place—and rate the risk based on their answers, just as they do with other practitioners. Concern about keeping up with legal developments should not be an issue in states with mandatory CLE requirements; in states without such requirements, the insurer could simply refuse coverage to lawyers who hadn't attended enough recent courses.

Insurers could inquire about outside interests and other ventures. Most contract lawyers we interviewed were not running businesses on the side. They were involved in the same activities as full-time practitioners: parenting, writing, art, travel, continuing education and sports. They either wanted to live more balanced lives than the current standard of practice permits, or were doing their best to earn a living in a tight job market.

Carriers' assumptions about the law firms and lawyers who delegate work to contract lawyers are also faulty. Partners in large law firms may supervise a dozen associates subject to high annual billable-hour requirements, but the carriers express no concern about supervision and control in those situations.

What is more, in today's fluid market the assumption of a cohesive law firm is questionable at best. Firms have never been less stable. According to a recent survey by the National Association for Law Placement, 43 percent of any associate class has departed within three years of joining the firm.[10] Do carriers exclude those lateral hires from coverage when they move to the next firm, or tell the firms that an infusion of laterals has destroyed their cohesiveness? Do they cancel policies when firms merge or experience high turnover? Do they refuse to extend coverage to spin-offs?

The notion that hiring lawyers present a high risk could not be farther from the truth. Lawyers with out-of-control practices seldom have the perspective, good sense, or cash flow to hire contract lawyers. With rare exceptions, only savvy lawyers with successful practices recognize the need for outside assistance and take the time to find it. Many of the lawyers we interviewed who relied on occasional or regular contract lawyer services are counted among the stars of their professional communities.

---

10. NALP Foundation for Research and Education, *Keeping the Keepers: Strategies for Associate Retention in Times of Attrition.*

We heard only two well-founded statements from carriers. One is the concern that insured contract lawyers working under the supervision of uninsured hiring lawyers would be unfair targets. The solution to this potential problem is to specifically exclude from coverage any claims stemming from a relationship with an uninsured lawyer, thus placing the onus on the contract lawyer to assure qualification for coverage. The second true statement is that most contract lawyers are working under another lawyer's direction and control, and wouldn't be liable for professional negligence anyway. This fact is now used to deny coverage, but it is equally persuasive as an argument to extend it, if only to offer contract lawyers some protection against the costs of defense.

ASSURING COVERAGE AS A CONTRACT LAWYER

The most important point for contract lawyers to remember is that minimal exposure to liability does not necessarily translate into minimal exposure to lawsuits, and that insurance companies pay out more in defense fees than they do in awards to claimants. Relying upon hold harmless agreements and coverage through the hiring lawyer's policy only works when the hiring lawyer is fully insured at the time you do the work and, when dealing with claims-made coverage, maintains the policy *into the future.*

Maureen Carden worked as a contract lawyer for several years while developing a guardianship and estate planning practice for low-income clients. Many of her assignments were referred through Quo Jure, a legal research and writing service in Northern California. She also accepted occasional assignments directly from hiring lawyers, including one lawyer who "stiffed" her for $1,000 in fees at the same time she became concerned about his out-of-control practice style. Even though there have been no claims from this work, her contract experiences have come back to haunt her. The only full coverage she can get costs her $6,300 annually. Other carriers have offered to insure her for a more reasonable premium only if they exclude all claims stemming from her work for Quo Jure and the problematic hiring lawyer.

We hope that as contract lawyer arrangements become more widely accepted, it will be easier for contract lawyers to obtain their own coverage—and for hiring lawyers to purchase extended coverage. In the meantime, most contract lawyers who seek coverage can secure it by describing themselves as sole practitioners. Those who do not purchase their own policies will have to rely on a combination of hold harmless agreements and extension of the hiring lawyer's coverage.

Insurance companies assess risk by looking at specific categories and expectations for office systems and practice areas. Any contract lawyer who decides to obtain coverage should therefore try to learn in advance what safeguards underwriters want to see and what types of practices are rated as high risk. For example, a carrier might refuse coverage to a solo practitioner without a full-time secretary or religiously-used computerized calendaring system.

Carriers also charge higher premiums to lawyers with high-risk practices, and for those who represent themselves as being able to handle any type of project in any subject area. A contract lawyer who handles projects in a high-risk subject like securities work should calculate precisely what percentage of his income derives from that work as opposed to lower-risk areas; small differences in ratios can translate into large differences in premiums. Those who have been holding themselves out as capable of accepting any and every assignment must narrow their focus and indicate limited expertise on their application. (Chapter 6 outlines the steps for defining your market. Chapter 8 explains why this approach makes good marketing sense as well.)

LOSS PREVENTION FOR THE CONTRACT LAWYER

Whether or not you've decided to purchase malpractice insurance, you don't want to be sued. Both insured and uninsured contract lawyers need to be vigilant about loss prevention.

First, screen hiring lawyers and their cases as you would any other paying clients. Don't be afraid to say "no" to lawyers whose practice styles or personalities make you uneasy. Decline assignments that trouble you ethically. Think long and hard about accepting a project when the hiring lawyer tells you this client previously hired and fired four other lawyers on the case. Stay plugged into your local legal community through bar and other activities, so you'll be aware of lawyers' reputations, especially for dealing fairly with contract lawyers.

Second, *be sure that every hiring lawyer carries malpractice insurance* and is a member in good standing of the state bar. Ask to see a copy of the hiring lawyer's liability insurance policy, specifically the portion that covers acts of independent contractor, temporary or contract lawyers. Look for any notification requirements and make sure the law firm follows through in contacting their insurance company. You may want to check for pending malpractice claims or disciplinary actions as well. If you suspect that all is not as it should be with a lawyer who wants to hire you, call the appropriate licensing authority for a status report. Be certain, as well, that you inform the hiring lawyer of your uninsured status.

Contract lawyers might also follow Oregon's law clerk exemption guidelines to structure a relationship in which the hiring lawyer assumes most of the risk, but they must be diligent in assuring that the hiring lawyer is insured and that the hiring lawyer's policy will cover them individually—that is, will pay costs of their defense as well as liability—for all claims stemming from their work for the hiring lawyer. (See discussion about carrier policies starting at page 229.) If the hiring lawyer's policy will not cover them individually, they should purchase their own coverage, if they can, or turn down assignments when they will be (1) minimally supervised by hiring lawyers, (2) responsible for meeting court deadlines or communicating status or developments to clients, or (3) responsible for proper and timely service. Contract lawyers should always obtain individual insurance coverage if they are retained as consulting lawyers because of their expertise in particular areas or are heavily involved in key strategy decisions. They should turn down assignments without a second thought if the hiring lawyer is "going bare" or not likely to remain insured well into the future.

Third, make it clear between you and the hiring lawyer who is responsible for what tasks. If you're expected to make a court or deposition appearance, *confirm in writing* the date, time and subject. If you're drafting a complaint, answer, motion to dismiss, reply memo, or anything else with a firm deadline, make sure that (1) you know when it must be filed and when the hiring lawyer must have it, and (2) the hiring lawyer understands his office is responsible for filing and service. Always send a written memo to the hiring lawyer noting deadlines and confirming responsibilities like service and filing. As a corollary, include clear language about indemnification in your retention agreement or letter

Fourth, take appropriate precautions the minute you suspect you should have said "no" to a particular lawyer or case assignment. Inform the hiring lawyer about conflicting statements or outright lies you've heard from the client. If you're concerned about legal arguments so weak they border on bad faith, tell the hiring lawyer how you see it—preferably in writing—and don't sign any pleadings. Once you've undertaken an assignment, you have a contractual obligation to complete it, but if you feel strongly about problems with the case you should convey your feelings to the hiring lawyer. If you're in the midst of a time-sensitive project, make certain that both your file and that of the hiring lawyer reflect your timely completion of the work, and don't accept further projects.

Sometimes the warning sign will be a delay in payment. A hiring lawyer who doesn't pay you may have problems in addition to cash flow—like substance abuse, alcoholism, or a messy divorce—that could lead to malpractice.

Fifth, always do a conscientious and thorough job, whether the assignment involves research into a murky area of the law or a routine appearance. Tell the hiring lawyer as soon as you know that you won't be able to do a complete job in the hours allotted to the project. Let him know immediately if the witness in the deposition you defended made a damaging statement.

Finally, apply rules for good client relations to your relations with hiring lawyers. Return telephone calls promptly, explain things clearly, both orally and in writing, and encourage realistic expectations.

LOSS PREVENTION FOR THE HIRING LAWYER

Your most important task is to choose contract lawyers with care. Conduct a personal interview whenever possible, ask for writing samples, check current references, or use an agency that does the screening for you. (Chapter 13 outlines a strategy for hiring.)

When hiring a contract lawyer with special expertise or one who you will minimally supervise, confirm that the contract lawyer is individually insured or that the agency has its own liability insurance that covers negligent placements of legal personnel (some E & O policies exclude "legal personnel"). If you both have coverage, review your policy for its treatment of "multiple coverage." To prevent being penalized by "multiple coverage" provisions, ask your carrier to exclude from your coverage primary liability for the negligence of the independent contractor lawyer (without removing coverage for your own negligent hiring or supervision).

Second, be aware of your insurance company's policy toward contract lawyers. Make certain you provide any required notification to the carrier before you give work to a contract lawyer. Consider formalizing an "of counsel" association if coverage will be extended only on that basis. When working with a contract lawyer who does not have his own coverage, make sure your office handles the high-risk parts of the project (timely filing and proper service, for example).

Conduct a thorough conflicts check before hiring the contract lawyer. If the contract lawyer works as an independent contractor, or is working as a contract lawyer in more than one firm, continually update your conflicts check and take screening precautions.

Notify your client of your intent to use a contract lawyer and obtain his or her consent and approval, preferably in writing. Notification and consent can be added to your standard retainer agreement. (See sample language in Chapter 14 at page 174.) If you're planning to use a contract lawyer with special expertise, however, you're better off getting specific consent to the arrangement. You can let your client know the benefit and perhaps pass along some cost savings.

Practice the same rules for good relations with your contract lawyer as you do with clients and staff. Remember that—as with attorney employees and non-attorney staff—the contract lawyer will do better work if he's treated with respect. Return his calls promptly. Make sure his bills are paid on time. Let him know if you think he's done a good job—and don't hesitate to question his conclusions if you have doubts about them. Keep him informed of developments in the case.

Be aware that faulty or inadequate research *can* result in malpractice liability. If you hire contract lawyers primarily for research and writing, spend time discussing the legal issues with them—the results of their research, the sources they consulted, additional angles to try. If you suspect that any conclusions reached by the contract lawyer are wrong, spend an hour or two checking them. Richard Kaplan of San Francisco truly believed a contract lawyer was mistaken about the law. Rather than simply follow his instincts or judge the contract lawyer incompetent, he checked the sources himself. In fact, the contract lawyer was right. But it's always possible that a contract lawyer has erred; checking his results will protect against your potential liability for failure adequately to supervise the contract lawyer.

If you are concerned that a contract lawyer has a personal problem that interferes with his functioning, take action. Switch to another lawyer. Don't entrust him with time-sensitive assignments. And try to help. If you don't know of an appropriate local organization, call the ABA Commission on Impaired Lawyers (312-988-5359) for the telephone number of the lawyer assistance program nearest you.

Every lawyer should avoid accepting problematic clients or cases, but we've all fallen into the trap. If you've taken on a bothersome client or one who looks like trouble, you may be tempted to delegate work in that client's case to a contract lawyer. Don't fall into that trap either. Doing anything that makes the client feel underserved could increase the likelihood the client will bring a claim.

CONCLUSION

In spite of murky issues and unenlightened insurance carriers, lawsuits and claims arising from the contract lawyer relationship are pretty much unheard of. Be cautious, but don't let uncertainty about ultimate liability—or difficulty finding the right insurance carrier or coverage—discourage you from working as a contract lawyer or with contract lawyers.

20

THE AGREEMENT

Follow the advice you give your clients: confirm your oral contracts in writing to assure a meeting of the minds. We provide a checklist of discussion points, as well as sample engagement letters and retention agreements to tailor to your needs and style.

Robert Thomas has seen contract lawyering from all sides. He founded a contract lawyer placement service in Seattle and administered it for four years; he obtained an associate position in the firm in which he is now a partner by accepting a contract assignment; now he works with other contract lawyers regularly. He has learned from his unique perspective to insist on a written memorial of the agreement whenever he begins a relationship or gives a new assignment.

A variety of misunderstandings may result when there is no written agreement. Here are a few examples:

- *Hubert, a hiring lawyer in Cincinnati, asked Penelope to do a "thorough job" on a legal research project. Hubert's unspoken standard of thoroughness would have taken about five hours to achieve. Penelope interpreted "thorough" to mean "reconstruct the history of this issue no matter how long it takes." After 35 hours, she presented a progress bill; Hubert was horrified. Hubert and Penelope negotiated a compromise fee of 50 percent, but will not work together again.*

- *Arnold, a contract lawyer in Philadelphia who maintained his own home office and worked simultaneously for several other lawyers, handled three big projects in succession for one firm. He submitted the bills, but the law firm delayed paying them, citing its concern that he might be considered an employee of the firm rather than an independent contractor. To get his bills paid, Arnold had to research and write a detailed memorandum supporting his status as an independent contractor.*

■ *Laureen, a hiring lawyer in Minneapolis, asked Philip to research the application of the Fair Credit Reporting Act to a specific set of facts. Philip spent two hours fruitlessly searching state and federal codes before concluding that the Act did not apply. Laureen had misspoken — she meant to refer to the Unfair Debt Collection Practices Act—but she did not recall misstating her reference. She blamed Philip for misunderstanding the assignment and refused to compensate him for the time spent researching the wrong issue.*

In a perfect world, a clearly written agreement would govern every assignment or long-term contract relationship, and every area of potential conflict or misunderstanding. In the real world of rush assignments, reluctance to "waste" time on details, and a naive denial that misunderstandings can and do occur, agreements are usually oral and often incomplete. We recommend that any agreement be confirmed in writing, but at a minimum, take the time to discuss all necessary terms.

DISCUSSION POINTS

RATES

Settle on the rate for this project or assignment. Establish at the beginning of the relationship whether the rate will vary depending upon the type of work or substantive area of law, timing or size of the project. Finally, discuss what costs are anticipated and decide which will be reimbursed. (Chapters 7 and 14 address the art and science of setting rates, from both the contract and hiring lawyers' perspectives.)

BILLING

Ascertain whether the hiring lawyer expects time sheets as well as bills, and agree on the time for submission of both. Will payment be made at completion of the project, at the end of each month or at some other interval? For any contingent fee arrangement or payment over time, make sure both parties understand and agree on the terms. Clarify that the hiring lawyer pays regardless of whether the client pays, unless the agreement is one for contingent payment. If fee splitting will be involved, confirm the client's consent within the agreement.

AVAILABILITY

Confirm that the contract lawyer is available to complete the project within the anticipated time frame. For a longer term assignment (filling in during family leave, for example, or until a new lateral hire can start work), agree on the number of hours per day or week that the contract lawyer will be available, as well as the duration of the assignment. If the project requires the exclusive attention of the contract lawyer for any period, the agreement should so state.

SCOPE OF ASSIGNMENT

Confirm that both parties understand the assignment by describing it fully, preferably in writing. For example, if the project is to draft a summary judgment motion, clarify whether the contract lawyer is also expected to draft supporting affidavits. If so, will he be working from the hiring lawyer's notes or talking directly to the witnesses? When the hiring lawyer asks for research on a subject, discuss whether she wants an immediate oral answer, a written memo within two days, or both. If a written memo is part of the assignment, should it be addressed to the hiring lawyer or the client? Make certain that the contract lawyer has access to any background information needed to complete the project.

TIME EXPECTATIONS

Raise the subject of any applicable deadlines, whether set by the court, the client or the hiring lawyer. Is a statute of limitations a concern? The hiring lawyer should specify how far in advance of a filing deadline he wants to review the work product, and whether he expects the contract lawyer to be available to make revisions or do additional research thereafter.

The hiring lawyer should also express his expectations about the time required for the project, either prescribing—"I'd like you to spend no more than two hours on this"—or asking, "How long do you think this project will take?" The contract lawyer cannot assume that silence on this subject means there are no expectations. If the hiring lawyer does not raise the subject, the contract lawyer *should*, saying, for example, "This looks like an eight-hour project to me. Does that sound about right?" Or, "I'll talk to you if it looks like it will take more than five hours."

RESPONSIBILITIES

Clarify overall whether the hiring lawyer will supervise or oversee the contract lawyer's work, or whether the hiring lawyer will rely on the contract lawyer's expertise in a specialty area. Then, define specific responsibilities. For example, if the contract lawyer is preparing a complaint, motion, response or other court paper, specify whose office will be responsible for copying, filing and service, and providing copies to the client. If the client is to review and comment on a document before it is finalized, specify whether the contract lawyer or hiring lawyer will be responsible for getting it to the client and responding to the client's comments.

TAX STATUS

No agreement is complete without addressing the issue of independent contractor versus employee status. The terms of the agreement will not be dispositive in the event of an IRS audit, but it helps if the agreement addresses and clarifies the nature of the relationship. (See Chapter 18 for a full discussion of the employee/independent contractor distinction.) If the contract lawyer is treated as an independent contractor, confirm he will pay his own taxes. If the contract lawyer is to work as a temporary employee, the hiring lawyer should provide a written contract that outlines the terms of the engagement.

MALPRACTICE INSURANCE AND INDEMNITY

Address both the malpractice liability and coverage questions. First, refer back to your agreement as to the split of responsibilities. Then ascertain insurance status for both parties. If the contract lawyer will be working under the supervision of the hiring lawyer, the hiring lawyer should agree to hold the contract lawyer harmless from any resulting claims and, if possible, arrange for the contract lawyer's work to be covered by the firm's professional negligence policy. If the contract lawyer is providing services in an area in which he claims expertise that the hiring lawyer does not have, the agreement should acknowledge that the contract lawyer has been hired because of his expertise, confirm that the hiring lawyer is not expected to check the work, and contain the contract lawyer's promise to hold the hiring lawyer harmless from any problems arising from his legal work.

If the hiring and contract lawyers are separately insured, read the policy language carefully to determine if there are any "other insurance" or "multiple coverage" clauses that could void coverage altogether. If there are, decide which insurance will be primary and notify the carriers.

See Chapter 19 for an in-depth look at these issues.

CONFLICTS

The hiring lawyer should disclose to the contract lawyer the names of all parties and potential parties *before* divulging client confidences. The agreement should confirm such disclosures and the absence of real or possible conflicts of interest. Both contract and hiring lawyers should confirm their intent to screen the contract lawyer from all other office matters. (An in-depth discussion of conflicts issues appears in Chapter 17.)

DISCLOSURE TO CLIENT

A contract lawyer working independently from the hiring lawyer should confirm in writing that the client has consented to the arrangement. The same applies if the contract lawyer will receive a percentage or division of the fees paid by or on behalf of the client.

GOOD STANDING

If this is the first time the parties have worked together, both should affirm their active licensed status. They may also want to ask about past or pending ethics or malpractice complaints.

COPYRIGHT

Copyright will be an issue whenever a document is prepared for distribution beyond filing in a specific case. In this situation, specify the holder of the copyright *in writing.* A contract lawyer who helps prepare materials for publication or inclusion in a CLE course should, at a minimum, receive acknowledgment or credit. In certain circumstances the contract lawyer should also be an official copyright holder. Copyright may also be an issue if the contract lawyer prepares a comprehensive memorandum, the distribution of which either or both parties would like to control.

CONTRACTUAL OBLIGATIONS

In general, when working with an independent contractor, each party is obligated to perform according to the terms of the contract. That is, the contract lawyer must complete the project or fulfill the time obligations specified.

If the contract lawyer performs according to agreement, the hiring lawyer is obligated to pay at the agreed rate, even if he is unhappy with the work. If the contract lawyer fails to deliver, the hiring lawyer can either refuse to pay or negotiate a fee adjustment, and then never call again. But whereas an employee can give a month's notice and leave at the end of that month regardless of what projects are left unfinished, a contract lawyer cannot walk off the job in the middle of a project he has contracted to complete. Similarly, if a hiring lawyer asks a contract lawyer to write an appeal brief, but a week before it's due he decides to write the brief himself, he'll still have to pay for the contract lawyer's time.

SAMPLE AGREEMENTS

It is important for every agreement to be complete; it is also important that the agreement reflect the personal styles of the parties, as well as relevant firm or corporate policies and concerns specific to the situation. We offer sample agreements, therefore, not as models for you to follow slavishly but as examples of different approaches, ranging from informal and friendly to formal and meticulous.[1] Use our checklist and consult our samples, but create your own agreement to meet the requirements of your situation.

ENGAGEMENT LETTER FROM HIRING LAWYER TO CONTRACT LAWYER

Donald Barton
1100 Pine Street
Vermillion, SD 57069

Re: Research Project

Dear Donald:

I am retaining you as an independent contractor to complete the following research for a total fee of $250 plus reimbursement for photocopying expense. I expect the project to take up to 6 hours. If you complete the research adequately in fewer hours, so much the better for you!

The research involves two parts. First, I'd like you to Shepardize the 15 cases listed on the attached sheet and provide me copies of any from our jurisdiction or that take the law a step further. Second, I'd like you to complete nationwide research on "of counsel" employment arrangements and non-equity partnership agreements with law firms. Please limit your research to articles and cases from 1985 to the present. I am not looking for arcane or esoteric interpretations of these terms, or for information about arrangements outside the United States. Please provide the original research only. I do not need, nor do I want, a memorandum summarizing or analyzing your findings.

As we discussed, I'd like your research by next Friday. I understand that you will be working on several other projects and will get the research to me sooner if you can. *Since this is a time-sensitive project, I will not compensate you for your time if the research is delivered late.* Thank you for your prompt attention to this project.

Very truly yours,

Andrea A. Litwak

---

1.   The July/August 1995 edition of *Law Practicement Management,* published by the ABA, also contains two sample retention agreements.

ENGAGEMENT LETTER FROM CONTRACT LAWYER TO HIRING LAWYER

Sarah Patterson, Attorney at Law
Schmidt, Patterson & Perkins
2100 Metropolitan Plaza
Newton, MA 02159

Re: *Best v. Elfstrom*

Dear Sarah:

This will confirm our agreement for me to perform legal services for your firm at the rate of $50 per hour. I will prepare a response to the plaintiff's motion to dismiss in the case of *Best v. Elfstrom*, including reviewing your file, performing all necessary legal research, drafting the memorandum in opposition, submitting a draft for your review and comment, and producing a final version incorporating your suggestions.

We anticipate the project will take me no longer than twelve hours to complete. I will discuss any additional time requirements with you before spending more than 12 hours on the project. I understand the memorandum must be filed and served by November 15. I will provide a draft for your review and comment no later than 5:00 p.m. on November 13, and will deliver the final version, in hard copy and on disk, to your office by 9:00 a.m. November 15. Your office will be responsible for finalizing, filing and serving the memorandum.

I will bill your office and provide time sheets within five days after completing the project; my payment terms are net ten days from billing date. You are responsible for my fees whether or not the client pays you. I absorb the cost of copying as a business expense, but if it is necessary to use Lexis or Westlaw I will bill your firm for those costs. I will obtain your prior authorization for any such costs in excess of $35. We do not anticipate that this assignment will require any extraordinary travel time or mileage.

I operate as an independent contractor with my own business, and therefore your firm should neither withhold nor pay on my behalf income tax, social security or any other payroll taxes. I understand that payment of taxes is my responsibility, and that I am not entitled to employee benefits or statutory mandates like workers' compensation or unemployment insurance.

I do not carry my own malpractice insurance. I understand that your firm's insurance will cover any work I do at your direction on behalf of your firm's clients.

You have disclosed to me all parties and potential parties to *Best v. Elfstrom*. I have checked my records and confirm that no conflict of interest prevents me from undertaking this assignment. Your firm agrees to ensure that I do not have access to files, documents or other information about firm clients other than Elfstrom.

If this letter is consistent with your understanding of the terms of our agreement, please sign a copy and return it to me. Please let me know immediately if you have a different understanding of any of the terms. Thank you for calling on me to help with this project. I look forward to working with you.

Very truly yours,

Carol Kramer

Agreed:

_____

Sarah Patterson

SAMPLE RETENTION AGREEMENT
(Independent Contractor Subject Matter Specialist)

This Agreement is entered into this 10th day of February, 1999, between Ralph Touchett ("Hiring Lawyer") and Isabel Osmond ("Contract Lawyer").

1. Hiring Lawyer retains Contract Lawyer to render legal services in the matter of the purchase by Goodwood & Stackpole (Clients) of the assets of Warburton, Inc. The work will consist of: research on general partnership law in California, New York and Delaware; review and amendment of the Goodwood & Stackpole partnership agreement; draft of the asset purchase agreement; review and comment on financing and security agreements; the coordination of revisions to all agreements; arranging for and attending closing; and any other drafting or review of documents necessary to conclude the transaction (together, the "Services").

2. Hiring Lawyer agrees to pay Contract Lawyer the sum of $1,500 cash, as a retainer, against which applicable costs expended and services rendered shall be charged.

3. Hiring Lawyer agrees to compensate Contract Lawyer for the Services at the rate of $80 per billable hour. This rate is effective through June 30, 1999, and may be increased thereafter with prior notice to Hiring Lawyer.

4. Hiring Lawyer agrees to reimburse Contract Lawyer for costs expended by Contract Lawyer specifically on behalf of Hiring Lawyer or Clients. Such costs may include, but shall not be limited to, long distance telephone charges, photocopying, long-distance fax, overnight delivery, computerized legal research up to $250, and parking. Contract Lawyer shall be responsible for costs associated with maintaining an office, travel to and from Hiring Lawyer's office, and other general costs of doing business.

5. The transaction closing is anticipated to take place on or before June 1, 1999, and Contract Lawyer agrees to be available until that date for as many hours as are required to perform the Services. In the event closing is delayed beyond June 1, this

Agreement will be modified to provide for continued performance of the Services by Contract Lawyer consistent with her continued availability.

6. Contract Lawyer agrees to submit time records to Hiring Lawyer at least once a week, and in any event to submit all current time records by the last working day of each calendar month. Contract Lawyer shall submit bills to Hiring Lawyer for Services every two weeks.

7. Payment of all bills shall be due within 14 days from the date of billing. Interest at the rate of twelve (12) percent per annum shall be charged on all accounts unpaid 14 days after the date of billing, computed from the date of billing. Statements paid in full in less than seven days shall receive a ten (10) percent discount.

8. It is agreed that because Contract Lawyer is an independent contractor, Hiring Lawyer has no obligation to provide worker's compensation, unemployment insurance coverage, or any other statutory employment benefits for Contract Lawyer. It shall be Contract Lawyer's responsibility to make required payments for FICA, FUTA, income tax withholding and other legally required payments, and to provide Hiring Lawyer with evidence of the same whenever requested.

9. Hiring Lawyer has disclosed to Contract Lawyer all parties involved in the matter for which Contract Lawyer will provide Services. Contract Lawyer has undertaken a conflicts check and has no conflict of interest or other ethical concern under applicable rules of professional conduct. While actively engaged in this matter, Contract Lawyer will neither undertake nor pursue any matter for Hiring Lawyer or any other client of Contract Lawyer that would create or be reasonably likely to create a conflict of interest.

10. Hiring Lawyer has disclosed to Clients that Contract Lawyer will be handling this matter and has obtained written consent to the arrangement from Clients.

11. The parties agree that Hiring Lawyer is relying upon Contract Lawyer as a subject matter expert. Contract Lawyer agrees to bear responsibility for legal services rendered to Clients and to indemnify and hold Hiring Lawyer harmless from any claim, loss or liability, including malpractice liability arising out of or related to any service, work product or action of Contract Lawyer. Contract Lawyer represents to Hiring Lawyer that she currently maintains malpractice insurance coverage with policy limits of $1,000,000.

11. If suit becomes necessary to collect unpaid fees, the prevailing party shall receive court costs and reasonable attorney's fees, to be paid by the losing party. If the matter is forwarded for collection, Hiring Lawyer agrees to pay all reasonable collection fees and costs in addition to the amounts due Contract Lawyer.

12. This Agreement constitutes the entire agreement between Contract Lawyer and Hiring Lawyer as to the above matter and there are no oral agreements or understandings that modify this Agreement. Any modification to this Agreement must be in writing and signed by the parties to be effective.

Hiring Lawyer   Contract Lawyer

_____   _____

Ralph Touchett   Isabel Osmond

SAMPLE RETENTION AGREEMENT
(Employee Relationship)

This Agreement is entered into this 10th day of February, 1999, between Ralph Touchett ("Hiring Lawyer") and Isabel Osmond ("Contract Lawyer").

1. Hiring Lawyer will employ Contract Lawyer on a temporary basis to assist in rendering legal services in the matter of the purchase by Goodwood & Stackpole of the assets of Warburton, Inc. This assistance will consist of: research on general partnership law in California, New York and Delaware; review and amendment of the Goodwood & Stackpole partnership agreement; draft of the asset purchase agreement; review and comment on financing and security agreements; the coordination of revisions to all agreements; arranging for and attending closing; and any other drafting or review of documents necessary to conclude the transaction (together, the "Services"). Contract Lawyer will perform all Services under the supervision and control of Hiring Lawyer.

2. The transaction closing is anticipated to take place on or before June 1, 1999, and Contract Lawyer agrees to be available until that date for as many hours as are required to perform the Services. In the event closing is delayed beyond June 1, this Agreement will be modified to provide for continued performance of the Services by Contract Lawyer consistent with her continued availability.

3. Hiring Lawyer agrees to compensate Contract Lawyer at the rate of $60 per billable hour. This rate is effective through June 30, 1999. Contract Lawyer agrees to maintain complete and accurate time records and to submit them weekly to Hiring Lawyer. Hiring Lawyer will issue to Contract Lawyer a paycheck for each week's time the Friday of the following week.

4. It is agreed that because Contract Lawyer is a temporary professional employee of Hiring Lawyer, Hiring Lawyer will be responsible for FICA, FUTA, income tax withholding, worker's compensation, unemployment insurance coverage, and any other legally required payments or statutory employment benefits for Contract Lawyer. Contract Lawyer will not, however, be entitled to any other benefits of permanent employment including, but not limited to, vacation pay, sick leave, overtime, health, life or disability insurance, or participation in any profit sharing or retirement programs.

5. Hiring Lawyer agrees to reimburse Contract Lawyer for costs incurred by Contract Lawyer specifically on behalf of Hiring Lawyer or Goodwood & Stackpole outside Hiring Lawyer's office. Such costs may include, but shall not be limited to, long distance telephone charges, photocopying, long-distance fax, overnight delivery, computerized legal research up to $250, parking and transportation.

6. Hiring Lawyer has disclosed to Contract Lawyer all parties involved in the matter for which Contract Lawyer will provide Services. Contract Lawyer has undertaken a conflicts check and has no conflict of interest or other ethical concern under applicable rules of professional conduct. While actively engaged by Hiring Lawyer, Contract Lawyer will neither undertake nor pursue any matter for Hiring Lawyer or any other client of Contract Lawyer that would create or be reasonably likely to create a conflict of interest.

7. Hiring Lawyer agrees to bear responsibility for legal services rendered by Contract Lawyer to Hiring Lawyer's clients and to indemnify and hold Contract Lawyer

harmless from any claim, loss or liability, including malpractice liability arising out of or related to any service, work product or action of Contract Lawyer. Hiring Lawyer represents that he has notified his malpractice insurance carrier of Contract Lawyer's work on this matter and warrants that coverage has been extended to Contract Lawyer for Services rendered pursuant to this Agreement as a temporary employee of the firm.

8. This Agreement constitutes the entire agreement between Contract Lawyer and Hiring Lawyer as to the above matter and there are no oral agreements or understandings that modify this Agreement. Any modification to this Agreement must be in writing and signed by the parties to be effective.

Hiring Lawyer   Contract Lawyer

_____   _____

Ralph Touchett   Isabel Osmond

OPTIONAL RETENTION AGREEMENT PROVISIONS

REPRESENTATIONS OF THE PARTIES

a. The parties warrant that the information they have provided to each other regarding their education, experience, malpractice insurance coverage, licensing status and other credentials is complete and accurate.

b. Contract Lawyer is not restricted by any agreement, law or regulation, or order, decree or ruling from performing the Services. Hiring Lawyer recognizes that Contract Lawyer is free to provide legal services to others during those hours that Contract Lawyer is not providing Services pursuant to this Agreement, provided such services do not create a conflict of interest with Contract Lawyer's Services for Hiring Lawyer.

STANDARDS AND GUIDELINES

a. Contract Lawyer will perform the Services diligently and in a competent manner using independent judgment and skill. Both parties will observe all applicable rules of professional conduct, including those related to privileged and confidential information of Hiring Lawyer and his clients.

b. Hiring Lawyer and Contract Lawyer agree to limit Contract Lawyer's access to confidential or privileged information possessed by Hiring Lawyer other than information related to the Services. Contract Lawyer will maintain on Hiring Lawyer's premises all such information duly received, and will remove such information from Hiring Lawyer's premises only with prior permission. Contract Lawyer agrees to return any such information (including all copies) immediately upon the earlier of request by Hiring Lawyer or completion of their use. Hiring Lawyer agrees to implement procedures and safeguards to screen Contract Lawyer from matters and clients other than those relating to the Services of this Agreement.

c. Contract Lawyer agrees to complete the Services within the guidelines provided by the Hiring Lawyer. Contract Lawyer will report the status of the Services to Hiring Lawyer on an as-needed basis, but not less than weekly.

21

CONTRACT LAWYER
PLACEMENT AGENCIES

*Throughout the book, we presume that most hiring and contract
lawyers will find each other and negotiate their contractual
arrangements directly. In many metropolitan areas, however,
contract lawyer placement agencies also serve those functions.
This chapter explores the practical and ethical issues triggered
by the involvement of an agency.*

Few realize that the entire temporary help industry is an invention of lawyers.
One day in 1948, two Minneapolis practitioners needed secretarial help to prepare a
legal brief. One lawyer, Elmer L. Winter, remembered a former secretary who had
married, then left the firm to have a baby. He called to ask if she would be willing to
work for a day or two. The woman agreed and the crisis was averted.

Later it occurred to Winter and his partner, Aaron Scheinfeld, that their experience
was not unusual. A check with friends in other industries and colleagues within the
law confirmed their hunch. The two founded a company to provide temporary clerical
help to business and industry. Thirty-five years later, that company—Manpower—
surpassed General Motors as the largest private employer in the United States.

Temporary lawyer placements evolved more recently. Even though lawyers
have shifted temporary assignments to other lawyers for decades through office
sharing and other arrangements, it wasn't until 1984 that the nation's first contract
lawyer placement agency was founded. When Janis Goldman's children were small,
several firms approached her to ask if she would help with their overload on a temporary basis. Later, she learned of colleagues reentering the profession who wanted
to work in the same way. In 1984, she started matchmaking in Washington, D.C.,
under the business name Lawyer's Lawyer.

Selling the concept to law firms was harder than selling it to the lawyers who wanted to practice that way. Many firms resisted the idea simply because it hadn't been tried before. Large firms thought Goldman wouldn't be able to provide the kind of lawyers they wanted—those of "high enough caliber." So her first placements were for solo practitioners who were going on maternity leave or vacation, or were just overworked. Eventually, Goldman placed ten temporaries with a spin-off from a large firm that had taken major clients but not much staff and didn't want to hire permanent associates prematurely. From there her business took off.

Goldman was the first to found a contract lawyer placement agency,[1] but others had the same idea at about the same time. Robert Webster founded the Lawsmiths in San Francisco in early 1985. Another agency opened its doors in Southern California later that year. Others followed in the next ten years; some flourishing, some not. By the mid-1990s, business for a select few appeared to be booming. For example, in 1994, New York City's Special Counsel claimed an international clientele and revenues exceeding $10 million when it was purchased by national temp agency, Accustaff.

The agency market only a few years later has exploded. Today Special Counsel, now the legal staffing subsidiary of Modis Professional Services, boasts 22 branch offices across the United States plus six in Great Britain. Every major legal market in the country supports at least two or three competing temporary placement companies that serve lawyers throughout the region. Most of the major players in office temporary staffing have joined the field—Interim, The Affiliates, Kelly Services—and they are aggressively marketing their contract lawyer placement capabilities. Legal headhunters have responded to the agencies, and their temp-to-perm arrangements, by offering temporary placements as well.

HOW AGENCIES WORK

Practices vary somewhat among agencies, but the operating theory is essentially the same. The agency gathers a list (also referred to as a "pool") of lawyers available for temporary or project work. Typically, the agency will screen the applicants by verifying law school graduation and bar admission, checking references and conducting personal interviews. Some agencies choose to represent only lawyers

---

1.   Many agencies refer to themselves as temporary lawyer placement agencies, temporary staffing services or legal staffing services. For the sake of consistency with the rest of this book, we apply the name "contract lawyer placement agency" to all businesses that place lawyers in temporary or project-based assignments with legal services providers.

with good law school credentials and some law firm experience. Others accept all résumés but find work for only a small percentage of the many lawyers who apply.

Most agencies concentrate on placements with in-house legal departments and law firms, although placements are also made with solo practitioners and government agencies. Lawyers (or law office administrators) call the agency to request a temporary placement when they need help—usually at the last minute! The agency reviews the hiring lawyer's requirements and searches its database for appropriate candidates. Typically, the agency provides the hiring lawyer with résumés from several candidates and the hiring lawyer makes the final selection. As Robert Webster, founder of California's The Lawsmiths, describes the process, "We tell law firms we are able to screen people about as well as they could on an initial pass if they were looking for associates, and we always expect the law firms to do their own [further] screening."

To receive payment, the contract lawyer submits to the agency time records that have been pre-approved by the hiring lawyer. Some agencies pay contract lawyers as independent contractors; an equal number pay them as employees; and still others will go either way, depending upon the circumstances. If an employee, the contract lawyer is paid on a regular schedule; contract lawyers paid as independent contractors often must wait to get their money until the agency is paid by the hiring lawyer.

The hiring lawyer pays the agency for its placement and screening services by paying more per hour to the agency than the agency pays the contract lawyer. The *Wall Street Journal* reported in September, 1994, that "Temporary agencies typically charge companies and law firms between $45 and $125 an hour for lawyers, depending on the city and the difficulty of the assignment; temps get roughly $30 to $100 an hour, with the remainder going to the agency." The *National Law Journal* reported that, as of July 1, 1996, agencies typically paid contract lawyers from $25 to $30 per hour at the "junior" level (that is, one to four years of experience) to as much as $90 per hour for a specialist. Hourly wages have stretched a bit more since then. Agencies now place more new law school graduates at the lowest rates ($18 to $25 per hour). Experienced contract lawyers with hot specialties—e.g., intellectual property, real estate, employment law—can command hourly rates exceeding $100.

The agency's markup may be a flat hourly figure (we've heard of rates as low as $5 per hour) or an added percentage of the total. Our off-the-record survey indicated typical surcharges of 25 to 100 percent; the lower the rate paid to the contract lawyer the higher the agency's percentage increase. Some agencies charge more if the search is an arduous one. When lawyers are easier to recruit, or the assignment is expected to last longer than a couple of months, the markup may be less.

THE STATE OF THE MARKET

What can you expect from a contract lawyer agency? When we wrote the first edition of this book in 1995, it was a buyer's market. All agency owners we talked to confirmed the ease of finding lawyers willing to sign on for contract assignments, and the challenge of persuading firms and businesses to hire contract lawyers. As a result, most agencies had more lawyers willing to take assignments than assignments ready for them to take.

Things have changed since then. As Allen Barteld, co-founder of Portland's The Associates, notes, "The contract lawyer market is very reflective of the permanent attorney market." With shortages of qualified associates across the country, agencies are having a harder time finding the kind of well-credentialed contract lawyers who flooded their offices a few years ago. Says Jodi Nadler, co-founder of Law Pros Legal Placement Services in New Jersey, "There are not as many available, flexible workers right now because we're operating so close to full employment." Placements have shifted as a result. Lawyers with solid, mid-sized to large law firm experience in intellectual property, real estate, employment law and other in-demand areas are rapidly scooped up and can almost name their price.

Unlike the permanent attorney market, however, temporary positions for new law school graduates have also shot from zero to sixty. Nadler places many entry-level lawyers in temporary positions with corporate legal departments, handling contract administration, compliance and regulatory matters. Other agencies have noticed an explosion in placements involving the review, analysis and coding of documents in complex lawsuits.

Most of the larger agencies report an increase in extensive project management assignments. Special Counsel put together a team of 500 lawyers and paralegals, located in two sites, to handle claims processing for one corporate client. David Gelbanski of Michigan's Contract Counsel predicts that the use of outside assistance in the discovery phase of document-intensive litigation will increase for the simple reason that it relieves law firms and corporate legal departments of the physical constraints of large-scale litigation management.

The majority of placements in law firms for experienced lawyers are litigation-related. Assignments might involve attendance at depositions taken by other defendants, legal research and writing, or other pre-trial preparation, in large, multi-party lawsuits. But while temporary assistance for litigation matters in law firms is now well-accepted, in-house law firm recruiters report continued resistance to contract lawyers among their transactional lawyers. The basis for their opposition is twofold: skepticism about contract lawyers' ability or willingness to work demanding hours, and concern about preserving the confidentiality of sensitive transactions if "outsiders" are involved.

In-house legal departments, on the other hand, have fully embraced the use of contract lawyers to handle the more run-of-the-mill aspects of major transactions: due diligence review, drafting purchase agreements and routine counsel within the corporation. By hiring contract lawyers for these matters, they save considerable money and allow their in-house and outside lawyers to concentrate on the more high-risk, high-impact work.

Although agencies no longer have to introduce many clients to the notion of staffing with contract lawyers, getting business in today's erratic economy can still be a challenge. For example, law firms responded late to the booming financial market, waiting until the 1997- 1998 season to increase their recruitment and hiring of permanent staff lawyers. The stock market drop in the summer of 1998 left some firms overstaffed, yet facing the influx of huge classes of associates in the Fall. Some contract lawyer agencies reported a slowing in demand for their services as a result.

A second challenge stems from the fact that, for the most part, the lawyers in agency pools do not match the impressive credentials of those they represented in the early 1990s, when hotshot associates from prestigious firms were laid off en masse. Today's experienced contract lawyers tend to be competent lawyers who did not fit into their prior practice arrangements. They may have been "riffed" from an in-house legal department, told they were not on partnership track, suffered a personality clash with a supervising partner, or hated the billable hour pressure, perhaps because of parenting responsibilities. At this point, they are either over-experienced for one of the many openings for associates with two to five years experience, or reluctant to commit blindly to another firm.

Mark Neumann, chief operating officer of Special Counsel, believes there's an assignment in his company for virtually any law school graduate who might apply. "Not every assignment needs a Harvard Law School graduate with big firm experience," he says, "and not every client wants to pay for one." Despite Neumann's attitude, licensed lawyers without impressive credentials or "in demand" experience would be well-advised to regard agencies as potentially attractive traps. Sign up with them but don't expect them to provide a magic answer to your employment difficulties.

WHERE AGENCIES OPERATE

In mid-1995, only a few of the largest legal markets—New York, Washington,

San Francisco, Los Angeles, Dallas and Houston—supported several thriving agencies. Most had none at all, or, like Seattle and Portland, Oregon, had seen agencies come and go.

By the end of 1998, agencies were thriving in mid-sized to large cities across the country. Seattle's legal market supported five agencies. Portland had three. This growth trend should continue. Pat Comeford, founder of The Esquire Group in Minneapolis, noticed two definite trends in the last half of 1998: employers had increased their use of contract lawyers and more were using agencies rather than handling the recruitment, screening and paperwork themselves. In the face of continued economic uncertainty, and the growing acceptance of temporary legal staffing, we expect the number, size and influence of agencies nationwide to multiply in the next ten years.

If several agencies compete for business in your area, you may be able to select from among them. Consider local custom, though. It is common for contract lawyers in the San Francisco Bay Area to sign up with, and for hiring lawyers to call, all agencies in that region. Agency placement personnel compete to match the right lawyer with the right assignment. If that's the case in your area, you could be at a disadvantage by limiting yourself to a single agency.

WHAT TO LOOK FOR IN AN AGENCY

If you have a choice of agencies, investigate all options before deciding to work with one. If you don't have a choice, evaluate the available agency according to the factors that follow.

REPUTATION

First and foremost, put your ear to the ground to learn how the agencies you're considering are perceived within your legal community. Are contract lawyers treated courteously, no matter what their chances of being placed by the company? Have hiring lawyers been satisfied with the quality, responsiveness and cost of the services they've received? It shouldn't take you long to root out the agencies you should avoid. When customers receive good service from a company, they tell one other person; if the service was bad, they tell ten.

EXPERIENCE OR EXPERTISE

How long has the agency been in business, and *how long has it been placing contract lawyers*—as opposed to placing paralegals and secretaries, or finding candidates for permanent positions? Like so many issues, this one cuts both ways. The agency with an established track record in contract lawyer placements may be more reliable; it's a known quantity. But the new one trying to break into the market may work harder to please. Ask for names of satisfied customers who will speak honestly of their experience with the agency. You're well-advised, however, to retain only agencies that concentrate on the legal market, whether they handle contract lawyer placements exclusively or offer a full range of temporary and permanent staffing services.

Who are the placement personnel? Most successful agencies are staffed by experienced lawyers who know the legal profession and communities in which they operate. A former practicing lawyer with experience in the same general area as that of the hiring lawyer will be able to understand the hiring lawyer's needs and identify the profile of the best contract lawyers to meet them. A lawyer who is well-connected in the community may have an easier time finding qualified contract lawyers for unusual assignments—those involving esoteric subject matters or requiring many lawyers immediately, for example.

Some agencies are run by lawyers with little practice experience or by non-lawyers with experience placing only paralegals and legal secretaries. How do they compare? It depends. Some non-lawyer placement personnel—mostly those who worked as paralegals or secretaries before entering the industry—can pick up enough knowledge of the practice of law to be quite effective. Former contract lawyer placement specialist Liz Elliot believes it may even be better to work with a non-lawyer. A temporary placement specialist, she explains, should not "muddy the waters by exercising independent professional judgment in controlling the selection." She does admit there is some advantage to having a law background. "When you're very busy making placements it's nice to have an opinion of a lawyer to be sure you know what the client is requesting in the more complicated assignments." Elliott developed a circle of consulting lawyers who helped her when she needed more information or was dealing with a placement in a an unusual area.

Lawyers with little or no practice experience can be problematic (confirming the axiom that a little knowledge can be dangerous). The inexperienced lawyer might be less likely to check with an expert in the field before recommending a placement. More important, a recent graduate is not likely to have the contacts or perspective that inspire trust in the legal community. For example, two new law school graduates started a company in St. Louis; it didn't survive because the lawyers lacked credibility. The same thing happened in Seattle when two young lawyers who had just moved from Baltimore tried to start an agency.

On the other hand, well-respected agencies in New York, Michigan and Oregon were founded when the owners were still law students. Legal know-how isn't the only factor to consider. Several agency owners note that matchmaking inclinations and exceptional communication skills, especially listening and asking the right questions, are equally important. Be careful, but don't be a snob. One of the pioneering agencies, The Lawsmiths, was co-founded by an engineer. His lack of a law degree does not appear to have hurt the business.

BUSINESS STRUCTURE AND FOCUS

There are three types of temporary placement organizations: placement agencies, employment services and job shops. You'll find *placement agencies* among contract lawyer staffing groups; they act as intermediaries between independent contractors (i.e., contract lawyers) and law firms or in-house legal departments that need work done. *Employment services* pay their temporary workers as employees; most paralegal and legal secretarial placement agencies are in this category, as are many of today's contract lawyer agencies. Some of these agencies may simply process payment for legal employers that find contract lawyers on their own but need the intervention of an agency to protect them from IRS claims. (See Chapter 18 on independent contractor versus employee status.) *Job shops* are hired to complete a project and use their employees to perform the work. Litigation service providers generally use this organizational structure as do contract lawyer placement agencies that have expanded into project management services.

Permanent placement agencies, also known as legal search firms or headhunters, may also place temporary lawyers. Some began offering this service several years ago when market forces—that is, law firm hiring freezes—forced them to diversify in order to stay afloat. These temporary placements were seen only as a sideline because the fees earned were so much lower. In addition, the lawyers represented by those agencies often considered temporary assignments beneath them, accepted the assignment reluctantly and showed their resentment on the job.

Today, headhunters who wish to meet the needs of their clientele—both individual lawyers and law firms—must arrange occasional contract relationships. Darnell Shuart, founder of Shuart & Associates, Inc. in New Orleans, was faced with this reality when two well-credentialed lawyers who had just moved to the area would only agree to be placed in one-year contract "trial" periods. Neither would commit to a permanent arrangement until they had the opportunity to get to know the city and the practice environment.

A permanent placement agency that also offers temporary assignments can provide more flexibility to the firm that is considering, but cannot commit to, a permanent hire. It also appeals to contract lawyers who hope to find permanent jobs. On the other hand, most agencies that concentrate on temporary placements will also arrange permanent placements if the need arises. And virtually all will waive or substantially reduce their permanent placement fee if the contract lawyer works at least three months before converting to permanent status.

Only two agencies nationwide—The Lawsmiths in San Francisco and Assigned Counsel in Philadelphia—devote themselves exclusively to temporary lawyer placements. The others add permanent placements, temporary secretarial and paralegal help, deposition summaries, court reporting and other litigation services, or career counseling and outplacement functions to the mix. Again, circumstances will determine which kind of agency works best. A company that also places paralegals may be able to put together a more cost-effective package for a hiring firm with a massive discovery project, for example. But many of these multi-purpose agencies started as paralegal and secretarial placement services and added contract lawyer placements only as an afterthought. In some cases, they don't really know what to do with the lawyers on their rosters.

RESTRICTIONS

Look for an agency that does not restrict the ability of contract and hiring lawyers to work with other agencies. Avoid as well any agency that requires payment of a fee when a contract lawyer and hiring lawyer, both registered with the agency, find each other on their own. Be aware that some agencies protect their contract lawyer pool by restricting the hiring lawyer from giving the name of any contract lawyer to another lawyer. The restriction might be described in the written agreement as follows:

> *The Company agrees not to provide the identity of any lawyer with whom the Company has had Agency contact to another provider of legal services interested in obtaining contract services from such lawyer, unless approved in advance by Agency.*

Almost all agencies will require that they be notified if a hiring lawyer and contract lawyer decide to work together again within a year of placement. This requirement guarantees the agencies continued per-hour surcharges on any future contract work and lets them assess their placement fee should the relationship become permanent. The notice provision for a hiring lawyer might read as follows:

> *The Company shall, within two business days after any communication with which Agency is not involved regarding subsequent contract*

services or other legal work by a lawyer with whom the Company
has had Agency contact, inform Agency of the substance of each
such communication.

The notice provision for the contract lawyer might read like this:

If Contract Lawyer is engaged by a Hiring Lawyer or if Contract Lawyer is
referred to a Hiring Lawyer but not immediately engaged, Contract Lawyer
agrees that within one year from the date on which Contract Lawyer was
first engaged or referred to the Hiring Lawyer, Contract Lawyer will not
accept an offer of permanent employment, or accept a temporary
engagement, from that Hiring Lawyer without notifying and working
through Agency under the terms of this agreement.

FINANCIAL CONSIDERATIONS

Agencies make their money by marking up the fees they pay contract lawyers.
High agency overhead—fancy offices and a large staff—means either that the hiring
lawyers pay higher rates, or that the contract lawyers are paid lower rates. More
modest operations can charge less. The Lawsmiths adds a flat surcharge to whatever
the contract lawyer requests as an hourly rate. Says Robert Webster, "One reason
we've been successful is that we keep our prices down and our overhead at an
absolute minimum."

Which is better for you? Low-overhead operations can afford to charge less for
the same quality lawyer. Support staff and a large office suite may mean greater
emphasis on customer service. But don't decide to use an agency based only on
impressive brochures or classy office accoutrements. A solid track record is the most
important consideration. Interview the owners, ask for references, and learn all you
can about the issues that concern you.

Financial soundness is also a concern. Paychecks from a Dallas agency
reportedly bounced on one occasion. Many agencies have gone out of business.
If the hiring lawyer pays the agency but the agency, for whatever reason, does not
pay the contract lawyer, all parties will be unhappy. If you're working with a new
agency, learn what you can about its financial wherewithal.

INDEPENDENT CONTRACTOR OR EMPLOYEE

Our survey in 1995 indicated that the majority of agencies paid contract lawyers
as independent contractors. By 1998, more treated them as employees. (See Chapter
18 for a discussion of the distinction between independent contractor and

employee.) No matter which preference your agency expresses, the hiring lawyer and the contract lawyer should discuss the issue and decide at the beginning of the assignment whether the contract lawyer will be treated as an independent contractor or an employee. If the agency treats its contract lawyers as employees, this issue has been decided for you. But not everyone agrees that making contract lawyers employees of the agency is appropriate in light of rules of ethics. (See discussion below.)

At least one agency that treats its lawyers and paralegals as employees of the company touts its "labor expertise" as a selling point. The agency has an employee manual; it hand delivers checks to contract lawyers on site and holds office lunches. Another agency that treats its contract lawyers as employees pays them for sick leave and vacation days after they've billed a certain number of hours. An additional advantage, offered by at least one agency, is supplemental malpractice insurance coverage for liability stemming from the contract lawyer's work.

ETHICS ISSUES

The impetus for many state and local ethics opinions on the subject of contract lawyers has come from agencies. Two ethics issues have special application to the agency situation: the prohibition on fee-splitting with non-lawyers and the need to preserve the contract lawyer's independent professional judgment.

While the Model Rules *restrict* lawyers' ability to divide fees with other lawyers not at their firm, they *prohibit* the sharing of fees with non-lawyers. Courts and ethics committees have dealt with the fee-splitting issue in the agency context in two ways. ABA Op. 88-356 concludes that the typical agency arrangement "does not involve the sharing of legal fees by a lawyer with a non-lawyer in violation of Rule 5.4." The reason is that the fees paid to the lawyer are compensation for legal services, while the fees paid to the agency are compensation "for locating, recruiting, screening and providing the temporary lawyer for the law firm." Ethics committees in New York City, New Jersey and North Carolina have adopted this approach. (See Appendix 3.)

The second approach is to require that the client pay the agency and the temporary lawyer separately. Kentucky in *Oliver v. Board of Governors*, 779 S.W.2d 212 (Ky. 1989), prescribes this separation of fees, as does Connecticut. A California opinion advises that the agencies should not be paid a percentage of the fees collected from the client. (See Appendix 3.) Some California agencies believe this restriction means hiring lawyers must pay the agency and the contract lawyer with separate checks.

Note that many ethics opinions assume that non-lawyers own or control the agency. (In Florida, however, non-lawyers may be prohibited from ownership in agencies placing lawyers. See Appendix 3.) Presumably if licensed lawyers own and operate the agency, concerns about fee-splitting would be limited to those restricting division of fees among lawyers not in the same firm. (Those rules—fully discussed in Chapter 17—require prior notice to and consent of the law firm's client.) Be aware of your state's ethics rules and opinions and assure yourself that any arrangement you enter into with an agency does not violate fee-splitting prohibitions.

Concern with preserving the lawyer's professional independence is the source of the prohibition against division of fees with non-lawyers. ABA Op. 88-356 rejects the idea that an agency would be likely to exert influence on a contract lawyer's work for a hiring lawyer. Nevertheless, the opinion says that any agreement between an agency and a contract lawyer "should make clear in explicit legal terms that the agency will not exercise any control or influence over the exercise of professional judgment by the lawyer, including limiting or extending the amount of time the lawyer spends on work for the clients of the employing firm." The opinion further recommends that the hiring lawyer make certain the contract lawyer receives compensation that "is adequate to satisfy the firm that it may expect the work to be performed competently for the firm's clients." Several state and local ethics opinions—California, New Jersey, North and South Carolina—deal with the specter of influence by non-lawyers (i.e., agencies) similarly, by simply stating that agencies should not influence the contract lawyer's professional judgment.

What happens when an agency pays the contract lawyer as an employee—a status that implies supervision and control—while at the same time stating that it will not interfere with the exercise of the contract lawyer's professional judgment? Some agency owners believe that treating contract lawyers as employees can give rise to this and other ethical dilemmas. Rule 5.4(d) prohibits lawyers from practicing "with or in the form of a professional association authorized to practice law for a profit" if a non-lawyer is an owner, officer or director. An agency that treats the lawyers it places as employees might be considered an association that practices law for profit (usually a question of state law). Thus both agencies and contract lawyers would run afoul of the Rule if non-lawyers were owners, officers or directors. The response of agencies that *do* treat contract lawyers as employees might be that they are not in the business of practicing law.

Another concern is that, whether or not the agency is owned and operated by lawyers, treating contract lawyers as employees of agencies would create daunting problems in the area of protecting client confidences and avoiding conflicts of interest. For example, if the agency has placed contract lawyer Jolene with firm Black & White, which represents a corporate defendant in a products liability case, can it also place contract lawyer Rex with firm Smith & Jones, which represents a former employee suing the same corporation for discrimination?[2] What if the agency places its employees, Jolene and Rex, on either side of the products liability case? Has the agency created a conflict of interest? Will each contract lawyer's work product be protected from discovery by the other side? All of these concerns have been raised by agencies that pay their contract lawyers only as independent contractors.

As far as we know, no lawsuits, claims or bar association complaints based on employee status have materialized. But this does not mean the concerns are frivolous. Given the lack of clear guidelines or decisions on the subject, the most we can do is advise caution. If you work with an agency that treats contract lawyers as employees, ask for the agency's research and assure yourself that the arrangement does not violate applicable ethics rules or rulings. And stay tuned for future pronouncements by the ABA or your state ethics committee.

One last ethical consideration is the possibility of a conflict of interest when an experienced contract lawyer takes on an assignment from a law firm. Most agencies simply caution the hiring and contract lawyers that they need to conduct a conflicts check. Some agencies, though, coordinate the check themselves. As a precaution, though, hiring and contract lawyers should conduct their own conflicts reviews no matter what service the agency offers.

MALPRACTICE COVERAGE

Every agency is aware of the malpractice insurance coverage issue and either offers guidance to hiring and contract lawyers or discusses the issue with them. (See Chapter 19 for a complete discussion of malpractice issues.) No agency requires the lawyers it places to maintain their own professional negligence coverage. All discuss the issue with hiring lawyers before placement, often advising them how to obtain temporary coverage through their existing policies.

At least one agency owner, however, has found malpractice coverage to be a non-issue. When Susan Etheridge first opened Professional Placement Services, Inc. in Florida, hiring lawyers would demand that her agency provide malpractice insurance coverage for the contract lawyers it represented. She tried to obtain such coverage but was told by the insurance carriers, time and time again, that the firms' policies already provided coverage. She'd then ask the hiring lawyers to check with their own carriers. At that point, their demands would evaporate.

2.　At least one state ethics opinion (South Carolina Advisory Opinion 91-09) sees no conflict of interest problem in this hypothetical situation.

Most contract lawyer placement agencies operate with errors and omissions insurance that protects hiring lawyers from negligent placement of a contract lawyer within their office. These policies offer some comfort to hiring lawyers who ask agencies to find subject matter specialists to handle assignments without supervision. The hiring lawyer can seek indemnification from the agency for negligent placement and actually have some assurance of funds available to pay the claim. (The contract lawyer, on the other hand, will only be protected if he or she is still employed by the agency when the claim is made.) In actuality, however, these policies are mostly superfluous. The vast majority of agency placements are made with the requirement that the contract lawyer's work be supervised by the hiring lawyer.

Law Pros Legal Placement Services, Inc. in New Jersey is the only agency we discovered that has negotiated an insurance policy that covers the errors and omissions of both its in-house and external (i.e. contract lawyer) employees. This is great news for contract lawyers, who can find it almost impossible to obtain their own insurance protection. (See Chapter 19.) There is one caveat, however, for hiring lawyers: Law Pros only works with hiring lawyers who agree to supervise the work of contract lawyers and to acknowledge that the firm's insurance policy has primary coverage for professional negligence.

TYPICAL AGENCY ASSIGNMENTS

The majority of agency assignments are long-term (three months to a year), full-time, on-site placements with either a law firm or an in-house legal department. Increasingly these days, contract lawyers work in teams managed by someone from the agency, not a member of the law firm or corporate legal department. There are variations, however. An agency might connect a true independent contractor lawyer with a firm needing assistance with only one 10- to 15-hour research project, or several out-of-town depositions, in the hopes that an ongoing, agency-monitored relationship between contract lawyer and hiring lawyer would develop.

Remember, though, that agencies handle many types of assignments. Nancy Mitchell closed her solo practice in Jacksonville, Florida and moved to Tampa for personal and family reasons. Being in her late 40s, she found it hard to find work until she contacted Susan Etheridge of Professional Placement Services, Inc. Susan had received a frantic call from a young solo practitioner who'd lost the lead attorney he'd contracted with to handle a major piece of litigation. With the trial only eight weeks away, he desperately needed an experienced litigator who could run with the case. Nancy was selected to save the day, which she did with aplomb, winning a verdict of $1.8 million.

CONCERNS FOR HIRING LAWYERS

You're in the driver's seat; the market is biased in your favor. Use this advantage to ensure that the agency does the best possible job for you.

INTAKE
The agency should conduct a thorough interview to learn your needs, covering:

- *The scope of the contract services to be provided;*
- *The work product expected;*
- *Where you'd like the contract lawyer to work and what kind of support services you expect to provide;*
- *The approximate time frame for completing the contract services, including any deadlines;*
- *Whether you'd like a candidate appropriate for a permanent position if the placement works out;*
- *The responsibility for malpractice insurance coverage, if any;*
- *How weekly work-hour summaries will be handled and who will be responsible for review and approval; and*
- *What out-of-pocket expenses you expect the contract lawyer to incur.*

Consider also whether you are asked about ethical considerations relating to the contract services, including disclosure of potential conflicts of interests and protection of confidences. Confirm that the written agreement clearly explains the agency's procedures and financial terms.

PRESCREENING
Verify that the agency thoroughly screens all contract lawyers before placement. Thorough screening includes checking references, confirming law school graduation and bar admission, investigating disciplinary complaints, reviewing work product and conducting in-person interviews.

SIZE AND QUALITY OF POOL
Some agencies prescreen a relatively small pool of lawyers, but maintain a database of hundreds of lawyers. The advantage of such a system is that, for most matters, the agency can place its screened members quickly; for an unusual request, the agency has an extensive database from which to search for a lawyer with suitable qualifications.

GUARANTEES

Every agency we contacted either guarantees its placements (either by not charging for an unacceptable placement and finding a replacement, or by adjusting fees) or follows them up to confirm suitability and quality. But who knows—the agency you're talking to may have changed its policy or may respond inconsistently to complaints. Arco's Jess Womack discovered that "a lot of agencies place the contract lawyers and tell them they're on their own except for getting a paycheck from them. This can lead to problems with morale and work product." Ask the agency about its policy on follow-up and quality control, and look for an agency that works to ensure the satisfaction of both the contract lawyer and the hiring lawyer.

FINANCIAL ARRANGEMENT WITH HIRING LAWYER

Most agencies charge out the services of contract lawyers by the hour and submit bills to hiring lawyers weekly based on time sheets submitted by the contract lawyer and approved by the hiring lawyer. The fee charged the hiring lawyer, and the amount the contract lawyer gets paid, depend upon the experience of the contract lawyer and the nature of the assignment.

In addition, most agencies offer temp-to-perm arrangements. Terms for these placements are included in their written agreements. They generally credit their accrued temporary placement fees (that is, the agency's surcharge over the portion paid to the contract lawyer) against the permanent placement fee, or dispense with the necessity of paying a permanent placement fee altogether if the temporary placement lasts beyond a certain minimum time period.

Variations from these billing standards do occur. A few agencies bill bi-weekly, monthly or at the end of a project. Others will consider fixed-fee arrangements, assume all fees to be negotiable or set their fees by using a formula other than the experience of the contract lawyer and the nature of the assignment. In addition, some agencies require credit checks before placing a contract lawyer.

DISCOUNTS

If you contemplate hiring many lawyers over time, or you need an army right now for a megacase, ask about a volume discount.

CONFIDENTIALITY

No agency admitted to us that it discloses the names of its clients without their permission. But if secrecy is an issue for you, by all means ask about the agency's policy—and express your concerns.

CONCERNS FOR CONTRACT LAWYERS

SIZE AND QUALITY OF THE POOL

What is the nature of the pool? If the agency has restrictions in terms of years of practice or credentials, and you pass the test, fine. If the agency accepts all lawyers, try to learn whether it sees you as one who is likely to get work.

Whatever you do, don't inflate your credentials to satisfy a perceived standard. All but a few agencies require proof of law school graduation and bar admission before accepting a contract lawyer into their pool. Nearly all agencies check at least three references before adding a lawyer to the pool. One agency owner tells of a lawyer whom he would happily have accepted into his pool with her true credentials. Unfortunately, she had heard that his agency required "big firm" experience, so she added a job at a top San Francisco firm to her résumé. When he checked and found the firm had never heard of her, he eliminated her from consideration.

NATURE OF PLACEMENTS

Review the agencies profiled in Appendix 5 and you'll notice the wide range of placements they handle. Some tout "sophisticated" assignments or limit their placements to lawyers with significant experience; others concentrate more on large document review and due diligence projects and hire many new law school graduates.

Some placements for recent graduates actually constitute "high-end" paralegal work. David Galbenski of Contract Counsel encourages his law firm clients to pay the "few more dollars an hour" it costs to get the reliability of a new admittee for this type of work because quality can be an issue with those trained as legal assistants. At the same time, he encourages new graduates to take these temporary assignments, arguing that the typical graduate finds a first "job" six months after graduation. Why not earn good money doing document review until then?

Darnell Shuart of New Orlean's Shuart & Associates sees an additional advantage. She can cite four occasions in the last two years when new graduates accepted temporary positions handling paralegal duties but so impressed the firm with the quality of their work that they were offered permanent positions as lawyers shortly thereafter. Shuart says that new lawyers who are willing to "go out on a limb" cannot lose through these placements. You end up with experience to add to your résumé, another contact to use as a reference and the opportunity to prove yourself.

PLACEMENT RATE

How many placements does the agency typically make in a week? How many lawyers found work through the agency last month? What percentage of lawyers in the agency pool get placed in a year? How long is the typical assignment? The agency isn't likely to answer such questions, but you can always try.

U.S. News & World Report claimed in November 1993 that "the country's 140 or so executive-temp firms usually have a database of 5,000 to 10,000 names and place only 5 to 10 people a month." Contract lawyer placement agencies focusing on individual placements probably maintain smaller databases with comparable monthly placement rates. But those that staff large litigation or due diligence projects—either in-house or as outsourcers—may have hundreds or even thousands of lawyers employed at any one time.

STABILITY

How long has the agency been in business? Experience may not be an issue if it's the only agency in town, but ask anyway.

COMPENSATION

What will your hourly rate be? We talked to two agency owners who believe that contract lawyers should decide their own rates. This respect for the contract lawyer's professionalism is both unusual and commendable. Most agencies charge hiring lawyers substantially more for your time than they pay you. Ask what the agency's mark-up of your rate will be, but don't expect an answer: this information seems to be the most closely guarded secret in the business.

TAX STATUS

Will you be the agency's employee or an independent contractor? Many agencies pay contract lawyers exclusively as independent contractors. An equal number pay contract lawyers as employees so that all employer taxes are withheld and deposited; some even pay benefits. This designation has tax implications (see Chapter 18) and may have ethics ramifications as outlined above.

You're not likely to be kept in the dark about employee status. Those agencies that treat their contract lawyers as employees tout that advantage prominently in their promotion. The downside is that contract lawyers might be paid significantly less per hour than if they operated as independent contractors.

FREQUENCY OF PAYMENT

Agencies also vary in how they pay their contract lawyers. Those that consider contract lawyers to be employees tend to pay regularly (once a week, or once every two weeks, for example), regardless of when they are paid by the hiring lawyer.

Others pay their contract lawyers only after they have been paid by the hiring lawyers. This system usually goes hand in hand with independent contractor status. Also note that some agencies will pay you before they are paid—but then require that you reimburse them if the hiring lawyer defaults. This system may be more painful than one in which you are not paid until the hiring lawyer pays the agency.

TREATMENT

Some agencies treat the applicants they think they can place like aristocracy but give the brush-off to others. Liz Elliott believes that every agency ought to be courteous to all applicants. "I treated every applicant graciously and maintained their résumé in my file," says Elliott. "I never knew when I came in contact with a contract lawyer whether someday she might be a hiring lawyer, who would want me to find a contract lawyer for her." Allen Barteld of Portland's The Associates speaks with pride of his agency's policy of letting every applicant know up front his or her chances for placement.

PRIVACY CONCERNS

All but a few agencies will ask for your permission before sending out your résumé to a prospective hiring lawyer. Read their paperwork carefully. Those that ask for blanket permission to provide résumés to any prospective hiring lawyer will include that provision in their contract.

AGENCY ALTERNATIVES

In our research we came across several intriguing arrangements that, although not agencies, play a similar role: that is, they centralize the marketing function for contract lawyers, and the search function for hiring lawyers. Our research in this area was by no means exhaustive. You may find similar services in your locale on your own.

NONPROFIT REFERRAL SERVICE

In 1990, Oregon Women Lawyers started to maintain a list of lawyers available for contract work. Contract lawyers pay an annual $20 fee to be listed; the list is provided free to lawyers or firms seeking contract lawyers. A volunteer coordinator takes all calls and maintains the list. The coordinator does not screen contract lawyers or match lawyers up, although she will review the list and highlight appropriate candidates when specialized requests come in. The Referral Service can be reached at 503-228-0097.

Washington State followed suit in 1996 with its Washington Contract Attorneys' Group, a non-profit attorney cooperative. They publish a free directory of experienced attorneys available for temporary assignments in a wide variety of focus areas. They also meet for networking, education and discussion on the third Wednesday of every month in a conference room at the Washington State Bar Association. You can reach this organization at 206-224-4459.

Your city or town may have similar non-profit referral resources. If not, volunteer to get one off the ground.

INTERNET JOB POSTING SERVICES

The Internet offers dozens of sites that list job openings for lawyers. Most announce full-time, permanent positions, primarily those handled by legal recruiters and large law firms. You will, however, find some contract lawyer and temp-to-perm listings. The only sites that post openings specifically for contract positions are the well-respected Hieros Gamos Legal Employment Classifieds site at http://www.hg.org/temp-serv.html, and Emplawyernet at http://www.emplawyer-net.com, free to hiring lawyers and subscription-based for contract lawyers.

LEGAL RESEARCH SERVICES

Legal research services sell sophisticated research projects, mostly to corporations and law offices without sufficient staff or library resources to conduct their own in-depth studies. Fees are often project based, so the client knows beforehand exactly what the service will cost. Some large corporate clients are so impressed with the cost-effectiveness of this service that they now require their outside counsel to outsource all legal research to a particular firm, thus qualifying for discounted rates. Projects are frequently assigned to professors of law or experienced practitioners with expertise in a particular subject matter. The two best known services are Legal Research Center, Inc. (LRC), http://www.lrci.com, based in Minneapolis, and the National Legal Research Group Inc., http://www.nlrg.com, with offices in Charlottesville, Virginia and Chicago.

OUTSIDE GENERAL COUNSEL

In early 1985, around the same time that many agencies got started, Kent Larson went into the independent general counsel business in Minneapolis. At first he hired himself out to companies that were too small to need even one full-time in-house lawyer; he'd spend one day a week, or two days a week, or a few hours a week at their offices doing whatever needed to be done. As his business flourished, he hired other lawyers to serve the companies he couldn't fit into his schedule. Today his firm has eight lawyers, no office, and almost no overhead; it offers flexible schedules for all, legal work at bargain rates for its clients, and a decent income for both part-time and full-time lawyers.

Although the lawyers of The General Counsel, Ltd. are not "contract lawyers" as we define the term (see discussion of independent general counsel and part-time in-house counsel in Appendix 1 at page 274), and the firm is not an agency, there are similarities. By virtually eliminating overhead, the lawyers reduce their hourly rates to a fraction of what their conventional-firm colleagues charge. And they all participate in marketing the firm—under the direction of a contract marketing professional.

SOLE PRACTITIONERS

Many sole practitioners these days focus their marketing efforts as much on helping other lawyers as they do on developing their own lay clientele. The majority of the relationships develop through professional interaction—for example, renting office space in the same building, joining the same bar association committee or working together on a case or transaction. One contract lawyer agency owner admits that, even though several other agencies operate in his region, sole practitioners are really his prime competitors.

CONCLUSION

Agencies have legitimately sold the contract lawyer concept to untold numbers of law firms and corporations, and they are an excellent resource for contract lawyers working in the right places with the right credentials. But as Robert Webster observes, "much more than a majority of the contract work that goes on in the country is work that lawyers have found on their own, not through agencies." We definitely recommend that you contact the agencies in your area to see what they can do for you, but don't depend on them exclusively either to find work for yourself or to locate the perfect worker.

CONCLUSION

"The next ten years promise to be a time of massive risk and massive opportunities as the [legal] profession seeks a new paradigm," predicts Denver lawyer Ronald M. Martin in *Law Practice Management*. What might that "new paradigm" be? Just as the lawyers of the 1950s could not have anticipated the extent to which the AmLaw 100 would dominate the profession in the 1980s, and the lawyers of the 1980s did not suspect that technological advances would give solo practitioners and small firms the ability to compete with them in the 1990s, so today we have difficulty predicting precisely what shape law practice will take in the 21st Century.

It's easy to visualize the increasing involvement of technology in the practice of law: global teleconferencing for trials and hearings; motion practice through the Internet; negotiations by cell phone. But can you also imagine a future in which law firms concentrate on the pure practice of law and outsource all other roles, including practice development, to companies specializing in those functions? How about one in which firms consist only of rainmakers and rainmakers-in-training and assign all other legal services—research, writing, drafting, motion practice, trial preparation— to contract lawyers?

Developments outside the legal profession—like the dominance of Microsoft and Compaq over IBM, and Manpower's surpassing of General Motors as the largest employer in the United States—convince us that times are changing. And if we've learned any lesson from the past it is this: the strategies and techniques that are sensible in stable times become self-defeating in times of massive restructuring.

Rosabeth Moss Kanter contends in her book, *When Giants Learn to Dance*, that today's *worker*—read that, *lawyer, law firm* and *legal department*—can best assure a secure tomorrow by combining the "skill of the professional [with] the innovation of the entrepreneur." Contract lawyering does just that. It allows individual practitioners and law firms of all sizes to compete effectively in the new business climate. It enables firms to stay smaller and more flexible—to abandon the notion of a permanent staff (and the enormous overhead that supports it) capable of meeting any conceivable need. The *Connecticut Law Tribune* says, "The advent of temporary lawyers could be as big a boon to lawyering as the invention of the computerized . . . research system."

Although many law firms and lawyers today enthusiastically embrace the contract lawyer concept, others are sadly reluctant. Some cling to the antiquated notion that only poor quality, uncommitted lawyers would practice law on a flexible, impermanent basis; the resistance of others has more to do with a stubborn attachment to routine and convention. To thrive in the next century, lawyers and law firms must move beyond those outdated attitudes and embrace the law practice of the future. Taking advantage of contract legal services—by either hiring or working as a contract lawyer—is a wise first step.

APPENDIX I

CONTRACT LAWYERING AS DISTINGUISHED FROM OTHER ARRANGEMENTS

What distinguishes a contract lawyer who specializes in family law from a "consulting attorney"? How can you tell a contract lawyer who works with in-house legal departments from an independent general counsel? When does a contract lawyer relationship cross the line into an "of counsel," part-time or staff attorney association? What are leased lawyers? Are lawyers who work for legal research services or litigation services providers in any of these categories? This appendix explores these distinctions.

CONSULTING LAWYERS

Consulting lawyers are subject-matter specialists hired by lawyers who do not have sufficient expertise in the area to be able to handle a matter according to ethical and professional standards. Consulting lawyers will review and guide the work of another lawyer without taking over the case. Their fees are guaranteed and paid by the hiring lawyer, even if ultimately billed to the client.

Consulting lawyers have long entered into contract lawyer arrangements. Lawyers without expertise in tax often retain solo practitioner Brenda Smith to handle the tax ramifications of issues that arise in litigation or transactions. She charges the same $125 per hour to the lawyers who hire her as a consultant as she does to her lay clients. Penny Roberts drafts qualified domestic relations orders for matrimonial lawyers. Mark Reeve handles the environmental aspects of large business transactions for the primary lawyers. Lee Archer accepts appellate assignments from lawyers who maintain the client relationship. Consulting lawyers with established downtown practices do not hold themselves out as contract lawyers; those with home or space-sharing offices often do. All of them, however, may be considered contract lawyers to the extent that they enter into arrangements with other lawyers to work on a temporary or irregular basis.

OF COUNSEL

An "of counsel" arrangement, according to ABA Opinion 90-357, is a close, regular, personal relationship between a lawyer and a law firm, other than as a partner or associate. In the ABA's view, the term "of counsel" applies to four categories: (1) retired lawyers, (2) former partners or associates who want flexibility, (3) specialists who will never make partner, and (4) lateral hires.

The "of counsel" label as applied to retired lawyers is the usage most widely associated with the term and one historically considered a designation of honor. When a retired or semi-retired partner of a law firm wants to remain available for consultation, to handle an occasional case or maintain a few loyal clients, the addition of the lawyer's name to the letterhead as "of counsel" gives the remaining lawyers the advantage of his continued association while recognizing the former partner's contribution to the firm's reputation.

The other three usages of the term evolved in the 1980s to cover lawyers who didn't fit the conventional "partner" or "associate" categories. The term "of counsel" reflected the realities of the law practice environment where fewer associates were asked to join the partnership; where specialties went in and out of vogue and profitability; where some valued partners wanted to get off the fast track; and where highly-experienced but independent practitioners sought both autonomy and the sophisticated support services of a full-spectrum law firm.

The second usage of the term refers to "a part-time practitioner who practices law in association with a firm but on a basis different from that of the mainstream lawyers in the firm." These are associates or partners—usually women—who might have left the firm if it had not adjusted their compensation and billable hour expectations. They work part-time or flexible hours, freed from the pressure to produce more and more billable hours, and from liability for expensive leases or real estate purchases and malpractice lawsuits.[1]

The third use of the term has been described as the "no-man's land" of large law firms. These are the senior associates who will never make partner because they aren't client-getters, but whose legal skills and experience the firm values enough to want to retain. These lawyers, called non-equity partners at some firms, are usually well compensated on a salaried basis.

The last usage designates a lawyer who is, in effect, a probationary partner-to-be—perhaps a lateral hire with too much experience to be called an associate. He may have his own book of business but not be ready to commit to partnership, or he may practice in a specialty area the firm needs, but not badly enough to make a partnership offer. Some are salaried; others work for a mix of their own and firm clients and divide fees according to some complex formula. The "courtship" nature of these relationships makes them somewhat akin to our contract lawyer definition.

---

1. A consideration of particular concern to lawyers whose spouses have substantial income or assets that could, especially in a community property state, be subject to attachment.

Law firms have expanded the "of counsel" designation to embrace relationships even more like those with contract lawyers. A firm will hire a lawyer who specializes in a practice area such as matrimonial law, estate planning and probate, or criminal defense, in which the firm wishes to provide service to existing clients, but for which it does not wish to solicit new clients. In some cases, the firm's existing client base generates a steady but part-time workload for the "of counsel" lawyer. Some prefer this reduced schedule; others may take on outside cases that don't conflict with the firm's business. In other situations, the "of counsel" lawyer is called upon only sporadically to handle work for the firm even though he or she has on-site office space. The financial arrangement may require the "of-counsel" lawyer to share a specified amount of the business brought to the firm in consideration for use of the firm resources. In most cases, the "of counsel" lawyer, like a contract lawyer, is paid an hourly fee to work for the firm's clients.

The "of counsel" designation properly defines a permanent contractual arrangement between a lawyer and one or more[2] law firms. The key difference between "of counsel" and contract lawyer arrangements is the expectation of continuing as opposed to intermittent, and close as opposed to casual, association. Indeed, ABA Formal Opinion 90-330 (the predecessor to Op. 90-357) states that a relationship involving only occasional collaborative efforts among otherwise unrelated lawyers or firms, and the relationship of an outside consultant, are not properly called "of counsel." The "of counsel" designation, according to Op. 90-357, ought be "confined to relationships that in fact involve frequent and continuing contacts, not merely an availability for occasional consultations." Someone who meets our definition of a contract lawyer should not ethically be represented as "of counsel" to a firm.[3]

The "of counsel"[4] relationship, because it is not "temporary or irregular," should be easy to distinguish from the contract lawyer

---

2. ABA Formal Opinion 90-357 suggests that two law firms may be the maximum number with which a lawyer can associate consistent with ethical responsibilities. "A lawyer can surely have a close, regular, personal relationship with more than two clients; and the Committee sees no reason why the same cannot be true with more than two law firms. There is, to be sure, some point at which the number of relationships would be too great for any of them to have the necessary qualities of closeness and regularity, and that number may not be much beyond two, but the controlling criterion is 'close and regular' relationships, not a particular number."

3. Some firms obtain malpractice coverage for contract lawyers by defining them as "of counsel" to the firm. See Chapter 19 at page 225. This characterization does not violate ethical standards because the carriers define the term more broadly.

4. For an in-depth study of the term "of counsel," read Harold G. Wren and Beverly J. Glascock, *The Of Counsel Agreement: A Guide for Law Firm & Practitioner* (ABA 1991).

relationship. In practice, however, the line separating the "temporary or irregular" relationship from one that is "close [and] regular" is not always easy to see.

A relationship may begin as contract and develop into "of counsel." One 12-lawyer firm began working with Carl Maginnes, a contract lawyer experienced in securities work. At first there was no formal affiliation; Maginnes was paid by the billable hour and worked out of his own office. As time passed and the association continued, Maginnes and the firm decided they wanted a more formal and integrated relationship. Maginnes is now "of counsel" to the firm. The firm provides him with an office and secretarial support, and his name appears on the firm's letterhead. His compensation is based in part on the work he actually performs (billable hours) and in part on the work he brings to the firm.

Confusion may also result when the hiring lawyer intends the relationship to be temporary but acts as if he considers the relationship long-term. As one example, three lawyers who share space regularly assign projects on an hourly basis to four other lawyers for whom they provide rudimentary office space. The four "contract" lawyers have made long-term commitments to the three "hiring lawyers," letting them know in advance about vacations or other changes in schedule. The three hiring lawyers like having regular help but are unwilling to make long-term promises; they consider their four assistants to be contract lawyers. The four contract lawyers think of themselves more as part-time

associates or "of counsel."

The roles may be reversed when the hiring lawyer assumes there is more permanence to the relationship than does the contract lawyer. June Kobashigawa agreed to handle overload two days per week for the law firm from which she had resigned as a partner. In the years since her resignation, she has also worked for several other practitioners, but she now deals exclusively with this firm and is paid $65 for every billable hour she works. Kobashigawa is comfortable with the arrangement for now, but has no long-term plans and considers herself a contract lawyer. The law firm, however, sees the association as "permanent," and shows her as "of counsel" in their Martindale-Hubbell listing.

INDEPENDENT GENERAL COUNSEL

Also known as part-time in-house counsel, this is another variation on the contract lawyer theme. These are private practitioners who contract with a number of corporations to provide in-house legal services on a less than full-time basis. They charge hourly rates that are much lower than those of comparable outside counsel, or a guaranteed monthly retainer, and work on-site at the corporations. Some of their clients maintain an in-house legal staff; others have no other inside lawyers. See discussion at the end of Chapter 21.

"Those who want to become independent general counsels look for a long-term relationship with a company, and are not primarily interested in working on a series of temporary assignments or on single projects," says Robert P. Bigelow in an October 1994 column for *Law Practice Management.* He adds, though, that they are open to temporary assignments "if they have extra time, or if a specific situation appeals to them."

Independent general counsel may resemble contract lawyers, but they are actually a hybrid between in-house counsel and law-firm or solo practitioners. The independent general counsel is hired directly by a client, even though the client representative may also be a lawyer, and the parties usually enter into their relationship with the expectation that it will be long-lasting.

PART-TIME LAWYERS

Technically, a part-time lawyer is an associate or partner of a law firm or other legal employer who works on a reduced schedule in exchange for less money. Compensation may be a percentage of a comparable full-time employee's salary—usually 70 percent to 80 percent of an average full-time billable hour commitment—or may be calculated on a per-hour basis. Most part-time lawyers receive statutory benefits of Social Security and Medicare match, unemployment insurance and workers' compensation coverage. They may also receive health insurance, subsidies for bar membership and CLE expenses, and participate in the firm's retirement plan. As associates, they are subject to the control of the employer and are covered by the firm's malpractice insurance policy. As partners, they may or may not have voting rights. "Indefinite part-time attorney employment typically represents an accommodation to a present employee who may not be available full time for a variety of reasons," notes Philadelphia lawyer Samuel Frederick.

To distinguish between a part-time lawyer and a contract lawyer, consider whether (1) the lawyer's relationship with the firm has been long-term and unbroken, (2) the reduced schedule arrangement is permanent, and (3) compensation is fixed. If so, the lawyer is considered part-time. If, instead, the arrangement is short-term, contingent and flexible, it's contract.

STAFF ATTORNEYS

These are full-time law firm employees who enter into a contract for payment at an hourly, monthly, or annual rate. They tend to be "second-tier applicants," with less impressive credentials than the lawyers who are hired as associates. Their salaries are lower than those of associates with the same level of experience. As employees, they receive full benefits and work straight 40-hour weeks doing legal research and writing or litigation support. They may be the first to be laid off in a down market. In the 1980s, some law firms referred to these positions as "contract" rather than "staff" attorneys because the lawyers worked pursuant to an annual contract setting forth salary and benefits, work hours, and a procedure for renewal or cancellation.

The position has little in common with what we call contract lawyers. Staff attorneys are regular full-time employees of their firms; there is nothing intermittent or contingent about their relationships. Because they are not seen as "in the running" for partnership, they may work more reasonable hours than associates do; their status also frees them from certain aspects of office politics.

Contract lawyers who work mostly on discrete projects for a variety of hiring lawyers have nothing in common with staff attorneys. Even those who accept long-term assignments do so with the understanding that their stay is temporary. They also retain their independence—the ability to refuse further work for reasons other than lack of time.

LEASED LAWYERS

Some in-house legal departments avoid hiring another permanent employee or contract lawyer by entering into leased lawyer agreements. They bring in-house an associate of outside counsel for a monthly fee calculated according to what the firm pays the lawyer, including benefits, overhead, and sometimes profit. The leased lawyer remains on the law firm's payroll and receives the same benefits as other employees of the firm. The corporation avoids the cost and complication of filling a full-time position and is assured of receiving quality through its pre-existing relationship with the law firm. The law firm cements ties with an existing client and ends up with an associate well-versed in the client's special needs. Only the leased lawyer feels the drawbacks. Although he may appreciate the opportunity to learn more about the client's operations, he may also feel warehoused, isolated, and at a disadvantage in the competition for partnership. Obviously, a leased lawyer is not a contract lawyer even if serving subject to a contract between the employer and the client.

LEGAL RESEARCH AND LITIGATION SERVICE PROVIDERS

Two other temporary legal services providers warrant mention here: legal research and litigation support businesses. No one would confuse either of these service providers with contract lawyers, but some might want to characterize the lawyers who work for these services as contract lawyers. They are not.

LEGAL RESEARCH SERVICES

These service providers contract with law firms to produce memoranda on requested points of law. The research may or may not be generated by lawyers; sometimes a computer-research specialist or law student performs the services. Legal research services operate in many cities and regions across the country. Dov Seidman, owner of Legal Research Network, claims that doing legal research for other lawyers doesn't constitute the practice of law because the giving of advice is not involved. If he is correct, lawyers who work with legal research services are not practicing law and therefore are not contract lawyers. Even if Seidman's claim is wrong, however, they still don't fall within our definition of contract lawyer because they sell their services to the legal research service, not directly to other lawyers. More information about legal research services is contained at the end of Chapter 21.

LITIGATION SUPPORT SERVICES

Litigation support includes computerized document retrieval, organization and indexing; deposition summaries and indexes; and services such as video presentations, courtroom animation, model and mock-up construction, jury consulting, forensic accounting, asset location, billing oversight and case evaluation. Licensed attorneys may be hired to provide document organization and deposition services, but they are not practicing law because the services require only paraprofessional training.

APPENDIX 2

SETTING UP YOUR OFFICE

This appendix is for those who—as contract lawyers—plan to develop a contract practice for at least the next year or two. It is not intended for those who seek contract work until they obtain permanent employment, or those who intend to solicit only long-term, on-site assignments. If you're among the latter two, you won't need a fully-equipped office to perform your duties. (Keep in mind, though, that short-term solutions can turn into long-term career choices, and that you may experience gaps between on-site assignments, if you find them at all. You may want to revisit this discussion in a few months.)

Lee Archer, who once clerked for the Louisiana State Supreme Court, spent six years practicing in law firms before deciding to be her own boss. In 1992, she started her appellate practice in New Orleans by procuring contract assignments from other lawyers. Since then Archer has outfitted herself with both laptop and desktop computers, two laser printers, a scanner and fax/modem, accounting software, a photocopy machine and a serious CD-ROM library that includes state statutes and reporters, the USCA and some books, as well as access to Westlaw. What about the downtown office? Not for Lee. Her headquarters consists of two "cushy" rooms in her "big old southern Greek Revival house."

In the pages that follow we'll summarize what Archer and her counterparts did to establish their home offices, and what you can do to launch your own contract law business.

SELECTING A SITE

To begin, you need an appropriate work space, whether in the offices of your former colleagues, in your own home or in a rented space. The location will depend on three factors: your long-term goals, your financial resources and your reasons for taking on contract assignments.

THE HOME OFFICE

Working from home is a popular choice among contract lawyers. You can't beat the rent or convenience. Parents who don't want to put small children in full-time daycare, or who want to be around when the kids get home from school, can afford this option. Other candidates include those developing non-law careers, writing the great American screenplay or returning to school for a degree in psychology.

If possible, locate your home office in a room dedicated entirely to that purpose. (Note: Before you set up your home office, check all applicable zoning regulations.) Be creative if you don't have the luxury of a dedicated space. Contract lawyers establish their "headquarters" in unused entry halls, sun porches, back bedrooms, basements, even walk-in closets. Maybe your guest bedroom has space for a desk and file cabinet. Wherever it is, look for an area you can devote exclusively to work.

THE OFFICE SHARE OPTION

If, on the other hand, you plan to start a solo practice, or do contract work full-time, a "real" office is a better choice. Elizabeth Bottman's contract practice "really took off" when she moved into a downtown office. Denise Kuhlman has noticed that contract lawyers who set themselves up as solo practitioners are able to charge more per hour than those who don't.

A common arrangement is to share space with one or more solo practitioners, or with a law firm that has an extra office. Such arrangements are often inexpensive, and can include receptionist services, use of conference room and law library, and access to photocopy and fax machines, coffee makers and even kitchens. (Some contract lawyers work at home, but pay a law firm for such amenities as access to a small office or conference room for client meetings and depositions.)

The law firm or lawyer renting the space may be willing to trade a certain number of hours of your work for rent. Zoe Topsfield, who does contract work while establishing her own practice in Los Angeles, shares an office suite and pays the rent with her time. Another benefit of these arrangements is that—because you are on the spot and visible to other attorneys—you may pick up assignments that no one would otherwise think of you to handle.

ADVANTAGES OF A HOME OFFICE

- Ability to start your business immediately
- Minimal start-up capital needed
- Convenience, especially if you work unusual hours (e.g., late nights, early mornings)
- No rent or utility setup charges
- Reduced wardrobe expense
- No commuting time or expense
- Home office tax deduction
- Minimal exposure to office politics
- Flexibility and independence
- Low risk for trial and error

DISADVANTAGES OF A HOME OFFICE

- Motivation based 100 percent on your drive
- Many distractions close at hand
- Difficult access to clerical support
- Limited system for moral support
- More marketing effort required
- Isolation
- Limited work space
- Disruption of personal life
- The possibility of clients coming into your home
- Zoning restrictions

COMPUTER EQUIPMENT

According to recent surveys, fewer than half of small firm lawyers in the country have computers in their individual offices; they rely instead on their dictating machine and typists to generate output. (A survey reported in the October 10, 1994 *National Law Journal* found that fewer lawyers in small law offices than in larger firms personally use computers.) As a new business owner, you cannot afford to be ill-equipped; you must have your own computer set-up unless your assignments consist exclusively of covering hearings and depositions for other lawyers.

Welcome to the Byzantine world of computers, where almost every friend, relative, colleague, and neighbor—even the kids down the street—will convey (often fanatic) opinions about the best computer system (IBM-compatibile versus Apple), how much to pay (new or used), and where to make the purchase (computer outlet, consumer electronics store, office supply store, warehouse club, mail-order). If you've somehow managed to remain above this fray, get thee to a bookstore.

We recommend an ABA publication, *Flying Solo.* Chapter 38—"The Solo Computer"—provides a thorough discussion of lawyers' computer needs. In addition, there are two excellent magazines; *The Lawyer's PC*[1] and *Home Office Computing* (available on newsstands). The ABA Law Practicement Management section publishes *Law Practice Management* magazine as well

as books about law office computing (among them, *A Short Course on Personal Computers*, which explains hardware, and *Locate*, a directory of law office software vendors which also describes the software and its applications). For another helpful guide on computer purchasing, check the ratings in *Consumer Reports*.

COMPUTER HARDWARE

Before deciding on computer and software purchases, ask yourself which of the following tasks you're likely to perform:

- Writing and editing;
- Legal research;
- Document organization and retrieval;
- Conflicts checking;
- Law practice accounting;
- Client billing;
- Deposition summaries;
- Indexing depositions;
- Scheduling;
- Calendar and docket control;
- Spreadsheets; or
- Sophisticated calculations.

If your work will involve more than writing and accounting, you'll need a computer system that can comfortably handle the memory-hogging demands of the newer software. In 1998, experts recommend purchasing a computer with at least 32 megabytes of random access memory (RAM) (or even 64 megs with expansion as needed),

---

1. *Lawyer's PC* is available from Shepard's McGraw-Hill, P.O. Box 1235, Colorado Springs, CO 80901.

at least a one-gigabyte hard disk drive (preferably much larger), at least a 28.8 modem, and a built-in CD-ROM drive for your legal library (CD-ROM disks cost less than the books themselves, and can be more cost-effective than on-line legal research if you use them frequently).

How much money should you invest in a computer? It depends. If the purchase is part of a long-term office strategy, buy a computer whose RAM and disk drive are near-state-of-the-art (six months to a year old). If you can't afford this level of computing, explore the expanding used market through classified ads or the Yellow Pages. Whether you buy new or used, though, computers are evolving so fast that your purchase will be outdated within three to five years. So buy as much computing power now as you can afford.

A "desktop" computer is your best choice if you do a lot of writing. The full-size keyboard and screen are essential to prevent back, shoulder and eye strain. You should consider a laptop or notebook computer if you anticipate long hours in the library, or hope to work on-site for firms that can't provide you with your own terminal.

Laptops can give you an edge as a contract lawyer. You can leave your home office in the morning with a brief almost finished, stop in the library to Shepardize the cases you've used, input any changes, call the hiring lawyer for last-minute instructions (with your cell phone?), then drop by his office with the finished product.

If you absolutely must have the comfort of a desktop computer, but crave

the flexibility of a portable, don't despair. Most laptops permit the attachment of peripheral equipment like full-size keyboards and monitors. In the last few years, several companies have also developed 2-in-1 computers that convert laptops into desktop models.

OPERATING SYSTEM SOFTWARE

Most law offices own IBM-compatible systems operating in a Microsoft Windows environment. You'll encounter fewer compatibility problems if you do too. But don't worry if you're a loyal DOS system user or Apple computer lover. Just be conscientious in letting every hiring lawyer know what system you're using and in reminding them to provide files to you that have been translated into language your operating system can read.

WORD PROCESSING SOFTWARE

For many years, most law firms operated in a Word Perfect environment. According to a 1994 survey by the *National Law Journal*, 97.3 percent of lawyers used WordPerfect word processing software, 82.1 percent in a DOS environment. Upgrading to Windows was cited as the most commonly planned purchase for 1995. Now, most of those firms have converted to Windows. Many have also switched to Microsoft Word.

If you intend to draft documents for transfer to hiring lawyers by e-mail or on diskette—whether for revision or finalizing— try to install a relatively current version of WordPerfect or Microsoft Word for Windows. That way, you can convert your files to whatever format the hiring lawyer requires, and your software will be able to translate all but the most obscure computer languages.

Internet, that is, e-mail, transfers create an additional complication. You'll have to experiment with quirks of your and the hiring lawyer's service providers. As a general rule, you'll experience the least difficulty if you make it a habit of converting every file to rich text format (RTF) before transferring it.

To ensure easy transfer of your work product, use either Courier or Times Roman type fonts; almost all software programs recognize both. Avoid using macros (the custom-made codes that let you carry out complicated word-processing tasks like pleading captions and notary language with a single command) unless all of your work is for a law firm that relies on the same short-cuts. (The *National Law Journal's* Large Law Firm Technology Survey in August 1994 indicated that 32 percent of law firms use WordPerfect Macros as their primary document assembly system.)

OTHER SOFTWARE

Whether you invest in additional software depends on the nature of your practice, and how attached you are to your computer. For example, contract lawyer Steve Weinstein has a home office with a computer equipped to handle word process-ing, a fax/modem and a spreadsheet program. In contrast, Lee Archer uses word processing, a publishing program that creates professional-looking letterhead,

business cards and advertising pieces, a fax/modem, accounting software and CD-ROM research capabilities. Like most contract lawyers we interviewed, Weinstein and Archer manually perform timekeeping, calendaring and conflicts checks. As you'd expect, though, programs specifically designed for these functions do exist. You can add conflicts software to your collection if you'll be working on many small matters for a variety of clients, or if your past practice involved a large number of clients.

COMPUTER PRINTERS

The price of laser printers has dropped dramatically, but ink-jet printers still cost less while producing equally sharp print quality. Compare a black-and-white laser printer at $400 to an ink-jet at $200. Ink-jet printers do have some disadvantages: they are often slower than lasers; the print can smear if removed too quickly from the feed tray or if it gets wet, and it's possible that the ink will fade over time.

OTHER EQUIPMENT

Modem or no modem? A modem—that piece of computer equipment that allows you to use a standard phone line to send and receive data—will be essential for the future of your contract law business. Not only does it allow you to speed your computer files to clients, it also lets you send and receive e-mail, subscribe to Lexis or Westlaw, and take advantage of the myriad services on the Information Superhighway.

One of the modem's disadvantages is the cost of receiving on-line information.

Lee Archer's Westlaw bill averaged $1,000 per month; she halved the cost of computerized research by investing in a large CD-ROM library. Fortunately, she can bill most of the cost to her customers because the service makes her so much more efficient. She cites the example of Shepardizing through a West Publishing program called "West Check." The program extracts the citations from her briefs, logs on to Westlaw, automatically Shepardizes and Auto-Cites each case, then prints the results to her printer or hard disk in a matter of minutes. The same process done manually would take many hours.

Katherine Foldes, on the other hand, decided against using on-line research services for reasons other than cost. She feels that conducting on-line research from her home would deprive her of face-to-face contact with potential customers at the law library. In addition, she believes that computerized research is only cost-effective when you're very familiar with applicable key words.

FAX MACHINES

Most modems also allow you to send and receive faxes. In the beginning, a combined fax/modem might be enough. The problem is that you can send faxes only of documents already in your computer (unless you also invest in a scanner). A fax/modem is useless if someone sends you a draft by fax and asks you to mark it up by hand and send it back. Another problem with fax/modems is that you must keep your computer running and plugged into the phone line 24 hours a day to receive incoming faxes. This will be impossible if you've bought a laptop computer to take to the library, or if you don't have a dedicated phone line. With these caveats, a fax/modem has the advantage of providing some faxing capability in a relatively inexpensive manner.

A freestanding fax machine is not much more expensive than a fax/modem ($150 and up) and is far more convenient. The more expensive machines use plain paper instead of thermosensitive paper that fades in sunlight, and can double as photocopy machines; some—when hooked up to your computer—serve as ink-jet printers. You can install a separate phone line to take all fax calls, or hook up the fax to your regular phone line and screen fax calls as they come in. Better yet, add an inexpensive expansion line to your home telephone number, then purchase a switching mechanism (call director) that will discriminate between a fax call and a voice call.

Unless you have money to spare, delay purchasing a fax machine until you really need one. Until then, rely on a combination of the neighborhood office services—known as a "mailbox" facility—and a local messenger service. For the mailbox facility, simply introduce yourself to the owners and let them know you will be using their fax services. The facility will call you when you receive a fax. The cost is about $2 per page, and is less for receiving than for sending. (Of course, you should not use a mailbox facility to send or receive material that might contain client confidences.) A messenger service may seem expensive, but it is cheaper than what you would charge the hiring lawyer for your travel time to pick up and deliver. Keep track of the money you spend on this combination of services, as well as the hassle it causes. You'll know when it's time to invest in your own fax machine.

COMMUNICATIONS EQUIPMENT

If you rent an office in a law firm or in an office services suite, you probably have a satisfactory telephone arrangement. You have several decisions to make about your communications set-up, however, if you work out of your home.

BASIC EQUIPMENT

If you live alone, you probably won't require a dedicated business line, although you may still want one so that you can separate business calls from personal calls. You'll have to invest in a separate business phone number if others live with you (unless your housemates are well-trained in telephone etiquette and message retrieval). This need not be an expensive proposition. Most phone companies now offer "expansion" numbers that come in over the same telephone line but ring differently. You can hand out the expansion number to business clients and train your family to ignore the business ring. (You can even have two additional lines—one for your business and one for your fax line. The call director referred to above will distinguish among all three lines and direct each call to the right piece of equipment.)

Whether or not you order a second line, consider purchasing a headset for your office phone; it frees your hands to write, work at the computer, or leaf through law books while you're talking. Also, you'll want to consider adding call waiting, call forwarding and three-way conferencing options.

MESSAGING SYSTEM

To assure a business-like image, purchase a high-quality telephone answering machine or set up a voicemail service through your local phone company. Voicemail costs under $10 a month on a home telephone line, somewhat more for a business line. With voicemail, callers can leave a message when your line is busy and you never have to worry about a power interruption disabling your answering machine. Some lawyers combine answering machines with voicemail. When they're working on a project and don't want to be interrupted, they set the answering machine to pick up in one ring, overriding the voice-mail system, so they can screen the calls and answer only those relevant to the project.

No matter what system you use, hiring lawyers have a right to expect a business-like response. A simple "hello" may be fine for friends or relatives, but it is an awkward response for those who don't know you. During business hours, answer your phone with something like "Hello. John Jones speaking," or "Good morning. You've reached John Jones."

Likewise, any recorded message must make your professional status clear. Speak in your own voice and identify yourself by name and profession. A cryptic "You have reached 222-2222," or a greeting by a child or other family member will not assure hiring lawyers, their clients or their consultants that they are protected by confidentiality, or that their inquiry will even reach you. Clever messages and background music are also inappropriate.

It is important to convey to the caller that you are available. One lawyer even suggests updating your greeting *every day*, to let callers know whether you are in and when you expect to be able to return the call. Jackson S. White, Jr. suggested in the September 1994 issue of *Law Practice Management*:

The alternative, which I abhor, is the nonspecific or generic recorded message that says, "I cannot take your call now, but leave me a message and I'll get back to you as soon as I can." As a caller, I want to know when the return call is likely to come. During the next hour, or next week? It does make a difference. And recording a new message is so simple and quick. You owe as much to your callers.

If you are uncomfortable stating your name on your home telephone line, either install a second (business) line or pay for an answering service. This service for a low usage customer costs $25 to $35 per month.

FILING SYSTEMS

It may take a few months of work as a contract lawyer before filing becomes an issue, but if you are successful, it will eventually be of prime importance. Whether you worked as a secretary or relied on one in the past, now you'll need clerical skills of your own. But you're also

the boss—you can develop a filing system that takes into account the way you work, the habits of the lawyers you work for, and the kinds of projects you accept.

PROJECT INDEX

However you choose to organize the paperwork you generate as a contract lawyer, maintain an index to your files from the very beginning. Katherine Foldes keeps a complete project list in her computer, organized alphabetically and employing key words to assist with conflicts checks, legal research references, and subject matter similarities. You may choose instead to keep one index (and one file drawer) for form files, one for legal research, and one for completed projects. Arrange the files in the order shown on the index and you'll find what you need with a minimum of hassle.

PROJECT FILES

Keep all papers for each project in a separate file. Accordion files work well and are available in a range of lengths and widths. You may complete certain projects and never hear from the lawyer (or about the issue) again. More likely, at least once a month a hiring lawyer will call you with a question or follow-up assignment on a project you completed long enough in the past that you can't remember the details. Save yourself time and agony by keeping the projects separate and organized in a way that allows for easy retrieval—that is, by hiring lawyer, alphabetically, by date initiated or in any other way that works for you.

FORM FILES

Transactional lawyers usually retain files of the different kinds of agreements they've drafted. Most litigators, likewise, maintain files of frequently used pleadings, discovery forms, and other court papers. If you don't have form files, start compiling them. Keep your form files separate from your pending and completed project files.

LEGAL RESEARCH

If you do a lot of research projects, you'll find that some questions arise again and again. In the beginning, you'll probably store your research in the project file; make sure the file label gives a hint of the legal issues involved so you can retrieve old research without looking through all the files. Or, make your project index or list detailed enough to function as a legal research index as well, enabling you to locate your research by searching the computer file much as you would search on Lexis or Westlaw.

When an issue or area of law comes up for the second time, create a separate file for the research you've done on the subject. For example, in the area of debtor-creditor law, you might create a file on fraudulent transfers; in real estate, a file for adverse possession research. Then when you get an assignment on the issue, all you have to do is update what you already have in the file.

BUSINESS CARDS AND STATIONERY

Most computer programs these days can print professional-looking letterhead and envelopes. You can save on stationery this way, but if you want to look more official, get 500 sheets and envelopes printed at a quick-print company. The cost is minimal relative to the boost to your image.

Business cards are another matter. As a contract lawyer, you'll probably hand out your business card more often than you'll write business letters. Fortunately, nice-looking business cards are just about the cheapest investment you can make in your new business. This is an area where you can go all out by spending less than $50, and rack up some impressive marketing mileage. Just make sure that the card reflects your status as a contract lawyer. A new marketing trend is to use the back of your business card to specify the services you offer.

LIBRARY

Unless you're sharing space, your beginning office library will probably be minimal, but it does need to include more than the textbooks, hornbooks and *Black's Law Dictionary* left over from law school. First, purchase a complete set of state and local rules of procedure and any code (tax, bankruptcy, etc.) you use regularly.

Other resources depend on your practice. CLE materials can be useful additions to your library. One Oregon lawyer buys a CLE "season ticket" every year (for a one-time up-front fee you can attend any bar-sponsored CLE program at a cost of about $25). He doesn't go to many of the programs, but does order the written materials at substantial savings. Cindy Vranizan says that if she goes to the library more than once for a particular source, she'll consider purchasing it for her home office.

Finally, we will see more and more resources available on CD-ROM. The CDs are cheaper and take up less space than books. You'll need a state-of-the-art computer system and a high-quality monitor if you plan to develop your library this way though!

OFFICE FURNITURE

A proper computer desk is essential—low enough to permit comfortable use of the keyboard while providing enough height to place the screen at eye level. The right desk, with room for printer as well, is a good investment. Likewise, a good chair will make it easier for you to work long hours without undue fatigue.

These items can be expensive, but the right furniture is worth it. Even if you work only part-time, you will spend several hours a day using your desk and chair—probably more time than any other piece of furniture except your bed. Fatigue, irritability and even repetitive stress injuries can result from spending hours working at ill-fitted office furniture. Used office furniture stores may have what you need, but don't settle for something that's wrong for the sake of saving money. You'll probably end up getting rid of it at a loss and replacing it with more suitable furnishings later.

PAYING FOR YOUR INVESTMENT

Some would-be contract lawyers shrink from spending the $1,500 to $3,500 it takes to set up a complete office. If this is your attitude, you have two choices: You can market your services only to law firms and lawyers who want you to work in-house using their facilities (and thereby limit your prospects). Or, you can say to yourself, "I am investing in a business, not a job."

Another way to consider the investment is to imagine you just graduated from law school and have been hired by a prestigious firm. You have no money, and only the suit you wore to interviews. What do you do? Walk into Nordstrom, open a charge account, and buy enough clothing so you won't embarrass yourself at your new job? Or wear your one suit every day for the first six months? The clothing you buy to project the right image at a new job is not deductible on your income tax return, while the equipment and supplies you buy to outfit your office are.

"That's great in theory," you say. "But I still don't have the cash." Again, think of the expenditure as a vital investment in your professional future. You probably didn't have enough money to finance your law school education either, but somehow, on a combination of scholarships, student loans, part-time jobs, help from family and friends, credit cards—and guts—you did it.

A complete and comfortable office set-up has much to recommend it. It costs less than a semester in law school. The dollars expended usually come off the top of your income at tax time. (Some expenses must be amortized; check with your accountant or tax adviser.) Finally, being a fully-equipped contract lawyer adds to your sense of legitimacy and self-sufficiency. While there's no

STOCKING OUR RECOMMENDED BASIC OFFICE

Item	Used	New
computer bundled w/word processing & accounting	$750	$1,500
ink-jet printer	150	250
telephone/answering machine*	25	100
1000 business cards (low end to high end)	15	50
stationery (computer-generated v. quick-printed)	10	100
computer desk system	200	600
ergonomic chair	75	100
bookcase	50	150
file cabinet	75	125
supplies**	100	100
digital clock for time keeping	10	10
codes, statutes, etc.	100	300
Total	**1,560**	**3,385**

Optional:

	Used	New
thermal fax machine		150
plain paper fax machine		350
fax/modem	60	150

*We actually recommend a voicemail system. The $100 estimate would pay
for a residential phone system for one year.
**Includes pens, computer paper, a printer cartridge, yellow pads,
diskettes, stapler, staple remover, paper clips, accordion files, manila
envelopes.

guarantee that having an office will get you work, it's clear that not having an office will make it more difficult to do so. The decision is yours.

APPENDIX 3

STATE, LOCAL AND NATIONAL ETHICS OPINIONS ON CONTRACT LAWYER ISSUES

Note: These summaries are intended merely to inform lawyers of ethics opinions that may affect their contract lawyer arrangements, either lawyer-to-lawyer or lawyer-to-agency. Do not rely on our summaries, but read the full opinion yourself if you believe it applies to your situation. Our research is current through October, 1998.

AMERICAN BAR ASSOCIATION

Formal Opinion 88-356. Responds to a number of inquiries relating to the increasing use by law firms of temporary lawyers. *Definition:* Temporary lawyers typically are employed to meet temporary staffing needs of a firm or to provide special expertise for a specific matter. Temporary lawyers may work on a single assignment or more generally for a limited period. Temporary lawyers may or may not work in the firm's office. Temporary lawyers may work exclusively for one firm or simultaneously on matters for more than one firm.

Conflicts of Interest: Temporary lawyers cannot work simultaneously for clients of different firms with differing interests except as permitted by DR 5-105(c). Whether

a temporary lawyer is treated as being "associated with a firm" while working on a matter for the firm depends on whether the temporary lawyer has access to information relating to the representation of other firm clients. If a firm, through accurate records or otherwise, can demonstrate that the temporary lawyer only had access to information relating to the representation of certain clients, the temporary lawyer should not be deemed to be "associated with" the firm. Also, if a temporary lawyer works with a firm only on a single matter much like the collaboration of two independent firms, and the temporary lawyer does not have access to information about other firm clients, the temporary lawyer should not be deemed "associated with" the firm generally. If a temporary lawyer was directly involved in work on a matter for a firm's client and had knowledge of material information relating to the representation of that client, a second firm representing other parties in the same matter whose interests were directly adverse to those of the client of the first firm should not engage the temporary lawyer during the pendency of the matter, even for work on other matters. Firms should screen temporary lawyers from information relating to other clients and maintain complete and accurate records of all matters on which temporary lawyers work. Temporary lawyers working with several firms should avoid exposure to information relating to other firm clients. Temporary lawyers should also maintain their own records of clients and matters worked on.

Confidentiality: A temporary lawyer who works for a firm on matters of a firm client generally cannot reveal information relating to the representation of that client. The temporary lawyer also cannot reveal information relating to other clients of the firm learned as a result of working with the firm. If "associated with" the firm, the temporary lawyer cannot disclose information relating to the representation of firm clients regardless of the source of the information. If not "associated with" the firm, the temporary lawyer should not reveal (1) information relating to any client for whom the temporary lawyer is working, and (2) information relating to other firm clients obtained as a result of working with the firm. If "associated with" the firm, the temporary lawyer will be assumed to have obtained information relating to other clients in the course of employment by the firm. Supervising lawyers must make reasonable efforts to ensure that temporary lawyers conform to ethical rules, including those governing confidentiality of information.

Disclosure: The client must be advised of a temporary lawyer's work on the client's matter and the consent of the client must be obtained when the temporary lawyer will work independently, without the close supervision of the firm. Disclosure is not required when the temporary lawyer is working under the direct supervision of a lawyer associated with the firm. The firm has no obligation to reveal to the client the compensation arrangement with the temporary lawyer as long as the temporary lawyer is paid reasonably for services performed and the firm does not charge the payments directly to the client as a disbursement. Disclosure and consent are required if the arrangement between the firm and the temporary lawyer involves a direct division of the actual fee paid by the client, regardless of the extent of supervision. The requirement that the fee be reasonable must be satisfied in all events.

Placement Agencies: Paying a placement agency a fee for the services of a temporary lawyer and for its "locating, recruiting, screening and providing" of the temporary lawyer to the law firm does not constitute the sharing of fees with nonlawyers. Any agreement between a temporary lawyer and a placement agency should include explicit terms that the agency will not exercise any control or influence over the exercise of professional judgment by the temporary lawyer, including limiting or extending the amount of time the lawyer spends on the client's work. Law firms must also make certain that compensation received by temporary lawyers is adequate enough to believe that the temporary lawyer will perform competently for the firm's clients.

CALIFORNIA

Formal Opinion 1992-126. Issued in response to inquiries about the ethical propriety of attorneys organizing temporary attorney placement agencies. Advisory only. *Conflicts:* Both firm and contract lawyer are responsible for checking and avoiding conflicts. *Screening:* Law firm "must make a concerted effort to screen the contract attorney from confidential information that is unnecessary to the attorney's assignment at the firm." Refers to ABA Op. 88-356. *Independent judgment:* Agency should not attempt and contract lawyer should not allow agency to influence the contract lawyer's independent judgment in providing legal services to the actual client. *Agencies:* Recommends that hiring firm pay agency and contract lawyer separately. The client is entitled to full disclosure of amounts paid to each. Agencies should not collect a percentage of the fees collected from client.

Opinion 1994-138. *Division of fees; disclosure:* A lawyer who hires a contract lawyer must disclose the arrangement to the client if it is a significant development in the matter. Must comply with rules on fee-splitting if the contract lawyer is to receive a portion of the fee paid by the client.

L.A. County Opinion 473. *Division of fees; disclosure:* Same as Op. 1994-138. Outlines five factors (see page #) in making the determination of whether use of a contract lawyer constitutes a significant development in a matter, requiring disclosure to the client. Consent in writing is required for division of fees with any lawyer not a partner, employee or shareholder of the firm.

CONNECTICUT

Informal Opinion 88-15. Opinion requested by a lawyer wishing to act as recruiter of temporary lawyers. The proposed arrangement is that the recruiter and the contract lawyer will be paid separately. *Agencies:* No fee-splitting issues so long as fees are paid to recruiter and contract lawyer separately. Both lawyer recruiter and contract lawyer are bound by rules of ethics, must preserve client confidences, avoid conflicts of interest and be mindful of imputed disqualification problems.

DISTRICT OF COLUMBIA

Opinion 284. Written to respond to confusion among lawyers and clients as to ethical questions relating to temporary lawyers. *Disclosure:* Whether a lawyer must disclose to the client the use of a temporary lawyer on the client's matter depends on the nature of the work, the reasonable expectations of the client, and the nature of the relationship between the employing lawyer and the "temporary" lawyer. *Billing:* The employing lawyer generally need not disclose to the client the temporary lawyer's cost to the lawyer or law firm, and the lawyer may bill the client for the temporary lawyer's work at any reasonable rate mutually agreeable to the lawyer and client. Agency recruiting fees billed separately from hourly compensation for the temporary lawyer may not be billed to the client at greater than the amount actually disbursed or agreed to.

Opinion 255. Shareholder of firm to terminate association with firm but sublease office space and do contract work. *Conflicts, disclosure:* Mere association on ad hoc basis does not create relationship to trigger imputation of disqualification under Rule 1.20. Firm should not refer to lawyer as "special counsel" but rather as a consultant or contract lawyer.

FLORIDA

Opinion 88-12. Opinion issued in response to request of attorney contemplating involvement in a temporary attorney placement service. Opinion concludes the proposed arrangement is not ethically permissible, but offers guidelines for an arrangement that might be ethically permissible. *Conflicts:* The "primary burden of recognizing and avoiding potential conflicts" is on the agency and contract lawyers, rather than hiring lawyers. *Unauthorized practice of law:* Opinion raises but does not resolve the question of whether, if non-lawyers are owners or officers of the agency, the agency's activities could constitute the unauthorized practice of law. Also raises the question of whether, if the activities of the agency are considered the practice of law, the proposed corporate form would violate Florida law. *Fee-splitting:* Potential problems could be avoided by having no non-lawyer ownership, or by agency charging a flat fee rather than a portion of the amount billed for the contract lawyers' services.

ILLINOIS

State Bar Opinion No. 92-97. Opinion issued in response to question by firm wishing to hire solo practitioners on an occasional and hourly basis to cover court calls and depositions. *Disclosure:* A firm should advise its clients if it hires an outside lawyer for such matters. The firm must also obtain client consent to any fee-splitting arrangement with such a lawyer. Such hiring does not create an "of counsel" relationship. Both hiring lawyer and outside lawyer are bound by rules of professional conduct (referring to ABA Op. 88-356).

KENTUCKY

Oliver v. Board of Governors, 779 S.W.2d 212 (Ky. 1989). Lawyer who proposed to operate a temporary attorney placement service sought advisory opinion of Ethics Committee of Kentucky Bar Association. Ethics committee issued a formal opinion disapproving all temporary lawyer services. Kentucky Supreme Court accepted review and substituted its advisory opinion for that of the Ethics Committee. If a lawyer complies with guidelines in opinion he may operate a temporary attorney placement service. *Confidences and conflicts:* Adopts ABA Op. 88-356. *Disclosure:* Use of temporary or contract lawyers should always be disclosed to the client. The firm should also identify any placement fee it passes on to the client. *Agencies:* Firm must pay agency and contract lawyer separately. Contract lawyer should maintain independent professional judgment, free from improper influence by the temporary service.

NEW HAMPSHIRE

Opinion 1989-90/9. *Agencies:* Law firms may "lease" lawyer employees from leasing companies not owned by lawyers so long as the following conditions are met: (1) the arrangement is disclosed to the firm's clients, the leasing company's insurer, and the creditors of both firm and leasing company; (2) the firm maintains its independent professional judgment; (3) the firm does not divide fees with the leasing company directly or indirectly; and (4) the firm takes reasonable steps to comply with rules of ethics.

Opinion 1993-4/8. *Conflicts; disclosure:* A lawyer may offer pro tem services such as covering hearings so long as the client consents to the arrangement and the lawyer avoids conflicts of interest.

NEW JERSEY

Opinion 632. Opinion issued in response to inquiry by lawyer wishing to establish temporary attorney placement service owned and operated by the lawyer. Proposal is that agency will receive percentage of contract lawyers' fees as compensation but that payment shall be made separately to agency and contract lawyer. Advisory opinion concludes the lawyer may operate the agency under the guidelines set forth in the opinion. *Conflicts and client confidences:* Agrees with ABA Op. 88-356 on conflicts issues: need to assure no conflict exists, to maintain effective screening procedures, to maintain complete and accurate records of matters on which temporary attorneys work. *Disclosure:* Per ABA Op. 88-356, necessary only where temporary attorney works without close supervision. *Agencies:* The compensation arrangement

proposed does not constitute prohibited fee-splitting. The agency does not influence the professional judgment of the contract lawyers because they work under the supervision of the hiring firm.

NEW YORK

New York City Bar Opinion 1996-8. Discussion of whether a lawyer who works ten to fifteen hours per week on a non-exclusive per diem basis may be considered "of counsel" to the firm.

New York City Bar Opinion 1989-2. *Disclosure:* The opinion emphasizes the obligation of law firms using a temporary agency to make full disclosure of the use of temporary attorneys and obtain the consent of clients. *Agencies:* A law firm may compensate a temporary agency regardless of how the fee was calculated because the fee for the agency is not a "legal fee," but the agreement between agency and law firm should separately identify the agency fee, and the agency fee should not be included in the fee the firm charges its clients.

NORTH CAROLINA

Opinion 38. *Agencies:* A placement service for temporary lawyers that charges a placement fee is proper so long as the arrangement does not affect the lawyers' independent judgment and the contracts specify what firms will be charged and what lawyers' rates will be. Both firms and contract lawyers must guard client confidences and avoid conflicts of interest.

Opinion 104. *Agencies:* A law firm may lease associate lawyers from an employee leasing company operated by non-lawyers so long as (1) the fee to the leasing company is not tied to legal fees paid to the firm; (2) the public is not misled about the arrangement; (3) the leasing company does not influence the lawyers' independent judgment; (4) client confidences are maintained; and (5) other ethical obligations, including those for avoiding conflicts of interest, are met.

OHIO

Opinion 90-23. Advisory opinion issued in response to attorney's question whether proposed temporary attorney placement agency owned and operated by two lawyers is ethical. The opinion says yes, within the guidelines set forth. *Confidences and conflicts:* Agency must not breach lawyer's duty to preserve client confidences; agency must avoid conflicts of interest. *Disclosure:* There is a duty to disclose the relationship to the client if the client will be paying for the legal services. *Agencies:* Approves of ABA Op. 88-356. Adopts reasoning of City of New York Opinion 1989-2 with respect to fee division. The agency should not control the lawyer's time or professional judgment, including any attempt to influence the amount of time the lawyer spends. The agency also should not interfere with the traditional lawyer-client relationship.

RHODE ISLAND

Opinion 90-34. Opinion responds to questions of lawyer in private practice who also operates a temporary lawyer placement agency with a non-lawyer. *Agencies:* A

lawyer operating an agency may discuss ABA Op. 88-356 with clients without "practicing law." A non-lawyer operating an agency may discuss ABA Op. 88-356 with clients. A lawyer operating the agency may take assignments through it as long as the lawyers she works for are treated the same as other clients of the agency.

SOUTH CAROLINA

Advisory Opinion 91-09. A national employee leasing company presents questions about the leasing of lawyers to law firms. *Conflicts:* Lawyer employees can work for firms representing adverse parties in litigation without a conflict of interest if the lawyers and the firm exercise care to avoid conflicts of interest and maintain confidentiality of information, disclose the arrangement to clients "in some circumstances" and otherwise comply with ethics rules. *Agencies:* Adopts ABA Op. 88-356. Lawyers may work for an employee leasing company so long as the leasing company is the employer for all purposes, is not itself a law firm, and does not interfere with the lawyers' professional judgment. Fees charged to each client by the law firm must be reasonable.

TEXAS

Opinion 508. *Agencies:* A law firm may not enter into an agreement with an employee leasing company owned by non-lawyers. The arrangement does not violate proscription on fee division, but the potential for conflicts of interest among clients of different law firms to which lawyers are leased is too great.

APPENDIX 4

OPINIONS ON SCREENING TO AVOID IMPUTED DISQUALIFICATION

Note: Our list is not exhaustive; it covers only recent rulings and does not include all states. It is intended only to give examples of the approaches to screening taken by different courts and bar committees. Learn the rule in your jurisdiction before attempting to use screening to overcome imputed disqualification.

THE FOLLOWING STATES HAVE RULES OR OPINIONS THAT ALLOW SCREENING TO AVOID IMPUTED DISQUALIFICATION:

MASSACHUSETTS

A federal district court approved screening to avoid imputed disqualification when a lawyer who had previously worked on the same case for the opposing party moved to the firm. Screening procedures consisted of sending a memo to all firm lawyers telling them not to discuss the case with the new lawyer, locking the cabinet containing the case files, directing communications on the case be sent in sealed envelopes, and moving the new lawyer's office to a separate building. *Thomalen v. Marriott Corp.*, No. 90-40140, 10 *Lawyers' Manual on Professional Conduct* (ABA/BNA) 300 (D. Mass. 9/19/94).

NEW YORK

A federal district court held screening the lawyer avoided imputed disqualification of the firm. In addition to screening, lawyers at the new firm presented affidavits swearing that they had not discussed the case with the new lawyer, who had represented an adverse party at his previous firm. *In re Del-Val Financial Corp. Securities Litigation*, No. MDL 872, 10 *Lawyers' Manual on Professional Conduct* (ABA/BNA) 236 (S.D.N.Y. 7/29/94).

NORTH DAKOTA

A federal district court held screening mechanisms were sufficient to avoid imputed disqualification. Court also considered hardship that disqualification would impose at the late stage in case. *Ness,*

*Motley, Loadholt, Richardson and Poole
P.A. v. Aetna Casualty and Surety Co.*, Civ.
No. A3-88-157, 6 *Lawyers' Manual on
Professional Conduct* (ABA/BNA) 324 (D.N.D.
8/8/90).

OREGON

A rule describes screening procedures
that will avoid imputed disqualification
when a lawyer changes firms. Both the
lawyer changing firms and a member of the
new firm must prepare and serve on the
previous firm affidavits attesting that the
disqualified lawyer will not discuss or
participate in any case in which present
and former firms are involved. Oregon
DR 5-105(I).

UTAH

A court held that to be effective a
screening mechanism must be in place at
the time the potentially disqualifying event
(attorney joins firm or firm accepts case)
occurs. After-the-fact screening is not sufficient. *SLC Limited V v. Bradford Group West
Inc.*, No. 92-C-757A, 8 *Lawyers' Manual on
Professional Conduct* (ABA/BNA) 373 (D.
Utah 11/12/92).

SCREENING HAS BEEN DISAPPROVED
IN THE FOLLOWING STATES:

ALABAMA

The state supreme court did not permit
a firm to avoid imputed disqualification by
screening a lawyer previously employed by
a firm representing an adverse party.
Roberts v. Hutchins, 572 So. 2d 1231 (Ala.
1990).

ARIZONA

A court of appeals rejected screening
as a means to avoid imputed disqualification. *Towne Development of Chandler Inc.
v. Arizona Superior Court*, 173 Ariz. 364, 842
P.2d 1377 (Ariz. Ct. App. 1992), *rev. denied*
(1993).

KANSAS

A court rejected screening to avoid
imputed disqualification and held that
whether the new firm would be disqualified
depended on whether the lawyer moving to
the firm had acquired material confidential
information at the previous firm. *Lansing-
Delaware Water District v. Oak Lane Park
Inc.*, 248 Kan. 563, 808 P.2d 1369 (Kan. 1991).

NEBRASKA

A court said screening would not avoid
disqualification where newly hired lawyer
was deeply involved in the case on the
other side. *State ex rel. Freezer Services,
Inc. v. Mullen*, 235 Neb. 981, 458 N.W.2d 245
(Neb. 1990).

IN THE FOLLOWING STATES,
WHETHER SCREENING IS EFFECTIVE
MAY DEPEND ON OTHER FACTORS:

ARKANSAS

A case held that a new lawyer's prior
representation of an adverse party creates a
rebuttable presumption of imputed disqualification, which could be overcome by proof
of the lawyer's actual lack of access to
information about the client at previous
firm. *Burnette v. Morgan*, 303 Ark. 150, 794
S.W.2d 145 (Ark. 1990).

CALIFORNIA

A court of appeals held that screening will not avoid imputed disqualification where there is a "substantial relationship" between former and current representation. In this case, a firm that had represented the defendant in previous construction litigation represented plaintiffs after plaintiffs' lawyer joined the firm. *Rosenfeld Construction Co. v. Superior Court, 7 Lawyers' Manual on Professional Conduct* (ABA/BNA) 349 (Calif. Ct. App. 6/10/94).

GEORGIA

A federal district court refused to disqualify a lawyer in an "of counsel" relationship with a firm that employed a lawyer who had represented the opposing party while working at a different firm. The decision was based on the peripheral nature of the "of counsel" relationship rather than screening procedures. *Gray v. Memorial Medical Center Inc.,* 855 F. Supp. 377 (S.D.Ga. 1994).

APPENDIX 5

CONTRACT LAWYER PLACEMENT AGENCY PROFILES

What follows are profiles listed alphabetically of contract lawyer placement agencies nationwide that paid a small fee to be included. These dozen agencies represent the full spectrum of service providers you'll find across the country: international, multi-office enterprises to franchise operations to small regional companies; those that focus exclusively on contract lawyer assignments, to agencies handling the full range of temporary, permanent and project management legal staffing, to those that also offer individual career counseling and outplacement services.

We confirmed the information provided by the agencies by studying their websites, interviewing someone in management and asking each to review its profile and submit corrections. The "Business Profile" that introduces each listing includes our observations of what makes this agency distinctive from its competitors. The agencies offer their own marketing statements at the end of their profiles.

Assigned Counsel Incorporated · Wayne, PA

Business profile: Founded in 1992. One of only two agencies in the country that devotes 100 percent of its business to the placement of attorneys in temporary assignments. Named one of the 500 fastest growing privately-held companies in the US by Inc. Magazine in 1998. Created the first quality management program in the contract lawyer placement industry. Survey results show 97.7 percent of their placements meet or exceed hiring lawyer expectations. Current job opportunities posted on their well-developed website.

Placement personnel: Licensed lawyers with both law firm and business backgrounds.

Arrangements with hiring lawyers: Managing attorney (point person for the hiring lawyer) and recruiting attorney (behind-the-scenes to find the best candidate) work together to meet temporary staffing needs. Managing attorney follows up regularly to ensure complete satisfaction.

Financial arrangement with contract lawyers: Paid as independent contractors.

Contract lawyer pool: Accepts all lawyers into their pool. Most placements are experienced attorneys engaged in transactional, litigation and specialty area work for corporate law departments and law firms. Candidates include parents temporarily choosing project work or re-entering the workforce, private practitioners seeking to use their expertise in alternative settings, attorneys in transition due to marketplace changes, retirees and law professors with practice experience.

Agency statement: Assigned Counsel is the largest privately-owned, independent service providing exclusively contract attorneys to multiple markets nationwide. Experienced lawyers fill all senior operational positions as well as all professional positions involving client and candidate attorney contact. Offices, as of September 1998, are maintained serving Boston, Chicago, Cleveland, Houston, Philadelphia, Piscataway, Pittsburgh and Washington, DC. Additional offices are anticipated.

CONTACT INFORMATION:
Corporate Headquarters

950 W. Valley Road, Suite 2602 , Wayne, PA 19087

URL: www.AssignedCounsel.com

E-mail: info@AssignedCounsel.com

Telephone: (610) 964-8300

Fax: (610) 964-5709

Managing Director: Robert J. Murphy, Jr., Esq., President

Hiring Lawyer Contact: Mark Kudlacik, Esq., Vice-President

Contract Lawyer Contact: Ethan Cadoff, Esq, Senior Recruiting Attorney

The Associates — Portland, OR

Business profile: Founded in 1997 by two Willamette Law School JD/MBAs when one, Allen Barteld, had just graduated and the other, Ian Shearer, was in his last year of law school. A full service staffing company focusing exclusively on the legal profession; primary focus is the placement of contract lawyers. Contract lawyers receive employee benefits without a waiting period. Plan to open a Seattle branch office in 1999.

Placement personnel: Law school graduates.

Financial arrangement with contract lawyers: Paid as employees with benefits including health insurance, vacation pay, educational programs and coverage for workers' compensation and unemployment insurance.

Contract lawyer pool: Places new law school graduates in contract lawyer work and as JD Paralegals (those who are not yet members of the local bar). Typical placements are attorneys who have just relocated and those with significant experience who are making lifestyle choices. Placements primarily in the Pacific Northwest. Begin application process by submitting a résumé and a cover letter indicating the type of work you are seeking, your date of availability and salary requirements. You will be told whether or not the agency can help you.

Agency statement: The Associates is attorney-owned and operated. We provide contract attorneys to law firms, corporate legal departments and government agencies. We deal solely with the legal profession. Our commitment to the legal profession is to provide affordable solutions for its permanent and temporary hiring needs. Guaranteed.

CONTACT INFORMATION:

222 NW Davis Street, Suite 400, Portland, OR 97209

URL: www.theassociatesinc.com; www.contractattorneys.com   E-mail: info@theassoc.com

Telephone: (503) 464-9686; (888) 464-9686   Fax: (503) 464-9660

Managing Director: Ian Shearer and Allen Barteld, Esq.

Hiring and Contract Lawyer Contact: Allen Barteld, Esq.

Contract Counsel Headquartered in the Detroit area with two branch offices

Business profile: Founded in 1993 as AmeriClerk Temporary Legal Staffing by David Galbenski and Mark Adams just as they graduated from Wayne State University Law School. Started with a pool of 15 law students working as temporary clerks, but clients soon began requesting lawyers. Changed name in 1998. Plans in place to expand throughout the Midwest.

Placement personnel: Law school graduates with and without practice experience.

Arrangements with hiring lawyers: Staffing options include LawFirm+ (help corporations reduce outside legal fees by partnering contract lawyers with outside firms to handle the routine, labor-intensive tasks like document management and review); Rainmaker (assists firms with RFP's using contract lawyers to cut costs); Employee+ (an employment service); Platinum Partner (contract lawyers with 20+ years experience). Project+ (outsource large projects that are document and labor intensive without having to supervise the project in-house or incur the cost of sending it to outside counsel).

Financial arrangement with contract lawyers: Paid as employees with health insurance, vacation pay and unemployment and workers' compensation coverage.

Contract lawyer pool: Lawyers in pool range from new graduates looking for full-time employment to retiring attorneys seeking part-time work to caregivers juggling family and work commitments. New law school graduates are compensated for paralegal work at slightly higher fees.

Agency Statement: Contract Counsel is the Midwest's premier provider of contract legal staffing services. We consult with law firms and corporations of all sizes to design staffing strategies that are innovative, flexible, creative and responsible. We also work with lawyers, legal assistants and law clerks at all stages of their legal careers to locate job opportunities to meet their goals and objectives. Contract Counsel looks forward to working with you to help you revise your staffing strategy or explore your next career opportunity.

CONTACT INFORMATION:

Main Office

> 5700 Crooks Road, Suite 202,Troy, MI 48098
>
> URL: www.contractcounsel.com   E-mail: detroit@contractcounsel.com
>
> Telephone: (248) 879-6666; (toll-free) 877-KCounsel   Fax: (248) 879-1400
>
> Managing Director: David J. Galbenski, Esq.
>
> Hiring Lawyer Contact: Jonathan P. Bricker, Esq.
>
> Contract Lawyer Contact: Steven W. Hays, Esq.

Grand Rapids Office

> Direct written inquiries to the Main Office
>
> URL: www.contractcounsel.com   E-mail: grandrapids@contractcounsel.com
>
> Telephone: (248) 879-6666; (toll-free) 877-KCounsel   Fax: (248) 879-1400

Indianapolis Office

> Direct written inquiries to the Main Office
>
> URL: www.contractcounsel.com   E-mail: indianapolis@contractcounsel.com
>
> Telephone: (317) 706-0600; (toll-free) 877-KCounsel   Fax: (317) 705-0666
>
> Managing Director: Herman Foster, Esq.

Custom Counsel dba The Esquire Group   St. Louis, MO

Business profile: Founded in 1993. Places attorneys, paralegals, office administrators and legal secretaries in temporary and permanent positions nationwide, although the company tends to handle more temporary assignments. About 40 percent of placements involve lawyers. Number six on a 1998 list of the top 100 fastest growing, privately-held companies in St. Louis. Offers franchise opportunities to licensed attorneys in primary and secondary markets who are motivated, quality-minded and committed to their legal community. Custom Counsel will provide franchisees complete business development instructions including from how to select office space to equipment purchase to staffing. You'll receiving training materials, two weeks of training in St. Louis and the presence of a Custom Counsel representative for two days on your site.

Placement personnel: Former practicing lawyers.

Financial arrangement with contract lawyers: Paid as independent contractors.

Contract lawyer pool: Generally requires a minimum 2 years of experience practicing law. Prescreen, interview and check references for all prospective contract lawyers before considering them for placement. Periodically places new law school graduates in assignments.

Agency statement: We are an attorney-owned and operated service which places attorneys, paralegal and legal secretaries in temporary and permanent positions nationwide. Our clients include the most prestigious law firms and corporations in the nation. We have built our reputation on our ability to supply our clients with the highest caliber legal professionals while providing exceptional customer service.

CONTACT INFORMATION:

8860 Ladue Road, Suite 120, St. Louis, MO 63124

URL: www.esquiregroup.com

Telephone: (314) 862-1922

Managing Director: Lisa Collins Werner, Esq.

Hiring Lawyer Contact: Mark Ward, Esq.

Contract Lawyer Contact: Lynn Ann Whaley, Esq.

E-mail: esquiregroup@stlnet.com

Fax: (314) 862-7087

The Esquire Group   Minneapolis, MN

Business profile: Founded in 1989 when Patricia Comeford, then a practicing lawyer, realized that there were no legal search firms in the Twin Cities and decided to do something about it. Started with permanent lawyer placements; client demand led to the offering of temporary lawyer placements in 1994 and other career-related services. Now concentrates on "higher end" placements, that is, those involving more sophisticated legal work. Serves clients through two operating divisions, Esquire Search, Ltd., which recruits permanent and temporary attorneys, paralegals and legal assistants, and Esquire Consulting, Ltd., which offers outplacement services, individual attorney career counseling, comprehensive career testing and other career consulting services.

Placement personnel: Former practicing lawyers with law firm or corporate legal department experience.

Services for Hiring Lawyers: Able to assist local clients with national placements by using the services of affiliated agencies across the country. For example, a corporation headquartered in the Twin Cities could secure temporary staffing for its New York City division by working through The Esquire Group.

Financial arrangement with contract lawyers: Paid as independent contractor or as employee, depending on the wishes of the hiring lawyer and the circumstances of the contract lawyer. Offers educational programs, workers' compensation and unemployment insurance coverage.

Contract lawyer pool: Offers new law school graduates contract lawyer assignments. Most assignments, though, involve the placement of experienced practitioners in sophisticated areas of law, including corporate transactional work, contract drafting, mergers & acquisitions, litigation and intellectual property.

Agency statement: The Esquire Group is a full service legal placement firm providing permanent and contract/temporary placements for attorneys, paralegal and legal assistants. In addition, the firm provides career counseling and outplacement services. The firm is the recognized leader in the upper Midwest by law firms and corporate in-house departments for its placement services.

CONTACT INFORMATION:

501 Marquette Avenue, Suite 1800, Minneapolis, MN 55402

URL: www.esqgroup.com   E-mail: esqgroup@aol.com

Telephone: (612) 340-9068; (800) 755-7779   Fax: (612) 340-1218

Managing Director: Patricia A. Comeford, Esq.

Hiring Lawyer Contact: Robert E. Harrer, Esq.

Contract Lawyer Contact: Timothy P. Mahoney, Esq.

Law Pros Legal Placement Services, Inc.   Short Hills, NJ

Business profile: Founded in 1994 by two lawyers. A full-service strategic staffing service for law firms and corporate legal departments that places lawyers and paralegals in temporary and permanent positions. About half of business devoted to contract lawyer placements.

Placement personnel: Primarily former- or non-practicing lawyers.

Arrangements with Hiring Lawyers: Offers the assurance of an insurance policy that covers the errors and omissions of both its in-house and external employees. Hiring lawyers receive protection, therefore, for negligent hiring or placement, as well as secondary coverage for professional negligence. (The hiring lawyer's professional negligence policy has primary coverage since contract lawyers are placed only with the contractual understanding that their work will be supervised by the hiring lawyer.) Available by beeper 24 hours a day, 7 days a week.

Financial arrangement with contract lawyers: Paid as employees with workers' compensation and unemployment insurance coverage as well as 401(k) and profit sharing plans. Accrue vacation pay.

Contract lawyer pool: Places law school graduates and seasoned attorneys in litigation and transactional positions with law firms and corporate legal departments. New law school graduates might receive assignments ranging from legal research and document review to such non-traditional legal positions as contract administration or compliance/regulatory work.

Agency statement: Law Pros specializes in the placement of attorneys and para-legals throughout the New Jersey legal community. We assist law firms and legal departments in both their temporary staffing needs and permanent/direct hire recruiting efforts. Since its inception in 1994, the Law Pros staff has spent countless hours educating and consulting with law firms and legal departments about managing and staffing their departments to meet fluctuating caseloads. The Law Pros' staffing consultants pride themselves on their hands-on, personalized approach in both client and candidate relations. They understand the ever-changing legal staffing market and apply that knowledge to effectuate the best available staffing arrangements for both clients and candidates.

CONTACT INFORMATION:

511 Millburn Avenue, Short Hills, NJ 07078

URL: www.lawproslegal.com   E-mail: info@lawproslegal.com

Telephone: (973) 912-8400   Fax: (973) 912-8558

Managing Directors: Beth E. Richmond, Esq. and Jodi L. Nadler, Esq.

Hiring Lawyer Contact: Jodi L. Nadler, Esq.   Contract Lawyer Contact: Beth E. Richmond, Esq.

The Lawsmiths, Inc.   San Francisco, CA

Business profile: Founded in 1985 by Robert Webster, one of the earliest and most frequently quoted promoters of temporary lawyer placements. This agency has probably been around longer than any other in the country! One of only two agencies nationwide that devotes 100 percent of its business to contract lawyer placements. Serves the entire state of California. Webster consults with other lawyers who are interested in starting their own contract lawyer placement agencies.

Placement personnel: A licensed lawyer and a business professional.

Financial arrangement with contract lawyers: Paid as independent contractors. Agency compensated by a flat surcharge over the hourly rate requested by the contract lawyer. If able to get a higher rate than expected from the hiring lawyer, the difference goes to the contract lawyer.

Contract lawyer pool: Accepts all lawyers with "good" experience into pool. Make-up of pool constantly changes. Does not place new law school graduates.

Agency Statement: The Lawsmiths was one of the first contract attorney services in the country. We deal only with licensed attorneys, and we are known for our top-quality attorney placements throughout the State of California.

CONTACT INFORMATION:

2443 Fillmore Street, Suite 319, San Francisco, CA 94115

Telephone: (415) 929-1090   Fax: (415) 563-7004

Managing Director: Robert Webster, Esq.

Legal People, Inc.   Portland, OR

Business profile: Founded in 1995 by David O'Brien, a Willamette Law School graduate and contract lawyer, and Michael O'Brien, with a background in sales and marketing. (The two founders share the same surname but not the same family.) At first, concentrated on temporary lawyer placements; added permanent placement services later. Current business is now about 40 percent temporary placements. This agency claims the most unusual placement: A new law school graduate with a solo practice asked to be connected with a seasoned practitioner to obtain general case and office management advice. Legal People made the match, which lasted only an hour and never occurred again.

Placement personnel: Supervised by a licensed member of the Oregon State Bar.

Financial arrangement with contract lawyers: Usually paid as employees with coverage for workers' compensation and unemployment insurance. Will pay as independent contractor when applicable, for instance when a sole practitioner does contract work from his/her own office to supplement income.

Contract lawyer pool: Places new law school graduates in paralegal assignments. "Lead pool" members generally experienced lawyers who don't want to work full-time in law firms or lawyers at any experience level who can easily take last-minute assignments.

Agency statement: Legal is Portland's oldest contract lawyer firm. We provide a full spectrum portfolio of lawyers to corporate legal departments and law firms of all sizes. Our lawyer placement services include fast and efficient temporary, temp to perm, and permanent placements. invests a tremendous amount of time listening to the needs of our clients and adapting our business to better serve those needs.

CONTACT INFORMATION:

621 SW Alder Street, Suite 380A, Portland, OR 97205

URL: www.lawyerplacement.com

E-mail: lawyers@ipinc.net

Telephone: (503) 224-4507

Fax: (503) 224-7574

Managing Directors: David O'Brien, Esq. And Michael O'Brien

Hiring and Contract Lawyer Contacts: David or Michael O'Brien

Professional Placement Services, Inc. — Tampa, FL

Business profile: Founded in 1996 by former practicing lawyer, Susan Etheridge. Specializes in the temporary and permanent placement of attorneys, law clerks, legal administrators and legal nurse consultants. Touts its "thinking outside the box" approach to staffing. One of its contract lawyers recovered a $1.8 million verdict on assignment to a solo practitioner. A new division based in Miami offers career assessment and outplacement services. A third division works under the auspices of the Hillsborough County Bar Association to provide secretarial and paralegal staffing.

Placement personnel: Former practicing lawyers.

Hiring lawyer considerations: Completes an extensive questionnaire to document tax status of contract lawyer as employee or independent contractor.

Financial arrangement with contract lawyers: Paid as employees or independent contractors, depending upon the factual scenario surrounding the placement.

Contract lawyer pool: New admittees can find contract lawyer placements through this agency. Overall, though, pool members tend to be experienced lawyers with solid credentials. Placements range from several years to one day. Majority of placements with law firms.

Agency statement: Serving Florida and the entire Southeast. PPSI is completely attorney-owned and managed and in full compliance with Florida Bar Ethics Opinion 88-12. PPSI also has the largest verdict ever recovered by a contract lawyer and is the official affiliate of the placement office operated by the Hillsborough County Bar Association. In addition to temporary and permanent attorney placement, we have divisions which specialize in career assessment, career counseling, outplacement and other legal staffing.

CONTACT INFORMATION:

PO Box 130536, Tampa, FL 33681-0536

URL: www.ppsilaw.com

Telephone: (813) 831-2889

Owner: Susan Etheridge, Esq.

Hiring & Contract Lawyer Contact: Lisa Michael Imus, Esq.

E-mail: ppsi@ppsilaw.com

Fax: (813) 835-1400

Shuart & Associates, Inc. | Metaire, LA

Business profile: Founded in 1989 by partners Darnell and Devry Shuart. Temporary placements began in 1991. Company places full-time, contract and temporary lawyers, administrative and support staff. One of the few well-respected contract lawyer placement agencies in the country founded by and run by non-lawyers.

Placement personnel: Law firm or legal recruiting backgrounds.

Financial arrangement with contract lawyers: Paid as employees. Can purchase group health insurance through the agency. Accrue paid vacation and holiday bonuses.

Contract lawyer pool: Company prefers to check references before adding a lawyer to the pool. Will let you know if your experience level, skills or educational credentials do not match those required by their existing clients. Will market contract candidates with specific talents or needs to their clients. New law school graduates may be offered assignments that range from paralegal to law clerk to contract lawyer work.

Agency statement: Shuart & Associates, Inc. is a legal search and staffing firm which specializes in full-time, temporary and contract placement of attorneys, paralegals, legal secretaries, and administrative staff. We are headquartered in New Orleans and provide services in Texas, Louisiana and the Southeast United States. Our clients are high caliber law firms and corporate legal departments. Shuart's trademark, based on its depth of knowledge of the legal marketplace the past ten years, is for filling sophisticated positions with quality matches.

CONTACT INFORMATION:

3838 N. Causeway, Suite 2660, Metaire, LA 70002

URL: www.shuart.com

Telephone: (504) 836-7595

Managing Director: Darnell Shuart

Hiring & Contract Lawyer Contact: Devry Shuart

E-mail: shuartatty@aol.com

Fax: (504) 836-7039

Special Counsel   Baltimore, MD

Headquartered in Baltimore with 22 branch offices nationwide plus six in Great Britain

Business profile: Originally founded by Lesley Friedman in 1987, Special Counsel was acquired by Accustaff in 1995, shortly after it had purchased two other well-regarded agencies in Baltimore and Atlanta. The new company, run by the founders of the Baltimore agency, has grown to 22 offices in the US and six in Great Britain, primarily by acquiring other legal staffing companies. Modis Professional Services is the current parent company. Special Counsel recently acquired Legal Information Technology (LIT), to enhance its project management and trial consulting services. Serves lawyers nationwide and internationally.

*Placement personnel:*Former practicing lawyers.

*Financial arrangement with contract lawyers:*Paid as employees with full benefits including health insurance, vacation pay and disability insurance.

Contract lawyer pool: Lawyers compensated as contract lawyers all have "solid law firm or in-house experience." New graduates placed as "law clerks."

Agency statement: Founded in 1987, Special Counsel is the nation's largest legal staffing provider with offices nationally and internationally. With access to thousands of job opportunities, our professionals enjoy the distinction of working with leading law firms and Fortune 500 companies. In addition to competitive pay rates, we also provide outstanding benefits such as group health and life insurance, vacation and holiday pay, 401(k) and an employee stock purchase plan.

CONTACT INFORMATION:
Corporate Headquarters

1838 Greene Tree Road, Suite 350, Baltimore, MD 21208

URL: www.specialcounsel.com,

E-mail: laurab@specialcounsel.com or markn@specialcounsel.com

Telephone: (410) 415-6300 or (800) 737-3436   Fax: (410) 415-6301

Managing Directors: Laura B. Black, Esq., CEO; Mark D. Neumann, Esq., COO

Branch Offices:

Alabama

2340 Woodcrest Place, Suite 210, Birmingham, AL 35209

URL: www.specialcounsel.com   E-mail: nancy@amicus-staffing.com

Telephone: (205) 870-3330   Fax: (205) 870-3337

Branch Manager: Nancy Hagan

California

400 Corporate Pointe, Suite 755, Culver City, CA 90230
URL: www.specialcounsel.com
E-mail: tbowling@specialcounsel.com
Telephone: (310) 649-6389
Fax: (310) 649-6388
Branch Manager: Traci Bowling

44 Montgomery Street, Suite 1240, San Francisco, CA 94104
URL: www.specialcounsel.com
E-mail: smiller@specialcounsel.com
Telephone: (415) 392-9246
Fax: (415) 392-9250
Branch Manager: Stacy Miller

2901 Tasman Drive, Suite 100, Santa Clara, CA 95054
URL: www.specialcounsel.com
E-mail: smiller@specialcounsel.com
Telephone: (408) 980-1004
Fax: (408) 980-1036
Branch Manager: Stacy Miller

District of Columbia

1800 K Street, NW, Suite 1100, Washington, DC 20006
URL: www.specialcounsel.com
E-mail: jennifem@specialcounsel.com
Telephone: (202) 737-3436
Fax: (202) 776-0084
Branch Manager: Jennifer Myers-Bookoff

Florida

1551 Atlantic Boulevard, Suite 300, Jacksonville, FL 32207
URL: www.specialcounsel.com
E-mail: lorip@specialcounsel.com
Telephone: (904) 737-3436
Fax: (904) 398-5253
Branch Manager: Lori Phelps

1700 E. Las Olas Boulevard, Suite 103, Ft. Lauderdale, FL 33301
URL: www.specialcounsel.com
E-mail: robind@specialcounsel.com
Telephone: (954) 764-5474
Fax: (954) 764-5476
Branch Manager: Robin Dubowitz

Georgia

100 Colony Square, Suite 840, Atlanta, GA 20261
URL: www.specialcounsel.com
E-mail: dpark@specialcounsel.com
Telephone: (404) 872-6672
Fax: (404) 892-3180
Branch Manager: Donna Park

Illinois

150 N. Michigan Avenue, Suite 2115, Chicago, IL 60601

URL: www.specialcounsel.com

E-mail: elewis@specialcounsel.com

Telephone: (312) 814-0240

Fax: (312) 814-0241

Branch Manager: Elliot Lewis, Esq.

Louisiana

1100 Poydras Street, Suite 1260, New Orleans, LA 70163

URL: www.specialcounsel.com

E-mail: nick@amicus-staffing.com

Telephone: (504) 522-0133

Fax: (504) 522-0195

Branch Manager: Nicholas Liuzza

Maryland

16 S. Calvert Street, Suite 501, Baltimore, MD 21202

URL: www.specialcounsel.com

E-mail: valeriev@specialcounsel.com

Telephone: (410) 385-5350

Fax: (410) 385-5352

Branch Manager: Valerie Vadala

Massachusetts

40 Broad Street, 2nd Floor, Boston, MA 02109

URL: www.specialcounsel.com

E-mail: rosborne@specialcounsel.com

Telephone: (617) 338-7700

Fax: (617) 338-1777

Branch Manager: Rodney Osborne

Mississippi

633 North State Street, Suite 608, Jackson, MS 39202

URL: www.specialcounsel.com

E-mail: nick@amicus-staffing.com

Telephone: (601) 949-3000

Fax: (601) 949-3001

Branch Manager: Nick Luizza

New Jersey

10 Woodbridge Center Drive, Suite 740, Woodbridge, NJ 07095

URL: www.specialcounsel.com

Telephone: (732) 750-3331

Fax: (732) 750-3332

Branch Manager: Catherine Aveta

New York

20 W. 55th Street, 2nd Floor, New York, NY 10019

URL: www.specialcounsel.com

E-mail: brendap@specialcounsel.com

Telephone: (212) 245-5599   Fax: (212) 245-6010

Branch Manager: Brenda Pace

North Carolina

Building 5600 Vanguard Centre, 77 Center Drive, Suite 170, Charlotte, NC 28217,

URL: www.specialcounsel.com   E-mail: terri@amicus-staffing.com

Telephone: (704) 529-5590   Fax: (704) 529-5639

Branch Manager: Terri Williams, Esq.

Ohio

1000 Terminal Tower Building, 50 Public Square, Cleveland, OH 44113

URL: www.specialcounsel.com   E-mail: agarson@specialcounsel.com

Telephone: (215) 622-2100   Fax: (215) 622-2110

Branch Manager: Ann Garson

Pennsylvania

One Penn Center at Suburban Station, 1617 JFK Boulevard, Suite 810, Philadelphia, PA 19103

URL: www.specialcounsel.com   E-mail: stacyf@specialcounsel.com

Telephone: (215) 569-0999   Fax: (215) 568-0299

Branch Manager: Stacy Flickstein

Tennessee

PennMarc Centre, Suite 555, 6401 Poplar Avenue, Memphis, TN 38119

URL: www.specialcounsel.com   E-mail: memphis@amicus-staffing.com

Telephone: (901) 762-0111   Fax: (901) 762-0176

Branch Manager: Lawanna Love

Signature Center, Suite 425, 1900 Church Street, Nashville, TN 37203

URL: www.specialcounsel.com   E-mail: joe@amicus-staffing.com

Telephone: (615) 320-7700   Fax: (625) 320-7747

Branch Manager: Joseph Freedman, CPC

Texas

Center City Plaza, Suite 205, 1412 Main Street, Dallas, TX 75202

URL: www.specialcounsel.com   E-mail: david@amicus-staffing.com

Telephone: (214) 698-0200   Fax: (214) 698-8575

Branch Manager: David Maldonado, Esq.

Update Legal Staffing   Headquartered in New York City with four branch offices

Business profile: Founded in 1970. Joshua Schott joined the company in 1990 while still in law school and became president in 1993. The company focuses solely on placing legal professionals in law firms and corporate legal departments. First contract lawyer placements began in 1992. Generous employee benefits for contract lawyers who work a minimum number of hours in a three-month period. Agency works hard to make contract lawyers feel valued: e.g., publishes a quarterly newsletter for the temporary staff, and hosts events for contract workers.

Placement personnel: Law school graduates with and without practice experience.

Arrangements with hiring lawyers: In addition to a thorough background check, including verification of schools and bar standing, agency completes an extensive conflict of interest question-naire prior to placement of temporary staff. Client services representative acts as on-site manager for larger projects.

Financial arrangement with contract lawyers: Paid as employees. Benefits for those qualifying include health, dental, and disability insurance, 401(k), paid vacation, educational programs and coverage for workers' compensation and unemployment insurance.

Contract lawyer pool: Places new law school graduates as well as attorneys with years of work experience. Attorney candidates are evaluated to ensure that they possess the requisite knowledge for their area of practice and specific client requests. In many instances, applicants must submit writing samples that demonstrate the quality of their analytical thinking and their three months.

Agency statement: Update Legal Staffing partners with both our clients and candidates to create long-term staffing strategies. We foster close relationships with our permanent and contract attorneys, paralegals and litigation support staff to better match their needs to those of our law firm and corporate clients. And because we offer some of the best benefits in the industry— including medical, paid vacations and 401(k) plans—we attract the kind of dedicated professionals who are welcome additions to our clients' staff. We currently have offices in New York, Newark, Houston, Philadelphia and Boston and are expanding to select cities nationwide.

CONTACT INFORMATION

Main Office:

1140 6th Avenue, 6th Floor, New York, NY 10036

URL: www.updatelegal.com,   E-mail: mzamsky@updatelegal.com

Telephone: (212) 921-2200; (888) 354-8200   Fax: (212) 354-9480

Managing Director: Marc Zamsky, Esq.

Massachusetts

28 State Street, 17th Floor, Boston, MA 02109

URL: www.updatelegal.com   E-mail: pmasterson@updatelegal.com

Telephone: (617) 722-0100   Fax: (617) 722-0101

Branch Manager: Paul Masterson

New Jersey

One Riverfront Plaza, 14th Floor, Newark, NJ 07102

URL: www.updatelegal.com   E-mail: jherzog@updatelegal.com

Telephone: (973) 622-7575; (800) 635-5040   Fax: (973) 648-8692

Branch Manager: Jeff Herzog

Pennsylvania

1800 John F. Kennedy Boulevard, 4th Floor, Philadelphia, PA 19103

URL: www.updatelegal.com   E-mail: ecaufield@updatelegal.com

Telephone: (215) 981-0855; (800) 635-5040   Fax: (215) 981-0487

Branch Manager: Ed Caufield

Texas

Four Houston Center, 1221 Lamar, Suite 1136, Houston, TX 77010

URL: www.updatelegal.com   E-mail: sfox@updatelegal.com

Telephone: (713) 650-1000; (800) 466-1015   Fax: (713) 650-3204

Branch Manager: Sara Fox

TOPICAL INDEX

ABOUT THE AUTHORS

Deborah Arron is the author of two nationally-recognized books, *What Can You Do with a Law Degree?: A Lawyer's Guide to Career Alternatives Inside, Outside and Around the Law* and *Running from the Law: Why Good Lawyers Are Getting Out of the Legal Profession.* She has been featured in numerous legal and general interest publications including *Time,* the *ABA* and *National Law Journals, U.S.A. Today, Fortune,* the *New York Times,* and *Working Woman.*

A former civil litigator from Seattle, Washington, Arron now speaks widely on career development issues for lawyers. Sponsors of her seminars and workshops include scores of state and local bar associations, specialty bar organizations like the Council of Appellate Staff Attorneys, the Oregon Professional Liability Fund and the American College of Trial Lawyers, as well as dozens of law schools nationwide.

Arron obtained her B.A. degree from the University of Washington in 1971, where she graduated magna cum laude and was elected to Phi Beta Kappa. She graduated from UCLA Law School in 1975, and was a member of the *UCLA Law Review.* During the course of her ten-year legal career, she practiced as the first female associate of one of Seattle's large law firms, a partner in a small firm and a solo practitioner. She also chaired the (Seattle-) King County Young Lawyers Section and was elected to the Board of Trustees of the (Seattle-) King County Bar Association.

In the summer of 1985, Arron began a one-year sabbatical from the practice of law—from which she never returned! In 1988, she founded an information-and-support group for Seattle lawyers considering job or career change. The program provided direct and referral services to over 1,200 participants before it was incorporated into the Washington State Bar Association three years later.

Arron belongs to the National Speakers Association, and the Washington and California Bar Associations.

Deborah Guyol coordinates the Oregon Women Lawyers Contract Lawyer Referral Service. In this role, she provides information and assistance to scores of Oregon lawyers interested in becoming or hiring a contract lawyer. She also facilitates monthly support group meetings for the two dozen panel members and has been working with a committee to establish practice standards for temporary assignments.

Guyol obtained her B.A. from Reed College in 1968, and her J.D. from the University of Southern California in 1982 where she was executive editor of the *Southern California Law Review.* Her legal experience includes five years with New York City's Davis Polk & Wardwell where her practice focused on bankruptcy; and an additional five years handling bankruptcy and commercial litigation as an associate for three well-respected Portland, Oregon, law firms.

In 1992, she liberated herself from law firm life and began doing contract work for a variety of Oregon firms and solo practitioners. She belongs to the Oregon, Multnomah and American Bar Associations and is editor-in-chief of the *Oregon Debtor-Creditor Newsletter.*

What Can You Do With a Law Degree?

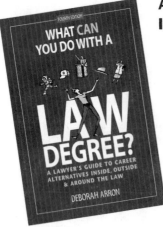

A Lawyer's Guide to Career Alternatives Inside, Outside & Around the Law

Do You Know . . .

- ▶ How to tell if you're better suited to the law or some other field?
- ▶ How to determine when to make the big break?
- ▶ How to analyze and overcome your barriers to change?
- ▶ How to transfer your legal skills to other professions?
- ▶ How to implement an effective job-finding campaign?

You must be able to answer these five questions if you want to develop a satisfying, long-lasting career. And here's the best resource to help you. Whether you're a veteran practitioner or a new law grad, this expanded 4th edition of Deborah Arron's career guide for lawyers will challenge and provoke you, while preparing you to move into any of the following fields:

ADR • Arts & Entertainment • Bar Association Management • Business • Communications • Consulting • Counseling • Education • Entrepreneurial Ventures • Environmental • Ethics • Foundations & Nonprofits • Government • Healthcare • Information Science • International Work • Labor Unions • Law Enforcement • Lobbying & Public Affairs • Private Law Practice • Publishing • Real Estate • Sports • Technology • The Judiciary

Here's what the critics say about What Can You Do With a Law Degree?

"Well-written, well-organized, optimistic and completely updated. An easy-to-follow travel guide for any attorney questioning career choices."
—*Massachusetts Lawyers Weekly*

"When those dark nights of the soul arise, this book is the beginning of the solution. Every lawyer, law student or aspiring law student will find this book useful." —*ABA's Law Practice Management Magazine*

"Take it from someone who has been there—Arron knows her stuff."
—*Women's Bar Association of DC Newsletter*